A GIFT *of* BARBED WIRE

America's Allies Abandoned in South Vietnam

A GIFT *of* BARBED WIRE

America's Allies Abandoned in South Vietnam

ROBERT S. MCKELVEY

UNIVERSITY OF WASHINGTON PRESS

Seattle and London

Library of Congress Cataloging-in-Publication Data
McKelvey, Robert S.
A gift of barbed wire : America's allies abandoned
in Vietnam / Robert S. McKelvey.
p. cm.
Includes bibliographical references and index.
ISBN 0-295-98224-1 (cloth : alk. paper)
ISBN 0-295-98225-X (pbk. : alk. paper)
1. Political prisoners—Vietnam.
2. Vietnam—Politics and government—1975.
I. Title.
HV8964.V5 M35 2002   959.704′4—DC21   2002016587

I give you a gift of barbed wire,
some creeping vine of this new age.

TRAN DA TU

CONTENTS

Preface   ix

Acknowledgments   xxi

1 / Introduction   3

PART I. Former Political Prisoners

2 / The Doctor   17

3 / The Engineer   31

4 / The Tailor   58

5 / The Spy   71

PART II. Former Political Prisoners and Their Families

6 / The Pilot   103

7 / The Pilot's Wife   123

8 / The Pilot's Daughter   132

9 / The Teacher   142

10 / The Teacher's Wife   169

11 / The Politician   178

CONTENTS

12 / The Politician's Wife   192

13 / The Politician's Son   201

14 / The Politician's Grandson   213

15 / The Politician's Daughter-in-Law   221

16 / Conclusion   229

Notes   242

Glossary   250

Index   258

PREFACE

Twenty-seven years ago we Americans walked away from our allies in South Vietnam and left them alone to face the North Vietnamese Army and the Viet Cong. After nearly a decade of massive intervention to save South Vietnam from "Communist aggression," our leaders decided that the political costs of sustaining the distant and unpopular war were too great. We "Vietnamized" the conflict, leaving behind our military bases and much of our equipment for use by the forces of the Republic of Vietnam. Belatedly, we had come to the realization that South Vietnam's struggle to preserve its fledgling democracy was really up to the Vietnamese. While we continued to send military aid to South Vietnam, the amount of such aid was steadily reduced, especially after Watergate and the furor surrounding President Nixon's resignation. The South Vietnamese continued to hope, however, that we would honor our commitments to them. "It was to this last hope that the armed forces and the people of South Vietnam desperately clung, and it was with the belief that somehow the additional aid would be provided that they stoically endured all privations and willingly shed more blood to make up for the missing rounds of ammunition."[1] Conditioned by the United States to fight a "rich man's war," replete with modern technology and massive firepower, the South Vietnamese increasingly found themselves without the sophisticated arms and equipment on which they had come to rely.

From time to time images of the catastrophe that followed our departure appeared in our newspapers and passed across our television screens. We watched helicopters leaving from the roof of the American Embassy in 1975 as Saigon fell and the war finally came to its disastrous end. We saw pictures of boat people fleeing Vietnam and heard horrific tales of drowning and starvation, assaults and rapes by pirates, and rescues at sea by passing freighters and tankers. We witnessed the growth of the Vietnamese refugee population in our country and responded with both resentment and admiration as these new Americans and their children put many of us to shame with their hard work and achievements. For the most part, however, when we thought of Vietnam it was to nurse our own wounds. Vietnam veterans marched and protested to gain some measure of respect and recognition for their sacrifices. A tragic and beautiful war memorial containing the names of the fallen was built in Washington, D.C. Politicians talked about bringing our prisoners of war and the remains of our dead home from Vietnam. We attended movies that showed the pain and futility of our suffering and the American lives that had been shattered by participation in the conflict. Very few of us, however, gave more than a passing thought to the shattered lives of those we had left behind. It did not occur to most of us that we had abandoned our former friends, the South Vietnamese, and even our children, the Vietnamese Amerasians, to our enemies. We had moved on with our lives; worked to renew our nation's prosperity; reinvested our military, political, and economic power in other parts of the world; and largely banished Vietnam from our consciousness.

This book is intended to show Americans what happened to our Vietnamese allies and their families after our troops went home. It chronicles the lives of former South Vietnamese government and military personnel who were incarcerated for many years by the Communists in "re-education camps," and the parallel experiences of their family members in postwar Vietnam. From World War II and the two Vietnam Wars—the first with the French, the second with the Americans—to re-education camps, refugee flight, and resettlement in the United States, these men and women faced recurrent trials and adversity. Their story is both a human tragedy and a testimony to endurance and courage.

Between 1969 and 1970 I served in Vietnam as a captain in the U.S. Marine Corps. I was assigned as a Civil Affairs officer, charged with "winning the hearts and minds" of the Vietnamese in our area of operations northwest of the city of Da Nang in central Vietnam. This work brought me into daily contact with Vietnamese civilians, most of them farmers, and provided me with a somewhat different perspective on the war than might have been the case had I been in an infantry platoon, an artillery battery, or an air wing. In a sense, I functioned more like an armed Peace Corps volunteer than as a soldier, making it easier for me to appreciate and empathize with the suffering of those Vietnamese who were caught between the warring armies.

After leaving Vietnam in May 1970 I returned home to begin a new career as a physician. I completed medical school in 1974 and finished my training as a psychiatrist and child psychiatrist in 1979. During those busy years I seldom thought about my wartime experiences. Then in the 1980s the many books, films, and discussions aimed at examining America's role in the Vietnam War reawakened my interest in, and memories of, Vietnam. I began to search for ways to return to Vietnam and to work with the Vietnamese, this time as a psychiatrist. In Ho Chi Minh City, at the Philippine Refugee Processing Center, and in the United States, I learned about the lives of the Vietnamese Amerasians, the children born during the war to American men and Vietnamese women.[2] I later broadened my focus to include other Vietnamese children in Australia, the United States, and Hanoi, capital of Vietnam.

In 1990, during my first return visit to Vietnam since my military service there, I purchased two beautiful lacquerware paintings.[3] They depicted abstractly drawn, ethereal women with long black hair clad in flowering purple and green *áo dàis*, the traditional Vietnamese dress. The sales clerk told me that the artist who had painted them lived nearby. I decided to pay him a visit. After searching for an hour or two through the crowded and dirty streets of Ho Chi Minh City, I finally found the tiny two-story apartment that served as both his home and studio. His wife answered the door and, after establishing that I was there to view and possibly to buy some of her husband's art, invited me in. She functioned as the gallery manager and showed me around, explaining how the works had been painted and describing some of the themes depicted in his art. As much as I admired her husband's work, several pieces of which I later purchased, I was even more captivated by the depth and beauty of her eyes. They seemed to me to be filled with enormous sadness and suffering. In asking about her husband's artistic background, I learned that he had served as an officer in the Army of the Republic of Vietnam (ARVN). After the Communist victory in 1975, the new government incarcerated him. When I asked why, she said that this had been the fate of many of those who had worked for the old government. She also spoke briefly of her own life during his five-year absence, describing the poverty and social isolation she had endured and their subsequent struggle to rebuild their lives after his release. Listening to her talk I began to understand some of the sadness in her eyes.

This was my first experience with Vietnamese former political prisoners and their families. I had been unaware that after the fall of Saigon on April 30, 1975, more than one million of our former South Vietnamese allies, out of a population of twenty million, were forced to enter re-education camps.[4] There they were put to work digging ditches and irrigation canals, raising crops, and constructing buildings and roads. They were fed starvation rations—two bowls of rice, some salt, and a little thin vegetable soup each day. In the evenings, after a full day's work, they were lectured on the errors of the old government and the Americans, on the theories of Marxism-Leninism, and on the glories of the new Communist regime, described by their jailers as "the best government in the world." They were also required to confess their past misdeeds as part of the re-education process that ostensibly would "transform" them into "new people."[5] It was not revealed to them until later that these confessions would form the basis for further accusations against them and an even longer imprisonment.

Finally released from the re-education camps after having been incarcerated from one to over twenty years, the former prisoners returned home as skeletal images of the men they had once been. They were exhausted, sick, and profoundly cynical about the new government and its true intentions. A very few, such as the artist I encountered, found employment approximating the work for which they had been trained. Most, however, had to settle for whatever jobs they could find, a despised underclass of highly educated and intelligent men with no prospects for a productive future in Vietnam either for themselves or for their children.

I encountered one of the many less fortunate former political prisoners during a subsequent visit to Vietnam. He had been a major in the ARVN, but by the time I met him in 1993 he was a lowly *cyclo* (pedicab) driver in Ho Chi Minh City. His work was to transport Western visitors by pedal power from their high-priced hotels around the central business district on shopping or sightseeing trips. During the making of the French film *Indochine* he had been the *cyclo* driver for the actress Catherine Deneuve. If asked, he would produce a laminated copy of the cover of *Paris Match* magazine on which he was pictured transporting Ms. Deneuve in his pedicab. He was the same age as I, and each day as I watched his slender, muscular frame struggling to propel the heavy burden of well-fed American and French tourists through the teeming streets of the city, I reflected on the differences in our fates.

In the years following their release from the re-education camps most of the former prisoners decided to leave Vietnam. Some escaped as boat people or overland through Cambodia and Thailand, while others left as part of the Orderly Departure Program (ODP).[6] Arriving in the United States they then faced the challenge, especially daunting for older people, of adapting to a country with vastly different cultural traditions. They usually spoke little English and often experienced racism, prejudice, and job discrimination. Unlike our own Vietnam veterans, few Americans knew or cared about their stories. No movies depicted their lives. The books they had written about their experiences were not on our best-seller lists.[7] There was no *Miss Saigon* to help us understand their suffering. Even the scientific literature contained only a few papers that addressed their problems.[8] How, I wondered, had they and their wives endured so many decades of protracted and repeated suffering? How had that suffering affected their personality development, their mental health, and their outlook on life? What remained of their youthful hopes and dreams? These were some of the questions I sought to answer in writing this book.

As I began to learn about the former political prisoners of Vietnam I anticipated that I would encounter broken and bitter people mourning for the past and resentful for all that they had lost. After many hours of meeting with them, listening to their experiences, and then reflecting and writing about them I have, to my surprise, found something different. While a few of those I got to know were bitter, none seemed broken, and almost all displayed an enormous resilience in the face of seemingly overwhelming trauma.

This book is based on a series of interviews I conducted over the course of a year and a half with ten former political prisoners and with several of their wives and children. I spoke with each person individually and face-to-face, usually with the assistance of an interpreter, but in those cases in which their English was fluent (the Doctor, the Politician's Grandson, the Pilot's Daughter, the Teacher, and the Tailor), without an interpreter. Two interpreters were used, depending on the geographical location of the interviews, which were conducted in Portland, Oregon, and Houston. I know both interpreters well and have worked with them previously on other projects. One is an older Vietnamese man, a former educational administrator in Vietnam who left his homeland in late middle age and has been in the United States for approximately ten years. He has worked extensively with Vietnamese refugees in Houston and has a sophisticated and charmingly humorous understanding of the cultural differences between the United States and Vietnam. The other interpreter is a young Vietnamese woman, born in Vietnam, who left there at age eight as a boat person and completed elementary school, high school, and college in Oregon. She has had considerable experience as a caseworker and mental health worker for Asian children and their families in Portland. Neither interpreter was in the re-education camps, although the woman spent almost a year in a refugee camp and many of the man's friends were former political prisoners.

Aside from the Tailor, whom I had known previously, the two interpreters introduced me to all of the former political prisoners and family members I interviewed. I had initially intended to write only about the former political prisoners themselves, but a friend and colleague in Houston, Thien Kim Pham, suggested that I also include the stories of their wives. As a caseworker and therapist in the Vietnamese community, she was aware that the former prisoners' wives had also suffered greatly both during and after their husbands' long incarcerations.

Interviews were conducted in the former prisoners' homes with two exceptions. The Doctor asked to be interviewed at a Vietnamese restaurant, and the Spy chose to come to my office at the medical school. Subjects were usually interviewed two to four times, with each interview lasting approximately three or four hours. Interviews with subjects who spoke English were generally briefer because an interpreter was not necessary.

Prior to conducting each interview I explained to the participants that it was my intention to use their life stories in a book describing the experiences of Vietnamese former political prisoners and their families in Vietnam and the United States. I told them that I would do my utmost to disguise their identities by not using their real names and by changing place names that might reveal who they were. (My reasons for doing so are explained below.) I mailed or had the interpreters deliver a draft of each participant's story to them and asked that they read it over for accuracy, correct any errors, adjust their "disguise," and add any supplementary material they wanted. Some chose to make no additions or corrections, saying simply that they trusted me. Others made corrections only, while a few were stimulated to write more about their experiences.

Although some participants told me they did not mind if I used their real names, most wanted to conceal their identities and certain details of their past lives. Their reasons for doing so varied. Some did not want to jeopardize the safety of family members and relatives still living in Vietnam. Others did not want Vietnamese authorities to know who they were in case they wanted to visit Vietnam in the future. The person I have referred to as the Spy was comfortable sharing the details of his adventures and did not mind if I used his real name. However, his wife and parents did not even want to be interviewed because they feared that they might somehow be identified and not allowed to return to Vietnam to see their relatives. Still other subjects wanted to conceal sensitive and controversial events in their lives that might cause embarrassment to themselves or to their family members. The Politician's Grandson, after talking with great openness about a painful situation in his family that continues to divide them to this day, later asked that I not include its details, but simply refer to a "family conflict." "Otherwise," he said, "when my relatives read the book they will be even angrier at us."

The anonymity that I have given to those who shared their lives with me for this book may diminish somewhat its vivacity. However, I was guided throughout by my desire, in the words of the ancient medical maxim, "To do no harm." I would prefer to have a slightly less colorful narrative than to risk some harm befalling either the participants or their families because of what I have written. I have spent many months in Vietnam at various times over the past ten years. Despite my love for the country, my occasional uncomfortable contacts with officials and bureaucrats there have made me very wary of bringing anyone to their displeased attention.

I also recognize that in the tell-all climate of the United States, where some private individuals are prepared to discuss the intimate details of their bizarre interpersonal adventures with talk show hosts and the tabloids, the low-key, reserved narrative style of those I interviewed may seem somewhat flat and dry. It may suggest to American readers that the Vietnamese I interviewed were not being completely truthful or forthcoming. However, as Vietnamese friends have often told me, "We Vietnamese do not wear our hearts on our sleeves. We carry a lot around inside our heads that we do not tell anyone, even our closest friends and family members." Traditional Vietnamese are uncomfortable with the very public self-examination and emotional openness that characterize many Americans. They have been taught to bear their feelings stoically and alone. In the Vietnamese cultural tradition a preoccupation with sharing one's emotions and inner experiences with others, and especially strangers, would be viewed as a sign of weakness or a lack of self-control. The Pilot's Daughter, who left Vietnam at an early age and spent most of her childhood in the United States, spoke very openly about her feelings toward her parents and her siblings. However, when she reviewed the draft manuscript of her story her acculturated Vietnamese reluctance to share too much took hold. In addition to making corrections, she asked me to soften, and in some cases to omit strong expressions of feeling that she or her parents had made toward one another or toward other family members.

Americans who have become acquainted with Vietnamese people in the United States or in Vietnam will recognize that they are socialized to be very sensitive to the impact of what they are saying on their listeners and to minimize interpersonal tensions. For an American reader not familiar with the Vietnamese I would characterize their inoffensive and charming style as somewhat akin to that found in the Deep South, the upper Midwest, or the Pacific Northwest of the United States. It is far removed from the very open and direct manner of, say, Boston or New York.

The modest, nonconfrontational style of the Vietnamese, and their reluctance to open their hearts and souls to strangers, may convey the impression that the people I interviewed did not feel deeply about the subjects being discussed. Nothing could be further from the truth. They felt passionately about the brutal treatment and the grievous injustices meted out to them by the Communists in Vietnam. They also greatly mourned the loss of their country. But they knew that they were telling their stories and expressing their feelings to an audience of strangers. They did not want to say too much or to offend their listeners. For example, the rather mild critiques of American policy and the behavior of American soldiers abroad provided by the Pilot and the Teacher should be read as representing much more anger and outrage than is actually being expressed. For older Vietnamese men such as these to criticize their listener's country while sitting with him in that country is very strong criticism indeed. An American must read carefully and often between the lines to recognize the depth of the feelings that are being expressed, turning up the volume on what is said to experience it in its true intensity.

Since the Civil War, Americans have enjoyed the great good fortune of fighting wars on other people's lands, not their own. Increasingly, America's wars have become distant and remote events, almost like televised sports or video games, in which tanks rumble across deserts and "smart" bombs penetrate bunkers while we watch from the comfort of our living rooms. We see affecting pictures of refugees moving along dusty roads, carrying bundles of possessions, and sometimes crying as correspondents interview them for our interest and entertainment. Occasionally we are shown the dead bodies or shattered limbs of war's victims, scenes prefaced by verbal cautions that what follows may not be suitable for younger or more sensitive viewers. However, unless we have been to war ourselves, or have experienced its searing and bitter wounds in the lives of our family and friends, the military conflicts of our country remain abstractions, interesting, but as unimportant to us "as the football scores of colleges other than our own."9

The same cannot be said for those who live in the distant lands where our armies fight, our planes drop bombs, and our ships fire cruise missiles. There war is real, and its effects devastating and lifelong. The lives of the Vietnamese former political prisoners illustrate for those of us who have always lived in peace what war really means for its victims. Their life histories provide a close-up documentary view, extending over a period of more than seventy years, of the effects of war and its aftermath on human lives. While unique in certain respects—especially in the length of their postwar incarceration in re-education camps— the prisoners' stories help us to understand and empathize with the suffering of other victims of war and may teach us how to help them once their immediate ordeal is over. Listening to them recount their life stories we learn about successful and unsuccessful strategies for coping with war trauma, re-education camps, the catastrophic loss of social and financial standing, and immigration at an advanced age to a country very different from one's own.

The tragedy of war devastates not only those who fight as soldiers or who become the direct civilian victims of the catastrophe, but also their families. The fathers, mothers, sisters, brothers, wives, and children of the combatants must learn to cope with their absence and with the loss of their emotional and financial support. They wrestle with fears for the safety and survival of their loved ones, with concerns about how the war will change them, and sometimes with their death. We often read about the soldiers who are sent away, but seldom about those who remain behind. That is why I have chosen to include in this book not only the life histories of the former political prisoners, but also those of some of their family members. The length of the prisoners' incarceration meant that their families were often separated from them for many years. After their departure for the re-education camps, their wives and children experienced an almost overnight descent from privileged lives into shame and degradation. They had to bear alone the enormous loss of status and its attendant poverty that were experienced by adherents of the former regime. And worst of all, they never knew when, or even if, their husbands and fathers would return. There was no due process or sentencing. Prisoners served until they died, were killed, or were released, "forgiven" at last by the Communist government.

In recounting their stories I have chosen to view the former prisoners' and their families' experiences not in isolation, but as a part of their overall life histories. I have done this for two reasons. First, I believe that it is important to understand traumatic events in context. Such experiences will have different effects on an otherwise healthy and stable person supported by family and friends and buttressed by educational, career, and financial success than on a person whose life has long been traumatic and who has few such resources. Despite sharing similar brutal treatment at the hands of the Communists, most American prisoners of war in Vietnam returned home to a hero's welcome and to a country rich in opportunities, where knowledge of their ordeal brought recognition and status.[10] Vietnamese former political prisoners, on the other hand, returned home to be reviled as "collaborators," socially ostracized and barred from entry into satisfying and rewarding professional careers. Their traumatic experiences continued for years after their release from the camps—as outcasts in Vietnam, sometimes as boat people, and later as older refugees struggling to gain a foothold in an alien and at times unwelcoming new country.

My second reason for portraying the re-education camp experience in the full context of human lives is the hope that this will help to close the empathic gap between non-Vietnamese readers and these slender, graying, dark-skinned people who might otherwise seem to come from a distant and unrelated universe. It can be difficult to recognize and appreciate the warm humanity and startling courage of people who appear superficially so different from ourselves. However, once one comes to know them for who they are, as I have been privileged to do over the course of preparing this book, one cannot help but hold them to one's heart. They are extraordinary and highly admirable human beings.

ACKNOWLEDGMENTS

I am deeply indebted to those former political prisoners and their family members who agreed to share their life stories with me. Without their cooperation this book would not have been possible. I hope that they will find the product of our work together a worthy reflection of their many years of suffering and of their courageous attempts to rebuild their lives.

Thien Kim Pham, who helped me with my previous book, *The Dust of Life* (Seattle: University of Washington Press, 1999), and with several other clinical and research projects with the Vietnamese community in Houston, suggested that the book also include the lives of the former political prisoners' wives. Their story has not, to my knowledge, been told before, and their long ordeal has gone largely unnoticed. I am very grateful to Ms. Pham for calling my attention to them.

Loan Huynh and Truong Nguyen introduced me to most of the former political prisoners I interviewed and functioned as both interpreters and cultural consultants. Their sensitivity and understanding have contributed immensely to this book. Although I cannot reveal their names, the two former political prisoners identified as the Spy and the Teacher each read through the entire manuscript, correcting mistakes that I had made in spelling Vietnamese words and place names. I owe them both a special debt of gratitude. Thanh Nguyen reviewed the final manuscript and added tone and diacritical marks to the Vietnamese words used.

Michael Duckworth at the University of Washington Press provided encouragement and very valuable assistance in carefully reviewing the manuscript and offering suggestions to make it a stronger book. Xavier Callahan, my editor there, has also been most helpful in her remarks and in kindly showing me the importance of certain revisions that I might otherwise have neglected.

Penny Harrison, editor of *Open Spaces Magazine,* reviewed the manuscript in its early days and helped me to clarify my thinking about the message that I was trying to convey. Several of my colleagues at Oregon Health & Science University provided moral support and suggestions for the manuscript's improvement. Nancy Winters in the Division of Child and Adolescent Psychiatry reviewed the introduction and offered thoughtful comments about how to strengthen it. Elizabeth Lynch cheerfully prepared countless revisions of the manuscript for review. J. David Kinzie helped to clarify my understanding of the different variants of Post-Traumatic Stress Disorder (PTSD). Ronald Rosenfeld, chair of the Department of Pediatrics, and Alfred Lewy, vice chairman of the Psychiatry Department, offered their interest and friendship throughout the project. The Tartar Foundation at Oregon Health & Science University provided a grant for interpreter services.

Most important, as always, has been the immeasurable contribution of my family and especially of my wife, Jill Roman, who tolerates my many weekends at the office, provides good-natured and continuous support, and generally makes life worth living. My son, Lowell McKelvey, and his fiancée, Christine Leech, have also provided non-stop encouragement and the great pleasure of their company.

A GIFT *of* BARBED WIRE

America's Allies Abandoned in South Vietnam

1 / Introduction

When the Vietnam War ended, thousands of former officials and soldiers of the Republic of South Vietnam fled their homeland with their families and whatever possessions they could carry. They were well connected, had foreseen the impending defeat of their country, and had laid plans to escape and create a future for themselves abroad. Most Vietnamese, however, were not so lucky. The precipitous collapse of South Vietnam surprised both the victors and the vanquished by its speed and totality and led to a period of great uncertainty immediately after the war during which neither side knew how the other would behave. Initially it was the avowed policy of the People's Revolutionary Government to deal leniently with its former enemies through a policy of "national concord and reconciliation."[1] It was stated that victory had been so complete, and the need for talented and well-trained people so obvious, that only a brief period of rehabilitation and "re-education" would be necessary for adherents of the former "puppet" (*nguy*) regime. Depending on their standing and importance in the South Vietnamese government or military, individuals would be required to participate in re-education ranging from three-day training sessions at locations near their homes to thirty-day stays at residential camps.[2] However, this seemingly humane policy turned out to be a masquerade for the new government's true intentions—to remove potentially subversive individuals from the fabric of Vietnamese society until it was deemed safe for them to return.[3] Instructed to bring along to the camps enough food and clothing for seven to thirty days, these men were separated from their families and incarcerated for up to twenty years.

The lives of the Vietnamese former political prisoners and their families portrayed in this book are linked by a number of common themes. All grew up against the backdrop of war and political turmoil in Vietnam. Most were well educated and came from relatively affluent families. They entered into the service of their country because they had to—the nation was in peril and all young men were being drafted. Serving in various capacities—as army officers, air force pilots, military doctors, politicians, and spies—they had a fairly comfortable lifestyle during the war, supported in part by American largesse. Following the fall of Saigon on April 30, 1975, however, their lives changed radically. The men were incarcerated in re-education camps, some in South Vietnam, others in the North. Many entered the camps, if not enthusiastically, at least initially believing the Communists' announced policy of "forgive and forget." They hoped that they would learn about, and be reconciled with, the new government and then be free to get on with their lives. However, they were quickly disillusioned and soon came to see the Communists as evil manipulators and liars interested only in controlling people for their own ends. This recognition, and the realization that they were in the camps indefinitely, led many into a period of depression and hopelessness.

Life for the prisoners in the re-education camps was very severe. "Most who endured would remember only an all-consuming hunger, maneuvering for a chance to drink the water their food had been cooked in, trying to catch birds and rats, scrambling to sneak a mouthful of wild berries on a work detail. . . . Many died in these camps. Many more were broken there, either mentally or physically."[4]

Following the men's departure for the re-education camps, their wives and dependents experienced a precipitous loss of social standing and a rapid descent into poverty. They were ostracized by former friends and neighbors and discriminated against educationally and vocationally by the government because of their connection with the old regime and the Americans. The wives, most of whom had led sheltered lives as stay-at-home mothers, often assisted by servants, now faced new and unaccustomed roles as the primary providers in their families. As their savings ran out they were forced to sell off their possessions on the streets, and when everything they owned was gone, to buy rice in one marketplace and then try to resell it for a small profit in another. They also faced a lengthy, if not permanent separation from their husbands, who were incarcerated without trial and detained until the government decided that they were ready to come home. Like their husbands in the camps, they too experienced periods of depression and despair.

Somehow, most of these resilient men and women found ways to cope with their bleak and uncertain future. Their strategies for coping varied. The wives struggled on for the sake of their children and to provide some emotional and material support for their starving, tormented husbands. The men tried to focus on the here and now, fought not to succumb to depression and suicide, and grasped at any shred of philosophy that might sustain them through the brutal monotony of the camps.

The men were released from the camps unpredictably and usually as a great surprise to themselves and to their families. The average length of stay in the camps was between seven and eight years,[5] and ranged from one or two years to over twenty years. Various factors appear to have influenced their release. If they became too sick to work, or if they had illnesses from which it appeared that they would not recover, they were released to go home and die. This spared the government the expense of their burial and also allowed it to claim that people did not die from being incarcerated in the camps. Sometimes external political concerns played a role. A number of physicians were released from the camps in the late 1970s as a precondition for French medical aid to Vietnam. Many other prisoners attributed their release during the late 1980s to General John Vessey's presence as the president's special emissary to Vietnam between 1987 and 1990 and to the subsequent improvement in relations between the United States and Vietnam. Internal reforms, such as the economic changes that occurred beginning in 1986 under the policy of đổi mới (renovation), also influenced life within the camps and may have led to the release of prisoners in order to transfer their upkeep from the state to their families. The government also released prisoners on special occasions, such as Independence Day (September 2d—the date in 1945 on which Ho Chi Minh declared Vietnamese independence from France and Japan), to demonstrate its magnanimity. At other times the prisoners' release followed no rationale or event discernable to them and may have been related to local or regional economic or political factors.

When the men finally were released they returned home to find a world turned upside down. The country was impoverished and isolated. Police were everywhere. Their wives were exhausted from the daily struggle to put food on the table. Their children wore rags and had often adopted the manners of the street, where many had been forced to raise themselves because their mothers were busy working. Some of the former prisoners' families had already left the country, fleeing as boat people or immigrating under the Orderly Departure Program (ODP) to the United States. Those former prisoners who were not too sick to do so tried to rebuild their lives. Some were relatively successful and able to return eventually to occupations similar to those they had pursued before the camps. Most, however, had to work as laborers or found no employment at all. Many of the men continued to experience symptoms of Post-Traumatic Stress Disorder (PTSD), a psychiatric condition that may develop after exposure to overwhelmingly traumatic events.[6] Hyperaroused, the former prisoners would be startled from sleep by a scratch at the door or the singing of a bird. They had nightmares about leading patrols against the Viet Cong or hearing the re-education camp's bell summoning them to work. They feared that at any moment the Communists might change their minds and come to take them back to the camps. Some remained quite depressed and hopeless, even considering suicide. Others recovered, at least in part.[7]

Eventually, almost all the former political prisoners came to the conclusion that there was no future for them or for their children in Vietnam. They began to search for ways to escape. Despite the dangers inherent in becoming boat people—drowning, death from exposure, starvation or thirst, murder or rape by pirates—many chose this desperate alternative. Others tried to secure the sponsorship of relatives already resettled abroad so that they could emigrate legally as refugees. Still others took advantage of a special subcategory of the ODP, officially designated as the Special Released Re-education Center Detainees Resettlement Program. Better known by its unofficial name, the H.O. Program,[8] this was an agreement negotiated bilaterally between the U.S. and Vietnamese governments and implemented in August 1989. It was reserved for those Vietnamese former political prisoners who had served during the war in the South Vietnamese government or military and who had spent at least three years in re-education camps. Under its terms eligible former political prisoners and their immediate family members were permitted to immigrate to the United States at U.S. government expense.

By the time they left Vietnam, the former prisoners and their wives were no longer young. Most were in their late forties, fifties, or sixties. They undertook a painful, often perilous migration, leaving behind the graves of their ancestors, their relatives, and their homes to find freedom for themselves and a future for their children. Once safely resettled in the United States, however, their difficulties were not at an end. They now had to turn their attention and remaining energies to survival. Most were too proud to see welfare as an acceptable option. They found jobs—sometimes two or three at a time—usually at levels far below their previous training and experience. Some were discouraged or embittered by underemployment and racial and age discrimination. Others were happy for any opportunity to support themselves and their families and to be independent. Whatever their feelings, most struggled on, pushing their children to attend college and graduate school so that the young might achieve the goals that war and its aftermath had denied their parents. In reflective moments they tried to come to grips with and accept their fate—"being born in the wrong time and place." Some were able to let go of the past and forgive those who had tormented them. Others held on to their hatred of the Communists and continued to denounce them.

Approximately 165,000 Vietnamese former political prisoners and their families live in the United States.[9] Now in late middle age or old age, the former prisoners and their wives are beginning to pass from the scene. The memory of what they have experienced and overcome is being lost, even to members of their own families. This book is an attempt to honor their courage and determination, to share their experiences with those who do not know them, and to learn what we can from their long ordeal.

The lives of the former political prisoners and their families played out against the backdrop of modern Vietnamese history. To understand their experience it is important to have some understanding of that history's main events. Americans are familiar with the Vietnam War, or at least the role of the United States in that distant, twenty-year struggle. However, we are often ignorant of anything prior to the war or of Vietnam's course after the departure of American troops in 1973. A large number of histories of modern Vietnam are available, including Joseph Buttinger's *A Dragon Defiant: A Short History of Vietnam* (New York: Prager, 1972) and Stanley Karnow's *Vietnam: A History* (New York: Viking, 1983). The following brief overview is derived from Nguyen Khac Vien's *Vietnam: A Long History* and the Federal Research Division's *Vietnam: A Country Study.*[10]

Prior to the French capture of the city of Tourane (Da Nang) in 1858, Vietnam was an independent country ruled by a feudal monarchy. Between 1858 and 1883, France conquered Vietnam and divided it into three administrative regions: Annam, Cochinchina, and Tonkin. These regions were administered separately as parts of French Indochina, which also included Cambodia and Laos, and not as parts of a unified Vietnam. France developed its three Vietnamese colonies economically, taxed their inhabitants, and established within them French cultural, educational, and political institutions. French power was supported by military force, including the Foreign Legion, African soldiers, and native militias recruited at the provincial level. The production of rice, Vietnam's principal crop and main export, was controlled by wealthy Vietnamese landowners. These landowners held more than 80 percent of Vietnam's agricultural land and exploited the labor of the landless peasant farmers, who comprised the majority of Vietnam's rural population.

Despite the appearance of nationalist movements against French rule, including the formation of the Indochinese Communist Party by Ho Chi Minh in 1930, French colonial domination of Vietnam continued until World War II. With the fall of France to Nazi Germany in 1940, the Vichy French colonial government was forced to sign a treaty with Japan permitting the Japanese military to transport troops across Indochina and to post an occupation force in Tonkin. In 1941 a number of Vietnamese nationalist groups, dominated by the Communist Party and led by Ho Chi Minh, formed the Viet Minh (formally *Việt Nam Độc Lập Đồng Minh Hội*—the League for Vietnamese Independence), to oppose both the French and the Japanese. In March 1945, as Japan's power over East Asia and the Pacific began to wane, the Japanese disarmed the French and allied with the Vietnamese Emperor Bao Dai, last representative of the Nguyen dynasty, to establish a puppet Vietnamese government under Japanese control. Following the bombings of Hiroshima and Nagasaki in August 1945, the Viet Minh organized and led a nationwide popular revolt (the August Revolution) against the Japanese and their Vietnamese government and established the Democratic Republic of Vietnam (DRV). On September 2, 1945, in Hanoi, Ho Chi Minh declared Vietnam an independent nation. "The

French have fled, the Japanese have capitulated, Emperor Bao Dai has abdicated. Our people have broken the chains which fettered them for nearly a century, and have won independence."[11]

The newly independent Vietnam was immediately threatened as France, with the assistance of Britain and the Nationalist Chinese, moved to re-establish its colonial authority. In September 1945 French military forces began to retake urban areas in southern Vietnam. By December 1946 they had retaken central Hanoi, the capital of the DRV, and in February 1947 they captured Hue, the former imperial capital. While the French came to control most urban areas in Vietnam, the Viet Minh held much of the countryside, where the majority of the Vietnamese population lived. In 1949 France granted Vietnam "associated statehood" within the French Union and established a Vietnamese government under Bao Dai.

Despite the appearance of independence, France retained ultimate control over Vietnam. In 1950 the United States recognized the Associated State of Vietnam, a move countered by the People's Republic of China and the Soviet Union, which formally recognized the DRV. Ho Chi Minh and the DRV continued the military and political struggle for independence from France (the First War of Resistance), decisively defeating the French in 1954 at the Battle of Dien Bien Phu. This victory led to the Geneva Accords of 1954 and a resultant cease-fire between the French and Viet Minh forces. Vietnam was divided provisionally at the 17th parallel, with a final political settlement of the conflict to be determined by a national election. French forces were withdrawn from the North, and Viet Minh forces from the South. The civilian population was given 300 days to migrate freely between the northern and southern zones, with many Roman Catholics and anti-Communists choosing to resettle in the South. In the North the DRV was established as an independent Communist-led government under the leadership of Ho Chi Minh. To counterbalance the Communist North, France and the United States supported the government of Bao Dai and his prime minister, Ngo Dinh Diem, in the South. Diem, a prominent nationalist, overthrew Bao Dai's government and in 1955 established the Republic of South Vietnam. He rejected the national referendum, called for by the Geneva Accords, which was intended to reunify Vietnam politically. His decision to do so was supported by the United States, by then Diem's main patron.

And so the lines were drawn for what Americans came to know as the Vietnam War and the North Vietnamese, the Second War of Resistance. For the next twenty years North Vietnam, working with Communist political and military forces in the South and supported by China and the Soviet Union, fought to overthrow the Republic of South Vietnam and to unify Vietnam under Communist control. U.S. military involvement in the conflict, which began in February 1955 with the arrival of American advisors to train the South Vietnamese army, escalated in 1965 with the landing of Marine Corps units in Da Nang. From this point on U.S. troops assumed an ever-expanding role in direct fighting against the North Vietnamese Army and the Viet Cong. This continued until 1970, when a lack of political support for the war in the United States led the Nixon administration to begin the gradual withdrawal of American troops and to shift the burden of the fighting back on to the South Vietnamese. The signing of the Paris Accords on January 27, 1973, led to the withdrawal of all U.S. forces by March 1973. Over the next two years the South Vietnamese military fought a losing battle against the North Vietnamese Army and Viet Cong, culminating in the final defeat of the Republic of South Vietnam and the fall of Saigon on April 30, 1975.

The end of hostilities, however, did not bring an end to the suffering of the Vietnamese people, who over the next decade experienced a painful social and economic transition as the Communist North sought to integrate the capitalistic South into a unified and independent country. Economically, Vietnam grew very slowly in the period after the war, becoming one of the poorest countries in the world and "one of the few countries in modern history to experience a sharp economic deterioration in a postwar reconstruction period."[12] This was the consequence of a number of factors: disastrous postwar economic policies, a series of natural disasters, and the Vietnamese invasion of Cambodia in 1978, which resulted in a loss of international aid. Private ownership was eliminated along with the Southern entrepreneurial class, consisting chiefly of ethnic Chinese living in Saigon's Cho Lon ("big market") section.

Socially, there was a concerted effort to develop a new order in the South resembling that in the North. Targets of this forced transition to a Socialist system were those considered exploiters of the peasants and workers, the large landowners and capitalists. A number of approaches to social control were utilized. Thought reform, such as mandatory "study sessions" for all adults and the much more intensive and extreme re-education camps, attempted to indoctrinate the Southern people in proper Communist thinking. The number of members of the former South Vietnamese elite who were still incarcerated in re-education camps in 1982, seven years after the war, has been estimated at about 120,000, with almost 40,000 still there by 1985.[13] The Hanoi government also instituted mass migrations of people from more densely populated areas such as Saigon to the remote and sparsely inhabited "New Economic Zones." While ostensibly an effort to reclaim unproductive land and ease overcrowding, resettlement to the New Economic Zones appears to have been applied more rigorously to those closely connected with the old regime and the United States. These included members of the former Saigon bureaucracy and army and the Amerasians, children of American men and Vietnamese women, and their families. The government also practiced extensive surveillance to detect counter-revolutionaries, who were interned in reform camps separate from the re-education camps and the New Economic Zones.

These economic and social changes were resisted by many in the South and led from 1975 onward to the mass migration overseas of over one million Vietnamese. Their principal means of escaping Vietnam were either walking overland to Thailand or taking boats onto the South China Sea and sailing to Hong Kong, Indonesia, Malaysia, the

Philippines, or Thailand. The migration of these boat people, often under deplorable conditions and with great loss of life, again brought Vietnam to world attention after the end of the war.

Militarily, Vietnam was threatened on its borders by the Khmer Rouge in Cambodia and by its former ally, China. In December 1978 the People's Army of Vietnam invaded Cambodia in response to border incursions by the Khmer Rouge. On January 7, 1979, the army captured Phnom Penh and overthrew the government of Pol Pot, bringing to an end the four years of the "Killing Fields" and the Cambodian genocide. In February 1979 China invaded Vietnam in response to a border dispute and to Hanoi's refusal to let Vietnam's ethnic Chinese community continue in its traditional role of commerce. The Vietnamese quickly defeated the Chinese, causing them to withdraw back across the border in March 1979. However, the conflict brought the loss of Chinese aid to Vietnam and increased Vietnam's economic dependency on the Soviet Union.

Prompted by the Cambodian invasion and by concerns over Americans still missing in action (MIA) from the Vietnam War, the United States refused for many years to establish normal diplomatic and trade relations with Vietnam, maintaining a stifling trade embargo that did much to keep Vietnam isolated and impoverished. The trade embargo was not fully lifted until 1994, and diplomatic relations between the United States and Vietnam were not normalized until 1995, twenty years after the end of the war. The first postwar American ambassador to Vietnam arrived in Hanoi on May 9, 1997.

For the people whose lives appear in this book, the Vietnam War was not an isolated, distant, or abstract event. War and its aftermath dominated their entire lives. During childhood or adolescence they experienced World War II and the fighting between the allies, the Vichy French, the Japanese, and the Viet Minh. In their late teens or young adulthood they witnessed, or participated in, the French struggles with the Viet Minh. Most then joined or were drafted into the fight between the Americans and the South Vietnamese against the North Vietnamese and the Viet Cong. As adults they experienced the defeat of their country and the subsequent vengeance of their enemies, who incarcerated them in re-education camps, drove them into poverty, and ostracized them socially. In late adulthood or old age they fled their homeland for the promise of freedom in the United States. It is difficult for those of us who have known only prosperity and peace to imagine lives filled with so much tragedy and loss. Yet somehow they endured, retaining their sanity and humanity under circumstances that many of us would probably not have survived. How did they do it? Perhaps those who were weaker or more vulnerable died along the way or did not have the courage and strength to leave their country in their late forties, fifties, or sixties. Perhaps there is something about the gritty Vietnamese character, accustomed to adapt to whatever fate offers, or the hardscrabble life of a developing country that conditioned them from an early age to survive regardless of the circumstances. Whatever its source, resilience, the ability to cope successfully with adversity, is one of the major themes illustrated in this book by the lives of the former political prisoners and their family members.

PART I

Former Political Prisoners

2 / The Doctor

*T*he doctor portrayed in this first chapter believes that he owes his survival in the re-education camps and his tenacious independence since then to philosophy. Surprisingly, the philosophy he follows is not an Asian one, but that of several French authors whose works he read in high school in Vietnam. They taught him to ignore the suffering of the moment and to keep his eye fixed clearly on the goal. As he put it: "To cry or to pray is cowardly. You just have to suffer and continue to work." His two experiences in re-education camps, totaling seven years, and his precipitous loss of social standing and wealth, first in Vietnam and then again in the United States, have tested his philosophy and left him wondering if he were born "at the wrong time and in the wrong place."

Tuan began by telling me about his parents. His father was born in a village in central Vietnam not far from the coastal city of Nha Trang. He and his family were landowners.

They worked hard and had a big house and lots of land in the countryside. My grandfather was sort of like a rancher here in the United States. My father was the only child in the family and his mother (my grandmother) died when he was three. For the first ten or eleven years of his life his family kept him at home, not sending him to school, but teaching him the old Vietnamese style of life, like learning to read Chinese characters [*Hán văn*]. When his cousin went off to high school in Hue he decided to follow him there. My grandfather did not want him to go, but he just hopped on a train and went, traveling without any money or clothes. He was a little spoiled. He had decided on his own that he wanted a French education even though he had no idea what that meant. My grandfather finally relented and sent him money for his tuition and clothing.

My father did well in school even though he did not know any French initially. Most of the teachers were French. There were very few Vietnamese teachers then, and all instruction was in French. Eventually, he learned to speak and write French fluently. In those days Vietnam was under the control of the French. During the 1930s there were a lot of political demonstrations against French rule. One of his classmates was Ngo Dinh Diem [first president of the Republic of South Vietnam and a prominent nationalist]. General Giap [a nationalist and later Communist who became commander of the North Vietnamese Army during the Vietnam War] was also a member of his generation. When my father was sixteen or seventeen he got involved in the political demonstrations and was expelled from school. He went home, but he was still under the control of the French government. They kept an eye on him. He did not need to work. His father exploited people, making them work for him for a little rice, kind of like serfs.

My father found the girl he wanted to marry by himself. She lived far away, in another village in his province. My grandfather did not know her. She was the eldest of twelve children. Her family were also landowners and wealthy. Her father was the village chief [Lý trưởng]. In those days a girl's job was to take care of the family. Girls in that generation did not get much education. My mother could not read or write, but she was very intelligent and, despite having no formal education, she could calculate as fast as people who had been to high school. My father's lifestyle was very different from the lifestyle of her family. He had been a student in a French school. He had lots of money, horses, and bicycles. He played around all over, including Saigon. I guess he was kind of like a playboy. He wore different clothes than the other people in the province—shirts, pants, and shoes instead of peasant dress. He ordered things from France, like the saddle for his horse. My mother's family had never seen anyone like him before! His family was wealthier than hers was. He was the only child of his parents, and his mother was dead. He was the boss of his family. He had some half brothers and sisters, but they were all afraid of him, even more than of my grandfather. My father had an open-minded lifestyle, unlike his father, who was very strict. When his half brothers and sisters asked my grandfather for things and he refused, my father would approve their requests. They looked at him like a god. They got everything from him. When he said something, they obeyed. Even now my aunts and uncles (my father's half brothers and sisters) obey me. It is because of my father's authority over them. My grandfather's fortune passed through my father to my brother and me. In Vietnam everyone follows the orders of the oldest son.

After my mother and father got married they moved into a house in my grandfather's compound. The compound consisted of two or three acres and had lots of houses, one for the cult of the ancestors, one for the kitchen, one for storing crops, one for my grandfather, and another for my parents. The compound was located in the village, not out on the land. The reason was safety. There were a lot of robbers in the region, so they built a fence around the village to protect it. The fence was made of living trees. My extended family had five or six compounds in the village and my family employed everyone who lived there.

We had a very good life, and everyone in the family got along well. There was no fighting. We were five children in all, three boys and two girls. My mother also had two or three miscarriages. I got my primary school education at home, learning to read and write. The school in our area had been closed because of the "nine-year war" between the French and Viet Minh [1945–54]. It was very dangerous in the countryside in those days. There was a lot of fighting in our area, and the public school was not secure. For high school my family sent me and my older brother and sister to a Catholic school in Da Lat [a city in the mountains northwest of Saigon where the French used to go to escape the heat of the coastal plain]. By then my father had become a province chief [similar to the governor of an American state]. He was the very first one under the regime of Bao Dai and Tran Trong Kim [Bao Dai, the former emperor, was head of state and Kim was prime minister of the Associated State of Vietnam established in 1949 and controlled by the French]. He recruited and trained soldiers to fight against the Viet Minh. In 1952 the French got Bao

Dai to relieve my father as province chief because he was a nationalist and against French rule. In 1954 he became province chief again and helped Ngo Dinh Diem come to power in the South.

My education in Da Lat was French, and most of the students were French. I started school there when I was ten or eleven years old, just like my father had done. I had to learn to be like a French student. After a year I could read and write in French, and I was soon the top student in the school, a position I held throughout my school years there. My friends were mostly Vietnamese, although I had a few French friends. We were always fighting the French students, but we did not let the professors see us doing it. I liked the school. It was the best school in Vietnam and very expensive. We did a lot of sports—volleyball, basketball, soccer—just like in France. I stayed at the school until 1954, then switched to a school in Saigon for a few years, completing my first *baccalauréat* there.[1] The reason for the change was that my family was not as rich as it used to be. My father was a friend of Diem's, but he fought with him politically because of Diem's family's control over Vietnam, so he had to quit the government. And we were not getting much income from farming because the Communists had been collecting the crops for the last twenty years! We still had a comfortable lifestyle out in the province, but there was not much extra money for education. After high school we kids had to pay for our education ourselves. In 1959 I returned to a different school in Da Lat and did my second *baccalauréat* there.

After I finished high school I went back to Saigon and attended the science faculty [of the public university there] for a year, studying basic science. You had to do that before you went to medical school. Then I entered medical school, attending from 1960 to 1966. In those days my medical school was the only one in Saigon. A few years later they opened a second one in Hue. Our professors were mostly Vietnamese, but all the instruction was in French. I did not have any money, so I had to let the army pay for my education. I was an officer during medical school, but I did not have to wear a uniform. I graduated as a doctor first lieutenant [*trung úy bác sĩ*] and went right into the army, serving as a battalion surgeon with an airborne division stationed in Saigon.

After two years of that I was sent to a medical company supporting a regiment, then to a hospital. In 1969 I became commander of a medical battalion. During those early years in the army I saw a lot of combat. I was at Khe Sanh, along the Ho Chi Minh Trail on the DMZ [demilitarized zone, a sort of no-man's land between North and South Vietnam], and at Dong Ha. I never had any PTSD [Post-Traumatic Stress Disorder] symptoms.[2] I think people who got PTSD were not strong enough in mind. They were not mentally prepared for war. I noticed the same thing in re-education camp. Some people could not control themselves. They went loose in their thinking.

You can endure suffering if you keep your mind focused on your goals. Otherwise you drown in pain. I learned this lesson from an early age. I was accustomed to suffer for something I wanted in the future, like getting an education so I could have a better life. Have you ever read *El Cid?* It is an example of the Corneillian personality, a strong personality that can overcome every difficulty. It became a role model for me. I read a lot of French seventeenth- and eighteenth-century literature about stoicism. Do you know the poem "The Death of the Wolf" ("La Mort du Loup") by de Vigny? I know it by heart. It says that you have to suffer and die without making a sound, just like the wolf who bears the pain of her own wound to protect her young. If she cries out, the hunter will hear her and come to get her little ones. This poem and my other reading of the stoics prepared me for suffering, for the war, and for the re-education camps. The Vietnamese people do not get much PTSD because they are used to suffering. They got their training from a war that lasted fifty years.

In 1973 I was sent to Cam Ranh Bay to open a 400-bed rehabilitation hospital to receive South Vietnamese prisoners being repatriated from North Vietnam after the Treaty of Paris in January 1973. But they never sent any prisoners, so it became a convalescent center for wounded soldiers. I was there for a year and a half. The general in charge of the medical units in the [South] Vietnamese army had told me that after doing that job for a few months he would send me to the United States for further training. All my friends had gone there. But when the time came for me to go he was not in charge anymore! So I was sent to the provincial hospital in Long Khanh near Bien Hoa. It was the very last place to surrender in 1975. My final rank in the army was major.

Looking back, how does he feel about his military service?

I did not benefit much from the army, but I served because of my love for my country. I believed that we were responsible for keeping our civilization alive. I hoped that in the future Vietnam would become a great nation. Our education gave us a broad perspective on the world. We trusted in the future of Vietnam after the war. We felt we could contain Communism and build a strong country. We were optimistic. After 1975 we lost our trust and hope in the future of Vietnam. We saw what was happening in Vietnam under the Communists. The country went backwards in terms of civilization. The way the Communists control people is archaic. They do it through their stomachs. They do not want them to be educated. They want to train them to serve the party, not the country. This is how the party does things; they control people's thinking. They do not care about educated people anymore. They want to use the illiterate people, telling them what they want them to hear. The illiterate group is very large. The party got them to take revenge on the educated people who had exploited them in the past.

What happened to him after the war ended?

The end of the war was a very chaotic time in Saigon. You could not go outside. Soldiers were shooting and looting. People had left everything they had in their haste to get out of the country. I spent the first couple of weeks after the war getting my family organized. There was only my father, mother, older sister, and me. Everyone else had left and was living in the United States or France. We were still living in Saigon. It was announced [on the radio and over loudspeakers] that all officers should present themselves for a four-week re-education program. You had to register or they came looking for you. They used kids to track you down. After the Communists took over Saigon the young people tried to get along with them and profit from the situation. The kids in my neighborhood knew that I was an officer. I had to present myself or they would have turned me in. They told us to come with enough clothing, food, and money for a month. The first night they took us to the re-education camp in a truck. The camp you went to depended on your rank. The majors and colonels were concentrated together. We did not know where we were going. The truck was covered and it was night. It was like taking pigs to the slaughter.

It may surprise non-Vietnamese readers, as it did me, that the former political prisoners I interviewed seemed to enter into and accept their incarceration in re-education camps without offering any overt resistance. One explanation for this behavior, offered by some of the former prisoners and their families, was that they initially believed what the Communists had told them about the purpose and the pro-jected length of the camps. They hoped that by cooperating over the course of a few days or weeks they would be taught about the new government and its policies, be reconciled with it, and then return home to get on with their lives and the job of rebuilding their coun-try.[3] Only those who had had extensive experiences with the Commu-nists in the North suspected that they might be being deceived. An-other explanation is the incredible speed and completeness of the South Vietnamese collapse at the end of the war, which neither side had anticipated.[4] As can be seen in several of the upcoming chapters ("The Engineer," p. 31, and "The Politician's Son," p. 201, for exam-ple), the rapidity and totality of South Vietnam's demise seems to have massively confused and demoralized many of South Vietnam's fight-ing men. A state of disbelief and near-paralysis appears to have over-come them as they retreated to their homes and waited to see what the victorious enemy would do. In addition, South Vietnam's final presi-dent, Duong Van Minh ("Big Minh"), as commander-in-chief of the armed forces, had ordered them to lay down their arms and to cooper-ate with the enemy. Supported by centuries of Confucian teaching to be compliant and obedient to authority, this directive may have been enough to discourage and undermine all but the most warlike. Had their final leader been a heroic, fight-to-the-death figure such as the Trung sisters or Tran Hung Dao,[5] and not a man who believed compromise with the Communists was both possible and necessary, a center of resistance might have coalesced and prompted more overt resistance to the re-education camps. Finally, the war had been very long and many on both sides were yearning for peace and home. After the departure of the Americans and the realization that they would not respond as they had promised to North Vietnamese violations of the Paris Accords, a spirit of quiet defeatism settled on many in the South. Most of the people I interviewed felt that the war was lost as soon as the treaty was signed. The final fifteen months of fighting led to what most seemed to see as a foregone conclusion. What purpose would further resistance serve?

We were taken to Xuan Loc, a camp left behind by the Red Cross. The Communists used all the old U.S. camps because they had barracks and empty buildings. They concentrated all the officers in one place so that they could control their families in Saigon. If something bad happened in Saigon, it would affect your status in the camp and vice versa. We got two bowls of rice a day. There was no meat, fish, or vegetables. During the first month we were not allowed any visitors. We spent our time digging holes, policing up the camp, and growing plants and vegetables. The "education" consisted of learning about their theories, about the history of the Communist Party, and that everything we in the South had done was wrong. It was a system of brainwashing. You had to use the new revolutionary vocabulary. The Communists were not literate. If they gave a speech they had to learn it by heart. They would speak nonstop for two hours. You had to stand there and listen to them make their pitch. They would talk and talk; pitchmen who knew nothing. They did it every day, and every day the person who spoke had no education.

Was there any torture or killing?

Yes, if you showed them you were against them. If they told you to do something and you did not do it, they would put you in a metal shipping container in an open area in the middle of the day when it was hottest. They would keep you there for a week. Some prisoners worked for them. But I saw that if they tortured you and you talked, they would just do it again or move you to another camp. So I learned to keep my mouth shut. They shot people who tried to escape from the camp. A couple of friends of mine tried to escape, and I never heard of them again.

How did the camp affect him? "If you were not prepared mentally you would do things you thought might get you released early, like be a spy. However, if your mind was strong you would think, 'If I become a spy I will only stay longer because they will know that they can use me and just move me around from one camp to the next.' " Does he ever dream of the camp?

No, not now. Sometimes I have dreams in which I feel I am still in Vietnam, even though I know I am not. I do not have any flashbacks.

I did not know when I would be released, but you had to keep your hope of being released alive so that you could survive. I would try to imagine a miracle happening, like the fall of Communism all over the world. I was never depressed for long. When I felt depressed I would think about how I was going to survive. I built myself up to get out of the depression. It is the only way to cope with a situation like that. You have to control your thinking and find a way to get your mind out of the situation you are in. For example, they once had a sixteen-year-old soldier standing guard over me. He acted like he was the boss and was very rude. I laughed to myself and told my friends about the stupidity of the situation. We swore to tell history about their stupidity.

The day you were released they called you over and you had to do all the paperwork to go home. In the camp you knew nothing, but the people in Saigon knew in advance the day that I was released. I do not know how they knew. They sent a car to pick me up and I went home. From there I was told to report to the Health Ministry. I know why I was released. Pham Van Dong [the Vietnamese premier at the time] had gone to France to ask for medical help for Vietnam. The French asked about all the doctors that were being held in re-education camps. As a condition of French aid they required the Vietnamese government to release all the doctors from the camps. So we got out early. I was only in for three years the first time. They sent me to work in a hospital in Saigon. There were no doctors in Saigon hospitals then. There were only nurses functioning as doctors, but with no medical training. They were party members who had been promoted to being doctors because they had some experience in the medical field working as nurses. As a doctor you worked under the supervision of laypeople—Communists—who knew nothing of medicine. After 1975 all the doctors looked so young! Even doctors who were fifteen years older than I was looked much younger than I did. That was because they did not have to bear any responsibility for their actions. Everything was a collective decision, not the decision of the individual doctor. You did not have to worry or care about your patients. If you were a patient, you got the kind of care that your status entitled you to. One person might be entitled to only seven medicines. A person with more status might be entitled to twenty. If you as a doctor prescribed a medicine that was not on your patient's list, they would not get it. If you were a higher-level party member, you were treated in a different, better-equipped hospital than other people. If you were the relative of a party member and the party member brought you to the hospital, it would help. They paid more attention to you.

All told I worked for about one year in an oncology hospital in Saigon. Then in 1979 I tried to escape by boat, but I got caught. I was put back in camp for four more years. This time it was a different camp, one in the Mekong Delta. In this second camp I was mixed in with laypeople, not just officers like before. There were a lot of boat people and kids. The other prisoners came and went, but I stayed. I had to work a lot harder than in the first camp. I was considered a possible leader of resistance or someone who might try to escape. I worked as a health care worker. There were no medicines, only herbs. In 1982 I was released again. I went back to Saigon. I was on probation, so I had to stay at home. I spent the time reading. Each week I had to stop in at an administrative office to tell them what I was doing. I had to write a report of my activities for them to review. Kids in the neighborhood tracked all my moves. The Communists wanted to know if I was doing anything that might harm the regime.

Then in 1984 my brother's family in France sponsored me and I was able to move there. I lived in Paris and worked as an intern in a hospital. I had a good life. I had had a French education [and so spoke French fluently], was able to get a job after only a month, and had enough money to rent an apartment in Paris.

In 1986 I came to the United States. I had a medical school classmate who had escaped from Vietnam in 1975 and was now practicing in the United States. She was divorced. I had been married before too. I had gotten married when I was thirty-three, had two sons, and then got divorced after three years of marriage. Both of my boys live in Paris. I do not have any contact with them anymore. Their mother's side of the family wanted to keep them for themselves. They were a wealthy family from Saigon with a city lifestyle and a very different way of thinking than people like me from central Vietnam. Anyway, my doctor friend and I had lived together in 1974 and 1975 and had planned to get married after she got back from doing some training in Europe. After 1975 we kept in touch through our families. We were separated for twelve years. She came to the United States, went to medical school here, and got a license through the ECFMG program [Educational Commission for Foreign Medical Graduates, a licensing exam for foreign medical graduates]. Then she did a residency in pediatrics. In 1986 she sponsored me to come to the United States.

We had a good life here. Her children knew me from before. They came to meet me at the airport when I arrived. She had a good practice. I worked as her office manager. I did insurance claims, Medicaid, and Medicare. I did not like the work, but she needed help. She was alone and had kids in college. We lived in a big house on a lake. In many ways I had it a lot easier than my friends who came here in 1975 did. They had to completely re-establish themselves. For me everything was settled. We had a big house and a Mercedes.

How did it affect him psychologically to work at a job so different from the one he had been trained to do?

27

I missed my life in Vietnam. There I had been a commander. I had a good living and a staff. Here I do not even work in the medical field. I could have gone off for further training and qualified to work as a doctor. There was a program in Connecticut where you went for three years and then were able to get a license. But my wife and I were concerned about the three-year separation and worried that even if I did the training I would not be able to practice. There had been a big scandal [involving some Vietnamese doctors] in 1984. About seventy doctors were accused of Medicare fraud. That had a big impact on the internship program for Vietnamese doctors.

My wife and I stayed together for ten years, then we got divorced. I had to get out of there. The problem was her children. She had three kids, two boys and a girl. She gave them everything. We never took a vacation because she had to work all the time to give them things. They lived at home and we had no privacy. I did not have a room of my own. I did not even have a table! Her children were so spoiled. They were even worse than American children are. They had independence but no responsibilities. Just to show you how spoiled they were, we once took her son to Las Vegas. On the way back he wanted to go rock climbing. We had to sit in the car in the hot sun for four hours waiting for him to climb his rock! Finally I decided, "I do not need this life." I had to cut off the relationship. If your mind is not happy, you are not happy. My friends said to me, "You must be crazy! You cannot practice medicine here. How are you going to make money?" But I was not worried. I had survived seven years in the re-education camps. Why then could I not survive in the United States? So I left her and moved here to [the city in which the interview was conducted] to live with my sister. I work for a company doing quality assurance and earn extra money doing some part-time interpreting.

My oldest sister is now sixty-six and lives in France. My oldest brother was sixty-three. He just died. He had coronary artery disease and died of a stroke during an operation on his heart. I am sixty-one years old. I also have a brother age fifty-five. He lives in France and works for the Ministry of Education. Then there is my sister who lives here. My older brother and I both got divorced after we left Vietnam. Our divorces were the result of psychological problems stemming from the war. We lost a lot of status after the war and had no money. Before we had had high positions, then we went to low positions. After the war it was hard to adjust because of the status changes. For example, my brother had been a lawyer in Vietnam. He was a member of the House of Representatives and chairman of [an important] committee. He was very rich and talented. In Vietnam he married one of his legal apprentices. After they left Vietnam they moved first to France and then to the United States. They got here in 1976 or 1977. He worked for a while in a grocery store, then as an accountant. They had no money and there were lots of fights. His wife did not support him. He was depressed because he had lost everything and did not have the energy to take the bar and become a lawyer again. He did not have enough time to build another life. Eventually he just gave up. I have a similar story. My wife was a doctor. I came here and we got married, but I got no support from her to get my medical license. So after ten years of marriage we got divorced.

Many of the former political prisoners are highly educated, well-trained men like Tuan who had already established themselves in professions or been high-ranking officers or officials prior to their incarceration in re-education camps. After their release, the new Communist regime in Vietnam made it impossible for them to regain their former professional and social standing. Many hoped that they would be able to resume their careers after their arrival in the United States. However, like so many refugees before them, they found numerous obstacles in their path. Most ended up in jobs far less prestigious than those they had enjoyed in Vietnam prior to 1975. Some were happy just to be alive and to have the opportunity to build a life here for their children. Others, like Tuan, experienced disappointment and resentment at not being able to practice their professions. Of the many challenges facing refugees, such declines in occupational and social status are among the most difficult and painful. They are especially burdensome for men in middle age, who may feel that they do not have the time and energy to restart their careers. It is also difficult if they come from countries with a strong patrilineal tradition, like Vietnam, in which it is expected that they will be the primary breadwinners for their families. In their new countries they find themselves unemployed or underemployed in unskilled or semiskilled occupations. As damaging as it may be for their self-esteem, they need to have their wives and sometimes their children work to generate enough income for their families to survive. Deprived of their former prestige and material well-being, such men may feel that they have lost face in the eyes of their families, who in turn may blame them for the catastrophe that has overtaken them all. As Tuan suggests, such psychological and material pressures undoubtedly contribute to the marital and familial tensions experienced by many refugees, including the former political prisoners.

As we concluded our interview I asked Tuan what lessons he had learned from his life experiences.

To explain my failure in the United States? That is what Buddhists call destiny. Or from a Catholic perspective, "Nothing happens without the consent of God." I miss my life in Vietnam. I was born in the wrong place at the wrong time. I have had to suffer along with the suffering of the Vietnamese nation. I had to give up everything I had and start anew. We Vietnamese believe that the suffering of this life is a consequence of your last life. What you do now affects your next life. It is hard for me to accept that you only get one chance at life on earth, then eternal life. I think you need more lives than just one to get it right. You probably need seven or eight. I agree with de Vigny's poem [about the wolf]. To cry or to pray is cowardly. You just have to suffer and continue to work.

3 / The Engineer

A former engineer and teacher, Kim is a reflective and emotional man who values education and the life of the spirit. After a career as an engineering officer in the Army of the Republic of Vietnam (ARVN), he was incarcerated in re-education camps for four years. He was released from the camps early because of severe health problems. After his release he was able to partially rebuild his career, but then suffered a number of health and financial setbacks before deciding to leave Vietnam in 1988. Now sixty-six years old and retired, Kim has recently earned a bachelor's degree in French literature and is working on his master's. He searches for simplicity, peace, and "the light [of humanity] in another's eye."

Kim lives far from the city center, in a transitional suburban neighborhood. Driving there through increasingly less affluent suburbs I was struck by how radically the lives of the former political prisoners and their families have changed. Once they were the elite of South Vietnamese society, sophisticated, well educated, and often rich. Imprisoned and impoverished after the war, many now struggle to get by in the United States and live among Americans who, at least superficially, appear far less sophisticated than they are. What do their neighbors know about these quiet, polite, and gracious people? Do they have any idea of the torments they have endured?

When I first met Kim he had just returned from school. He recently completed a bachelor's degree in French literature at a local public university and is now working on his master's degree. A photograph of

31

him receiving his degree is displayed in his living room along with silver-paper wall hangings celebrating "Baby's First Birthday." As we sat down to talk his one-year-old grandson ran across the room wearing a slightly askew baseball cap and carrying a baby bottle. Reaching his grandfather's knee he stood looking at me until his mother whisked him away.

Kim was born in 1933, the son of a wealthy landowning family in a province west of Saigon. He was the oldest of four children and had three younger siblings, a brother and two sisters. His parents farmed part of their land themselves and rented out the rest to tenant farmers, who repaid them with rice. Much of the land had been left to Kim's parents by his paternal and maternal grandparents. His parents subsequently enlarged their holdings by buying adjacent fields. Their primary crops were rice, coconuts, and bananas.

"Between 1943 and 1945 the Viet Minh grew increasingly powerful in our area. By the time I completed fifth grade [in 1945] they had taken over our province and it was no longer safe for people who owned land or were wealthy." What did the Viet Minh do to landowners and the wealthy? "It depended on how you got your wealth. If you got it by being cruel they killed you." What if you had simply worked hard? "It did not matter. They had a rule. Nobody is rich and nobody is poor. Everyone is equal." Kim's parents had heard stories of Viet Minh atrocities against landowners and decided to leave. They abandoned their house and lands and moved to a city in a neighboring province.

They took some money and jewelry with them. The people who had rented land from them were compassionate. They kept paying my parents for their land through an intermediary [even though they did not have to]. My parents had been kind to them, and now they were kind to my parents. My father had a younger sister who was married to a doctor. This doctor had two houses in the city. He let us live in one of them. We stayed there for ten years. Then, in 1955, after Vietnam had been divided by the Geneva Accords and the Communists had returned to the North, my parents moved back home. They repaired their land and began to farm it again. The people who rented land from them also continued to farm, but there was no fertilizer available. They could only raise enough rice to feed their own families and could not afford to pay the rent [to my parents].

During the ten years he and his family lived in the city Kim completed elementary school and enrolled in a French-language high school, where he completed eleventh grade and his first *baccalauréat*.

The teachers in my high school were French and Vietnamese and the instruction was all in French. I studied French from the second through the twelfth grade! There were a few French students, but most of us were Vietnamese. The school used to be named for a Frenchman who died in a war, I cannot remember which one, but in 1955 the French left and in 1957 the school was renamed for a Vietnamese poet, Nguyen Dinh Chieu.

In 1954, at the age of twenty-one, Kim moved to Saigon to complete the twelfth grade and his second *baccalauréat*. There he lived with an older cousin. I asked why it had taken him so long to complete his schooling. "The French system is different; there are a couple of extra years. Also I missed two years of school between 1944 and 1945 when there was so much fighting between the [Vichy] French, the Viet Minh, and the Japanese. In those days, with all the turmoil, it was hard to even find a place to live, so education did not seem all that important."

After high school Kim entered the École Supérieure des Trauvaux Publics to study civil engineering.

Sometimes I lived with my cousin, sometimes I chipped in and rented a place with other students who were my friends. I really liked engineering, but after two years of school I failed the test that would have allowed me to continue on with my studies. I thought I had passed it, but when the results were posted my name was not on the list of those who had passed. I was afraid to go home and tell my family the bad news. I was ashamed and thought I would lose face in the neighborhood. So I stayed in Saigon and got a job teaching in a private high school. After I had been teaching there for a couple of months my cousin told my family what had happened. They told my cousin to tell me that it was all right to come home and promised that they would not lecture or punish me.

I asked Kim why he had failed the exam.

There were a lot of reasons. First, I was not happy with my living situation. Sometimes I did not have enough money to pay the rent for a couple of months. My friends would get mad at me so I would move back in with my cousin. Then I would have a fight with him and have to move back in with my friends. There was a lot of conflict, and as a result I did not always do my homework or go to class. Second, I was lazy. Third, I wanted to have fun, so I went out a lot with my friends.

How did he get the teaching job?

In those days there were two public high schools in Saigon. There was one for boys, the Pétrus Ký High School, and one for girls, the Nữ Trung Học Gia Long. A lot of kids could not pass the qualifying exams for those schools and so there were a number of private high schools for kids whose parents could afford to send them there. I had had a lot of math. I showed my engineering certificate to the people at one of the private high schools, and they gave me a job. I did not have any other options. My family could not afford to keep sending me to school. I really liked teaching, and the students seemed to like me. In those days a teacher's salary was not very much. I was paid just enough to live on, but not enough to send money home to my family or to get married.

In 1961, when I was twenty-nine years old, Ngo Dinh Diem, president of the Republic of South Vietnam, issued a general mobilization order drafting all young men from eighteen to thirty-three years of age into the military. Everybody had to go: lawyers, doctors, everybody. If you had passed the first *baccalauréat* exam, you were sent to officer's candidate school in Thu Duc. They called us up for the school in groups of about a thousand each, starting with the oldest people first. My group was the thirteenth to enter. The training was divided into two parts. During the first period, which lasted three or four months, everybody received infantry training. Then during the second period you trained for the branch of the military in which you would be serving. I was put in the engineers because of my engineering background.

How did he feel about going into the military? "It was a totally different world from civilian life, and it seemed very strange. I did not know what to think. Some people I knew had finished the training school and then been killed in action [so it was pretty scary]."

After he completed his training Kim spent two years working as the adjutant, or S-1, of an engineer unit stationed in Hoc Mon, about 30 kilometers from Saigon. The unit spent most of its time building barracks and other buildings for the army. He was then sent to another engineer headquarters in Da Nang.

I was thirty-four years old at the time and still unmarried. Every evening after work I used to sit outside of my office looking out into the street and watching the students come and go. I was attracted to one of the girls I saw passing by every day. She was only seventeen at the time and in the twelfth grade. I liked her long dark hair and lovely white *áo dài* [the long flowing traditional dress worn by Vietnamese women]. I pursued that image for the next two years!

How did he arrange to meet her?

In my office there were about fifty soldiers and two hundred civilians. I asked the civilians about her and they told me what she was like. It sounded like a good match. The man in charge of the office, a major, went to her parents' home and talked with them about me. We kept visiting for the next couple of months, getting to know them. They were concerned because of the difference in our ages and because I did not have a family there in Da Nang. They wondered if I might already be married and have children. So they asked some of their friends to find out if money was being deducted from my paycheck and sent off to support a family. They also had some other people ask around about me in Saigon. After a few months they finally decided to let their daughter spend some time with me. At first we were not permitted to be alone together. We had to be with her older and younger sister. My wife's family was from Hue [the old imperial capital] and related to the nobility, so they were stricter and more traditional than many other families. Eventually, I got to go out alone with her. I used to borrow a jeep from work and take her to the movies, or to dinner, or to the ocean. Each time we went out I was careful to buy presents for her parents and her younger sisters and brother.

What attracted him to her? "I liked her long hair, her beauty, and her youth. I also liked her accent!" (The central Vietnamese accent is distinctly different from the accents of Saigon and Hanoi.)

Kim and his wife married in 1967. He was thirty-six years old and a first lieutenant of engineers in the ARVN. She was nineteen. "My father was paralyzed in one arm and one leg, and so my family was not able to come to the wedding. My commanding officer, the major who assisted me with the courtship, represented my family." Over the next two years the newly married couple had two children. By the time Kim was transferred to Da Lat in 1969, his wife was pregnant again. They stayed in Da Lat for four years and had three more children. "During those years all I wanted was peace and to be close to my wife and children. With five children, I guess it looks like I spent a lot of time with my wife, but I really did not. She and the children lived in a house on the base, not far from where I was living and working, but I was very busy and did not get to go home that often." Kim then added with a mischievous smile, "It seemed like every time I did go home I got a letter from her saying that she was pregnant again!"

In 1973 Kim was promoted to captain and transferred to the main engineer headquarters in Saigon. There he commanded the construction section that supported the army corps defending the nation's capital. I asked Kim if he had sensed that the South might lose the war. "No. In fact, two days before the Communist victory my commander told me that there was no way we could lose because we had support from the United States. You see I spent all of my time on base. I heard about our losing battles, but I never saw it. So when the war finally did end I was absolutely shocked!" I was struck by Kim's lack of awareness of the military situation during the last months of the war and by his and his commander's trust and faith in the United States. After America's massive intervention during the Vietnam (or Second Indochina) War, many South Vietnamese continued to believe until the very end that the Americans would return and rescue them.[1] The United States had, in fact, promised the South Vietnamese government as a condition of its acceptance of the Paris Accords of January 27, 1973, that it would respond to major North Vietnamese violations of the treaty. However, domestic political considerations in the United States, and especially the resignation of President Richard Nixon after Watergate, prevented the Americans from keeping that promise.[2]

Kim showed me an essay that he had written for one of his college classes describing his experiences on the last day of the war. In the essay, which I have edited with his permission, he describes his stunned surprise at learning of the fall of the Republic of South Vietnam on April 30, 1975.

During the last month of the war everyone was ordered to spend the night in their offices. In the last week of the month I got sick, and my commanding officer gave me permission to stay at home for a few days because my house was only about 300 feet away from the office. I stayed home, but I did not feel comfortable because there were explosions everywhere and rumors of public unrest. On April 30th I felt better and decided to return to work. When I arrived at my office around 11 A.M. there was nobody there! The only sound I heard was a song coming from a radio that someone had forgotten to turn off. Scattered about the office were books, papers, dishes, and food. People had clearly left in a hurry!

Suddenly from the radio I heard the warm, respectable, but discouraged sounding voice of President Duong Van Minh. He was saying, "The Communists have won. Vietnam belongs to them. All government employees, whether civilian or military, should not resist, but should wait for them to come and seize your offices. Then wait at home for them to decide our future." "That is enough!" I thought [turning off the radio]. I felt stupefied by the scene around me in the office and especially by what I had heard [President Minh say]. I never thought that the Communists would win in just a few days. Only a few weeks before they had been in the jungle and people in the capital were still living in peace!

I found myself sitting on the floor, my hands and head resting on a chair. I seemed to be unconscious for hours. I heard a bee buzzing around me. I was thinking about nothing. I had lost control—doing nothing, saying nothing, just sitting paralyzed and barely conscious—waiting. After coming to myself I had a bad headache. I was thirsty. I saw a bottle of Coca-Cola on the floor nearby, but I was so paralyzed by what I had heard and seen that I could not reach out and get the drink that might have revitalized me. Finally, I dragged myself home through the streets and lay down on the bed, covered with a blanket, not even looking at my wife and children. I just lay there thinking about how all this could have happened. Was it because of inflation or corruption in the government? Surely it must have had something to do with politics!

During the next few days of chaos and unrest people had to stay in their homes because there was no security. There were no office hours or markets and nobody was out walking around. The only people [on the streets] were skinny, strange-looking fellows in black clothes, canvas hats, and rubber sandals striding silently and curiously along with weapons in their hands [Viet Cong soldiers]. There were also looters everywhere. The Communists applied an iron discipline [to such people]—no trial, just an on-the-spot execution.

Staying at home waiting to see what was going to happen next was like a death sentence for me. After a few weeks the radio announced that all employees [of the old government], whether civilian or military, would be sent to re-education camps for ten to thirty days to learn about the Communist regime.

However, as it turned out, we were sent as prisoners, not as students, and we "learned" not for days, but for years and years.

Anyone with the rank of captain or below was told to bring enough clothing and supplies for ten days. Majors and above were told to bring clothing and supplies for a month. We were told to collect at locations near our homes. I was living in Saigon's District 10. We were told to go to a local school.

How did he feel when he arrived at the school?

I was happy. The country had been divided for a long time. Now it was united. I thought that I would be going to a re-education camp to learn about the new government and how to work with them.

They transported us from the school to the re-education camp in a large GMC truck. We were taken at night, and the truck was covered so that we did not know where we were going. By the time we arrived at the camp it was almost morning. The placed turned out to be an old civil engineer construction camp located 12 miles from Saigon. There were about one hundred of us, and when we arrived at the camp they divided us up into groups of ten. They gave us four or five days to settle in—to find a place to sleep, to get pots and pans, and to dig a well. Each day they gave us one day's ration of rice and salt. Then after we had been there for a few days they held a large meeting. High-ranking Communist officials came and talked to us. Their speech was divided into three parts. Part 1 was about our sin and guilt for preventing the Communists from doing their job of unifying the country. Part 2 was about re-education. The war was over. Now we had to be re-educated to understand the revolution. They told us, "Once you have been re-educated and have improved you get to go home." We had all assumed that we would only be there for ten to thirty days since they had told us to bring only enough clothing and supplies for that period of time. But during the lecture they pointed to the road behind us and told us to dig it up and plant tamarind trees [*cây me*] there for food. I thought to myself, "If we are only going to be here for ten to thirty days, why are they talking about planting tamarind trees for food? They take at least ten years to begin to grow fruit that you can eat."

Part 3 was a question period at the end of the speech. We were told we could ask questions about the speech, but not about anything else. One man asked the question everyone wanted to ask: "Captains and below are only supposed to be here for ten days. We have already been here for almost a week. When are we going to start learning about the new government and how long will it take?" They answered him: "We said captains and below should bring along enough clothing and supplies for ten days and majors and above should bring along enough clothing and supplies for thirty days. We never said that you would be in the camp for ten or thirty days." After we heard their answer we all felt really disappointed, hopeless, and confused. Why would the new government want to trick people with messages like that? When we left home we had told our families that we would only be gone for ten or thirty days. We had no idea that we would be gone any longer than that. Then I recalled what President Thieu had said about the Communists: "Do not listen to what they say, but look at what they do." The people who had resettled from the North to the South after 1954 had a much better idea of what the Communists were like. We in the South were very naive about what they were capable of doing.

After the first question there was a second: "If the announcement about ten or thirty days is not true, then how long will we be here?" They said, "When you have improved, then you will get to go home." Another person asked, "What if I have been here for two or three years and still have not made any improvement? How much longer will I have to stay?" They said, "You will stay until you have improved." Someone else asked, "You told us to grow tamarind trees for food. That will take at least ten years." They responded, "If you have not improved by the end of ten years, you can pick the fruit from the tamarind trees and make sweet and sour soup [*canh chua*]." As they spoke we began to realize that we were going to be there for a long time.

After that first meeting we all felt very disappointed in the new government. We had thought that re-education camp was to help us get to know the Communists and to repair the damage done by the war. But we learned that there was a barrier between the new government and the people. Now that I have been in the United States for a while and had the opportunity to think back on our situation and analyze it, I realize that what happened then was not unique to Vietnam. Things like that go on in other countries too. It is just what the winners do to the losers.

Kim's reflective analysis of the Communists' deceptive tactic of luring men into the camps by the promise of short stays and true re-education was much more philosophic than the reactions of most of the former political prisoners I interviewed. The majority of them were outraged by this lie, even after twenty-five years, and continued to chastise themselves for believing it. Doan Van Toai, a former Communist leader who became a prisoner himself after the fall of Saigon, echoes their outrage. "Once in jail, prisoners are taught that their behavior, attitude and 'good will' are the key factors in determining when they may be released—whatever crimes they may have committed. As a consequence, prisoners often obey the guards blindly, hoping for an early release. In fact, they never know when they may be released—or when their sentences may be extended."[3]

I asked Kim how he and his fellow prisoners had spent their days in the camp.

Some of us cooked, others went out into the fields and cultivated bindweed [*rau muống*]. We worked from the early morning until noon. Then we came home, took a shower, ate, relaxed a bit, and went back out to the fields to work. In the evening we came back, ate, and went to bed. A bell was rung every evening at about nine o'clock. That was the signal to get under the mosquito netting and go to sleep. If you were slow coming back from work or slow getting into bed, you had violated the camp policy. As a punishment the guards might tell you that the next day you would be sent to another camp. Then no one would ever see you again. That is just one example. Anything could happen. The prisoner always thought, "If I make one mistake I can be killed." A "mistake" might be trying to escape from the camp or writing a letter to your wife saying negative things about the new government.

Sometimes instead of going to work we were forced to attend a big meeting out in a rice field. The head Communists would come along and "re-educate" us. The prisoners had to stand up and confess their past wrongdoings. For example, there was a doctor in our group. He was the first person who volunteered to confess. He said, "I have no faults to confess. I worked in a hospital. I did whatever I could to take care of the patients. Some were badly injured and I had to amputate their legs. A lot of what I did was charity work." The Communists responded, "You have the biggest fault of all. If soldiers of the old government came in with problems, you would treat them. But if a Communist came in with a little scratch, you would amputate his leg!" Then they asked him again, "Do you have any faults?" He said, "If what you have said is true, then I am guilty. My fault is as the leaves in the forest. There are so many you cannot count them." He had no choice but to agree with them.

What happened if you did not agree with them?

There was one man in our group who had studied politics. He was very good at arguing with them. During one meeting he argued a lot. The next morning he was taken to another camp and never heard from again.

Let me give you another example. I was an engineer. I did not feel guilty. I had built roads, houses, and bridges for people to use and schools for soldiers' children. I was helping people out. But they said to me, "Your guilt is no less than the doctor's guilt. You built all those bridges and houses for soldiers to live in. You made it easier for them to fight against us. So you are guilty." Then they asked me, "Do you have a fault?" I said, "Yes, I admit that I have a fault." "How big is it?" "Just like the doctor's fault, like the leaves in the forest."

Meetings like that just made us more and more uncomfortable. We knew we had not done anything wrong, but we had to confess that we had! The atmosphere at those meetings was always very heavy and tense. Those of us in the camp were no longer Vietnamese citizens. That privilege had been taken away from us.

Aside from these re-education and confession lectures they left us pretty much alone. There were guards around the edge of the camp, but none inside.

42

When we went out to work in the fields or into the forest to cut down trees, the guards went along with us, but otherwise we were on our own. We did not get much to eat. There was no breakfast, only lunch and dinner. At each meal we got a bowl of rice and bindweed soup. I tried to eat very slowly to make the food last longer. When I was really hungry I drank water to try to quiet my hunger. I weighed 145 pounds when I entered the camp. Four years later when I left, I weighed 89 pounds.

During the first year in the camp I was not even allowed to write to my family to let them know where I was. After that they were permitted to come visit every two or three months and bring me 10 kilograms of supplies. They were not allowed to bring any rice, though. The guards were afraid that people would take the rice with them as [easily portable] supplies if they tried to escape. Some men did not get any visitors because they were from far away or their wives were dead or unable to come. Those who had visitors did not forget those who had none. We shared our supplies with them.

In the evenings after work I used to tell stories to my neighbors to entertain them. One day the man who slept next to me, a doctor, said, "Tonight we will have coffee and cookies while we listen to your stories. My wife is coming for a visit and she is going to bring them for us." That sounded great because it was during the wet monsoon and really cold at night. However, that evening after his visit the doctor did not come back to see me. I saw him sitting over in the corner of the room. "Why are you sitting over there so far away? Why do you look so sad?" He replied, "My wife came to visit today and brought a big bag, but all it contained was a blanket" [not the eagerly anticipated coffee and cookies]!

I asked Kim if he had ever seen people tortured or killed in the camp.

Personally, I did not see it, but I knew people were dying because some of the other prisoners had to bury them. They were not supposed to tell, but they did anyway. It is like that old story about the tailor who made clothes for the king. The king had big, pointy ears, but nobody knew it except the tailor. He was forbidden to tell his secret. He kept it inside for a long time, but it made him very uncomfortable. One day, to relieve the pressure, he dug a hole, stuck in his head, and yelled, "The king has big pointy ears!"

Did he make friends in the camp? "I made friends easily, but you had to be careful what you said to them. We did not talk about anything important, just [everyday] things like how our gardens were doing. We had to be careful because there were spies. We called them 'antennas.' " At this point, Kim interrupted himself.

I want to leave all that in the past. At the time I really did not like the spies, but now I realize that there are good and bad people everywhere. I have learned to accept [that some of my countrymen chose to become spies for the Communists]. When I was younger I read a book by a Frenchman, Sartre. It was about existentialism and it reminded me a lot of what Vietnam had gone through. It was about a poor third world country. Foreigners came and conquered it. The people fought the foreigners, got the country back, and tried to rebuild it, but they did not have any money. Foreign countries wanted to come in again and lend them money, but the country's leader would not permit it. Later you saw the leader sitting next to a bottle of whiskey. This meant that the foreigners had come in, taken over, and he had lost power to them.

Kim appeared to me to be working very hard to let go of the anger he had felt at the Communists and to move on to a new life focused on education and reflection. This ability to focus on the future and to leave behind the past was a characteristic that I noted in those former political prisoners who seemed most comfortable with their new lives in the United States. It was not that they had forgotten the past and their hatred of the Communists. Rather, they did not to want to dwell on things that they could not change or to focus energy on mourning for their past lives. On the other hand, those former prisoners who clung to the past appeared to me to be more bitter and unhappy. They

was being released, so there was no one there to help me. Fortunately, I had a little money saved up that a family member had given me secretly during a visit. I used it to pay for transportation home. At the gate of the camp I was able to hire a horse-drawn cart [*xe ngựa*] to take me out to the main street of the town. There I caught a bus into Saigon. From the bus station I took a *cyclo* home. When my children saw me they ran out, crying and calling to me "*Ba, Ba,*" [Father, Father]. By then the oldest was eleven and the youngest was seven. They ran up and hugged me so much that I could not get out of the *cyclo*. When I finally did get out and went into my house I saw that the only furniture left was the dinner table, a few chairs, two beds, and a clothes cupboard. Everything else had been sold, including the marble and tile from the floors! I asked the children where their mother was. They said that she was out selling things in the streets. She left early every morning and did not return until late at night. I looked at the children. They were dirty and their hair was long and unkempt. Their clothes were old. When I went out to the kitchen I noticed that it was cold, as if nothing had been cooked recently. I asked the children about it. They said that they did not usually have any breakfast. That was the reason the kitchen was cold when I arrived. In the afternoon before school they cooked lunch—rice and bindweed. They only went to school in the afternoon. When they got home from school they cooked rice and waited until their mother got home with the rest of the dinner. She bought whatever she could afford based on how much she had earned that day. By that time— 1979, four years after my incarceration—they had used up all of their savings. Other prisoners' families were in the same situation. They too had run out of savings and had to sell all their possessions to survive.

The children asked if I would like to go and see Mom. When I told them that I would, they said that she was out selling things with her older brother and his wife. Her brother had been a captain in the infantry and had also been to a re-education camp. I sent all of the children to school except for the oldest so that he could show me where his mother was. We hired a *cyclo* and rode out from Saigon to Gia Dinh, about five miles. She was at the market in an area called Ba Chieu. That part of town was considered a very spiritual place because a long-ago governor, Le Van Duyet, had lived there. He was very fair and helped the people. He believed in equality, fairness, and justice. After he died the people venerated him there.

When we got to the market my son told the *cyclo* driver to stop, got out, and went looking for her. When he saw her he cried out, "Mom, Dad is here!" When she heard him she looked up and saw me. She was measuring out some rice for a customer and was so startled to see me that she spilled it all over the place. She pulled me over to where she was standing and introduced me to the women next to her, who also had husbands in the re-education camps. I asked her about her business: What was she selling? She said that it was a very simple strategy. There was another market five or so miles away. She bought things wherever the price was cheaper and then sold them at the other market. That way she made a small profit just by buying and reselling. If she had a good day, she made enough money to buy dinner and to save a little. If she had a bad day, she had to use her small savings to buy food. My wife was so busy working that she had no time to educate or discipline the children. She turned that responsibility over to the school. Evenings when she arrived home she was so tired that it was all she could do to eat and go to bed.

I asked Kim to tell me about his readjustment to life after the re-education camp.

The first day home I worried about security. I had to get my release certificate from the re-education camp signed at the ward security office, the ward administrative office, and the city security office. For the first month after I got home I also had to attend meetings in my neighborhood every evening. They were just like the meetings in the camp. There were fifteen to twenty of my neighbors present and I had to stand up and confess. Each time I did I had to begin my remarks by saying, "I am grateful to the Communists." After a month of this I got a letter saying that I was a Vietnamese citizen again. It was very important to have that letter signed by the local police. The idea was that if you committed a serious crime, they would take [the letter and your citizenship] away again.

After I had been home for a few months I bumped into a friend of mine, a doctor, when I was downtown. When he saw me he said, "You look like a walking skeleton! I am taking you to the hospital." I was admitted there for a few months. I gradually gained weight, got better, and felt happier. Before that I had lost my smile.

The people at the ward security office did not like having us in their area. Saigon had a big population problem after the war, and they wanted us to leave the city and go back to our home village [nhà quê] or to the New Economic Zones. [These were sparsely populated, undeveloped areas where the Communist government tried to resettle people it considered to be surplus population or undesirables, like the former political prisoners or the Amerasians.] They promised people that if they went to the New Economic Zones they would have houses already built for them and schools for their children, but when people got there they found that nothing had been prepared. Some could not endure the very difficult conditions there and returned to the city, but by the time they got back their houses had been sold and they had to live on the street. There were seven of us in the family, so I really had to think matters through carefully. The security people came to our house every day and told us that we had to go. We did not trust their promises about the New Economic Zones, but we also could not stay where we were. Fortunately, I met a friend I had known in the army. He introduced me to the people at a construction engineering company. Since I had experience and had worked with some of them before, they offered me a job as a technical cadre. The money was not very good—not even enough to pay for public transportation to work—but having an official job and permission to work meant that we could stay living where we were. Another benefit was that we got a coupon to buy rice at a government discount. The company was half privately owned and half government owned. I rode my bike to work each day to save money. My initial duties were to supervise a sawmill where they made furniture and doors for use by another part of the company that built homes.

I asked Kim whether, after his four-year absence, he and his wife had experienced any difficulty adjusting to being back together again.

When we saw each other our love and shared memories were still there. We also recognized our shared concern for our children's lives and their future. This made our love and our bond even stronger. We shared the same ideals and expectations and the love for our children. This made me love her even more. It was not the strong physical love of our early marriage, but a finer, more compassionate love based on the children and our shared experiences together.

Did his experiences in the camp change him as a person?

Yes, definitely. I was a more difficult personality. I had lost hope in the future and for our children's future. At the time I did not notice the difference. Now looking back twenty years later I can see it. I had lost hope in our children's future because I could not help them with their education. Education in those days had so much to do with politics. For example, in school they would be given an arithmetic problem in which they were asked, "If a revolutionary soldier shoots three soldiers from the old regime and five Americans, how many people has he killed?" Also, the security people in our area kept coming and searching my home, so I really did not have any privacy. That was very hard to take.

I asked Kim's wife if she had noticed any changes in him as a result of the re-education camp. "He changed a lot. I first visited him after he had been in the camp for a year. I went with his younger sister. At first I did not recognize him because he had lost so much weight. I wanted to cry, but the guards said that if I did, they would not let me see him, so I had to hold back my tears." Did she notice any changes in his personality after he returned home from the camp? "I was too busy working to notice. I got up every morning at 5 A.M. and came home late. I did not spend much time with him. I focused entirely on making money while he cared for the children."

Kim did well at his job with the construction company and gradually secured positions of responsibility in which he could make more money. He began to work on a contract basis, keeping a portion of the profit on jobs he supervised. He made enough money so that his wife was able to stop working and stay at home, markedly improving conditions within the family. In 1983 or 1984 Kim had a contract to build the largest theater in Saigon. The contract stipulated that he would receive 80 percent of the profits. From his share he would have to pay the workers he hired, but the rest he could keep for himself. Presented with this opportunity to make a lot of money Kim worked on the project day and night. Unfortunately, the added stress was too much for his heart, and one day he collapsed at the job site. He was admitted to a hospital and stayed there for two months. Upon discharge the doctors told him that he could not return to work.

Despite his health, however, Kim could not afford to sit idly at home. "My wife had to return to work, and I set up a private business. I drew up blueprints for people who wanted to build houses. Then I hired the workers, built the house, and kept the profits." During this period his business was so busy that Kim's children had to quit school to help out. They attended private school in the evening so that they could continue with their studies. This was an expensive alternative to regular schooling, but Kim needed their assistance.

Kim and his family's roller-coaster fortunes in Saigon continued through the 1980s.

We put a lot of money into an investment scheme called a savings investment. We gave the company all of our savings, 3 million *đồng* [14,000 Vietnamese *đồng* at that time equaled approximately U.S.$1]. The company was to invest the money in making perfume and then pay us interest each month. We were supposed to get 15 percent interest in the first month, then 10 percent in succeeding months. We did it for three months, but then the government arrested the guy in charge of the scheme and kept all the money, not returning any to the investors. We lost everything. I think the guy had a connection with the government—he had been a security officer—and it is possible that it was just a scam for the government to get our money.

When did he decide to try to leave Vietnam?

Between 1983 and 1986 a lot of people were escaping by boat. You had to pay the person in charge of the escape one-third of the money up front and two-thirds after you got there. There were seven of us [in the family], and we did not have enough money for all of us to escape. My entire extended family chipped in so that I would have enough money for a down payment [to permit me to escape alone]. We gave the money to the person in charge. He took it, but the day before we were supposed to leave we learned that he was planning to leave without me. My wife went over to his house and tried to get the down payment back. He refused. She said, "If you do not give it to me, I will commit suicide right here in front of you." They gave the money back to avoid a scene.

I asked Kim's wife whether she really would have committed suicide. "Yes. I had borrowed all that money from our relatives. If my husband had been able to escape, I would have had some hope of repaying it. That was my only hope. I was desperate and would have done it."

Kim continued,

In 1987 I read in the newspaper about a program for people who had been officers or officials in the old government and had been in re-education camps for at least three years. It was called the "H.O. Program," and it allowed former officers and their families to go to the United States. At first I was afraid that it might be a trap and did not do anything about it until 1988. Then we began talking to other people who had signed up and asked them if anything bad had happened to them. When they said no, we decided to sign up too.

I asked what had prompted them to leave Vietnam.

Both of my older sons were at the age when they were eligible for the draft, but neither one had signed up. One night, at about 2 A.M. the police came to our house. My younger son was out, but they arrested my older son for not registering and took him to a camp in Loc Ninh. They sent young people there for discipline if they were caught doing things like using drugs or engaging in prostitution. When my wife got a note from the place saying that my son was there, she went to the ward administrative office to appeal because our son was not like that—he worked hard and went to school. She went to the office early in the morning and waited until late at night for a couple of weeks before the ward head would see her. He told her that he could not help. She left his office in tears. Out in the courtyard she met a man who had just succeeded in having his son released from the camp. He told her to try again, but this time to offer a bribe. She went back in and offered the bribe, but the ward head turned her down again. Then she said, "If you do not let him go, I will go downtown and sue you." He told her to come back tomorrow. The next day she returned and offered the bribe and he agreed to let my son go. She rode down to Loc Ninh in a hired car and from there rode a bicycle out into the jungle to the camp. Partway there a truck driver took pity on her and gave her a ride. When they got to the camp she asked him to wait. She went in and gave the guards gifts. After they brought my son out he and she got back on the truck. It was loaded with logs and people. On the way back it tipped over. Everyone fell off. Several people got hurt, but my wife and son just got a few scratches. It was my son's arrest and imprisonment in the camp that gave us the courage to apply for the H.O. Program.

I went to sign up in 1988. The paperwork was sent to Thailand, approved, and then the whole family had to have physical exams. There was a rumor going around that if a family had more than four members—we had seven— one of them would be found to have a disease and the whole family would be turned down. The Vietnamese doctors who did the exams told me that I had tuberculosis and denied our application. I knew that I did not have tuberculosis, so I bribed the doctors. They took the money, but it still took another six months before we were accepted. Then the U.S. Embassy representatives from Thailand interviewed us. They asked why we wanted to go to the United States. If you wanted to go for political reasons you were rejected. We left Vietnam on the 2nd of February, 1993, and arrived in the United States on the same day.

Kim explained that he has a lot of trouble remembering the details of his life between 1988 and 1993, such as the proper sequence of events in his application for the H.O. Program. "First there was the fall of Saigon. Then there was the re-education camp. After I got out of camp I felt disappointed and depressed about Vietnamese society. I saw no future for my children. Then my escape plan did not work. I lost hope and developed memory problems. I had all the symptoms of depression—lack of sleep, energy, concentration, and appetite." I asked if he had ever considered suicide. "No, mainly because of the children. I did not want to surrender and give up all hope."

Asked how he had felt about leaving Vietnam, Kim replied,

Even when I was sitting on the airplane I still could not believe that I was really going because of all that had happened before. It was only when I saw the ocean that I began to believe that I was really leaving. It was similar to the feeling I had when I left the re-education camp, a sense of freedom and relief. I had no restrictions. I could do what I liked. I felt free and light. There was nothing to limit me. I really liked the feeling. I did not even remember to eat until my wife reminded me. On the airplane my children were also in a dreamy state. In Vietnam they had little hope of getting an education. I was in a re-education camp. There was no real family life and no discipline. They had a lot of self-pity. Now they had hope. In Vietnam, even if they went to college they would have to be physical laborers. In the United States your job is equivalent to your education.

After our arrival here each member of the family got $250. The refugee center had an apartment ready for us. They gave us six months of English lessons and helped us get Social Security, Medicare, and a green card. The children learned English quickly. Because of my age and depressed mental state, I learned more slowly.

Did the reality of life in the United States disappoint him?

No. It was really sad to leave my ancestors and relatives, but here I get more educational and career opportunities for my children. I get the opportunity to educate myself and to enjoy my retirement. I do not have to go to meetings and lectures like I did in Vietnam. I do get homesick. I miss my neighbors, my relatives, and my country. The longer I live in a free country with a high standard of living, the more I feel compassion for the people of Vietnam who do not have these things.

I asked Kim about his health. "My health is good, but I am weak because of my age. I am much better than I was in Vietnam, where there is usually no medicine and when there is you do not know which medicine is real and which is not." Kim brought out his medicines and showed them to me, laying out an impressive array of bottles on the coffee table. "Taking all these medicines helps my health. Sometimes I forget to take all of them and then I worry. But if I forget that I forgot I am fine!" Is he still depressed? "No, I have not been really depressed since I got here. Of course, nothing is perfect."

How did Kim's absence in the re-education camp affect his children?

A lot. My wife had to work while I was in the camp. The children did not get any discipline from their parents. They went to school, but the rest of the time they were at home with no supervision. They learned from the street. They started using bad language, their hair was long, they were messy and dirty, and they went around barefoot. Even at school they did not get much discipline. The teachers were so poor that they had to sell candy and snacks to the students. They would not admit publicly that they were doing it because that would have been bad for their reputation. There are class issues. Teachers are from a different class than people who sell candy on the street. In the evening they had to take extra jobs as *cyclo* drivers. They were very stressed out, so even in school the children did not get proper discipline.

Now that he is in the United States does he ever have flashbacks to life in the camp? "I can never forget the camp experiences. Sometimes I think about when I had to cut down a tree with a dull knife. It was hard even for very strong people and especially for me because I had a weak heart. The guards told us, 'The revolutionaries in the jungle had no sharp knives, but they could cut down trees. Why are you not able to do it?' "

I asked Kim what lessons others might learn from his life. He reflected a long time before answering and replied thoughtfully and deliberately.

The Communists had two objectives. The first was to get the foreigners out. They achieved that. The second was to rebuild the country, exploiting the natural resources of Vietnam and strengthening its agriculture. They did not achieve that objective. In the camp they kept saying that the old government had prevented them from helping the people. But now they are preventing themselves from doing it. They did not rebuild the country; they destroyed it. They turned their backs on the people. They used manipulation and took bribes. [Corruption] went from the top to the bottom. There was no discipline, no justice, and no law. Even though Vietnam is overpopulated, it is next to China, and that makes it a weak country. There are fifteen Chinese for every Vietnamese. Vietnam needs to recognize this and find a way to unite with the rest of the world, not stand on its own. There is no utopia. Even people in the same family fight with one another. Vietnam needs to find a way to work in the world.

As an extension of what he had just told me, Kim handed me another essay he had written. In it he reflects on his life and tries to distill a philosophy for his remaining years. The essay is titled, "In God We Trust."

After grade school, high school, and college, I went to work. Because of the war against the Communists I had to join the army and do my duty. We fought side by side with the armies of brother countries to resist the Communists. When the Communists occupied South Vietnam they said that we were traitors and had to go to prison. There we were to learn about Communism, [which they referred to as] "the best regime in the world." When I got out of prison and went home I found that there was no furniture left. My family had sold it all because they were unemployed. So I went to work. I did any job I could find so that I could help to support my family. Then we came to the United States as refugees. One day, riding on a bus here, I was looking idly at a one-dollar bill. Suddenly, something caught my attention. It was the wide-open eye on top of the pyramid. The words "In God We Trust" flashed like beams of sunlight through my mind. It sounded so good and natural that it brought tears to my eyes. I distinctly remember two big tears rolling down my cheeks and falling onto my hands. To quote Henry Miller, "I felt safe again among human beings."

In the United States we never forget out native country, our little homes, our beloved relatives. We remember the ways to the market and to our offices. We never forget the wind that blew in the summer, the rains that knocked on the roof at night, or the dog barking at the moon. . . . The world belongs to promising young people, not to old men like me. My children have their plans. They are studying. In the future they will contribute to the development of our country. That is my only aspiration for them. My task is to simplify things for myself. I need peace and solitude and idleness. . . . Looking back on the past when I used to go out into society, I never knew a moment of peace and possessed not an ounce of faith—not in the corrupt Republican regime and not in the exhausted Communist regime. . . . When I saw that eye on the dollar bill I suddenly knew. I had to simplify things, to simplify my life. I do not travel any more. I need peace and idleness. The important thing is a warm handclasp and the light in a person's eye—especially the light in the eye. In God We Trust."

Three weeks after my last interview with Kim he died suddenly of an apparent heart attack. He passed away while working in the university library on a paper for his master's degree. When I heard the news of his death I felt immensely sad, as though I had lost a good friend. I thought of all his years of struggle, sacrifice, and suffering and searched for a meaning in them to somehow justify his loss. Kim seemed to me to be trying to forgive those who had tormented him in the past, to relinquish his bitterness and anger, and to move on to a simpler, more peaceful life. Did he gain anything from all those years of torment, war, re-education camps, poverty, discrimination, and loss of status and country? Perhaps he gained a sense of what is really important in life: to spend time with those we love; to participate in activities for the joy we gain, not for the profit we accumulate; and to appreciate one another's humanity. Or as Kim might have put it, "to look for the light in another person's eye."

4 / The Tailor

*B*ich, *a former colonel and commander of the Black Pajama Cadres, a South Vietnamese army unit that infiltrated villages to give early warning of Viet Cong (VC) attacks, spent twenty-four years as an officer in the Army of the Republic of Vietnam (ARVN) and the following thirteen years as a prisoner in re-education camps. He credits his survival to an independent spirit, a refusal to dwell on the past, and a lifetime practice of keeping busy. He taught himself to be a tailor in the camps, volunteering to repair the clothing of his fellow prisoners in his spare time "to remain sane." Two years after his release Bich came to the United States, where he continues to support his family as a tailor, working two and sometimes three jobs at a time so that his children can attend college and graduate school. In his limited spare time he undertakes volunteer activities, editing a Vietnamese community newsletter and teaching new immigrants and refugees how to operate computers and complete their income tax forms.*

I have known Bich for almost ten years. We worked together previously on a project to develop a mental health center for Vietnamese children and their families, and he later served on the center's advisory board. He is a slender, handsome man with a graying goatee. His active, energetic manner belies his age, which he says is "sixty-nine plus." I have always admired his quiet dignity and straightforward, yet courteous manner. During our interviews we sat together on a couch in the small front room of his home. The room is decorated with red and gold placards inscribed with messages in Chinese and Vietnamese and also contains the family's altar for ancestor veneration.

Bich was born in a province located four to five hundred kilometers south of Saigon. His parents' families were rice farmers who owned just enough land to support themselves.

I was the oldest son and had a younger sister and brother. My sister now lives with her husband in California. They are retired and live in Section 8 housing on Social Security. My brother is in Saigon and receives support from his children here in the United States. I keep in touch with both of them by e-mail. My father was a teacher and ran a private school in Saigon. He did not make enough money for us to live with him, so we lived in a provincial town. In 1947 the Viet Minh took over our province. Shortly thereafter my mother died, probably of hepatitis C. I was close to her and felt really depressed when she died, but since my father was in Saigon I had to take care of my brother and sister even though I was only about twelve or thirteen. We had food in reserve and were on our own for the next three or four months. I had a very independent life! We then moved to Saigon with my father and I entered the Pétrus Ký High School. I learned almost everything I know in high school—radio and television repair, mechanics, construction, typing, and shorthand. The high school was open for only half of each day, so I went to a commercial school in the afternoons. I did not want to be doing nothing! Ever since I was very young I have always liked being busy. When I asked my father for money to pay for the [extra] courses he was happy to give it to me. He was always busy with school.

In 1951 I was drafted into the military. The French had created a Vietnamese army to help them fight the Viet Minh. They drafted our entire class. I was in my last year of secondary school. I had finished the Baccalauréat I, but not the Baccalauréat II. They sent me for training at the officers school in Thu Duc. I planned to go back to school after two years in the military, but they never let me out!

How did he feel about going into the army?

Everyone had to go. I figured, "Why not go first, then come back in two years?" I did not like the army, but there was no way out. I did everything I was supposed to do, so I kept being promoted. I did all I could to accomplish my jobs, but I was not ambitious for promotion. I wanted out. After graduation [from officers training school] I was sent to France to become a signal corps officer. On my return I was sent to North Vietnam. One year later the Battle of Dien Bien Phu took place [the French defeat there led to their withdrawal from Vietnam]. I did not fight there. I was a first lieutenant in a mobile group of regimental size that consisted of infantry, artillery, and tanks. In 1964, when Vietnam was partitioned at the 17th parallel [by the Geneva Accords], my unit was moved to South Vietnam. We continued to move around a lot. I became a signal corps company commander, a battalion commander, and a signal corps officer in an infantry division. Later I held a similar position in II Corps Headquarters at Pleiku.[1] Finally, in 1954, I became chief signal officer for the entire army. I was a "bird colonel." Then I was sent to Fort Leavenworth for Command and General Staff College and after that to Fort Bragg for counterinsurgency training. When I returned to Vietnam in 1966 I was put on detached service with the government. I became director of the rural cadres program [the Black Pajama Cadres] and ended up the commander of the cadre training center at Vung Tau. I stayed there until the end of the war.

What did the rural cadres do?

We put the cadres into hamlets and villages where there was a possibility of the Viet Cong coming at night. They lived with and helped the people. It is like what I am doing here [in the United States] now. I organize computer classes, get free shots for low-income people, and help people fill out their income tax. I help others like I did then—"winning the hearts and minds of the people."

Was the rural cadre program successful?

Most people in Vietnam live in rural areas. The cadres lived with them and tried to wipe out the Viet Cong's base of support. We had one cadre for every nine hundred people. The cadres worked as a team outside of the regular [armed] forces. When they got information about the V C's infrastructure they would notify the Phoenix Program [a C I A-initiated program to "neutralize" the infrastructure of the Communists in South Vietnam] and they would go get them, mounting an ambush or conducting an operation. The cadres were very unpopular with the V C. That is why they kept me [in re-education camps] so long.

How did Bich meet his wife?

I met her in Hue. I was a captain then. I saw her coming out of school and followed her home. I did not court her; I courted her father. He was a government employee. I met him at his office. We became friends and he invited me home. I went there day after day, month after month. It took over a year. She knew what I was doing. Finally, I told her father the truth and asked to marry his daughter. My father's family was in Saigon. Traditionally, parents discuss the marriage of their children. In my case I had to set everything up myself. I wrote a letter to my father in Saigon, described the situation, gave him her father's address, and asked my father to write a letter to him. Then they exchanged letters. We got married in 1956. I was almost thirty, and she was almost twenty. Our first child was born nine months later. We had six children in all, three boys and three girls. My wife and my family had to follow me around most of the time [I was in the army]. She did not like it, but she did not have any choice. We lived in military housing initially. Later we got a house in Saigon.

What was he doing during the last days of the war?

The cadre training center was being used as a collecting point for refugees fleeing from central Vietnam in front of the North Vietnamese Army. My job was to care for the refugees. The center was built for 10,000 students, but we had over 50,000 refugees living there in tents. I could have left [Vietnam] with my family. They had been living in Saigon, but during the last month of the war they came to stay with me. I told myself that if I fled I would not know how people would care for me [as a refugee]. There [at the cadre training center] I had the power to care for myself. So I stayed until the last minute. On the last day the v c came in at the back of the center. My house was at the front, but by then there was no more transportation, so I hired a sampan to take my family and me back to Saigon on the Saigon River. I stayed there with my family until they called me up to the re-education camp.

How did he feel at the end of the war? "Depressed, but looking at the refugees I felt luckier than them. I had lost everything and thought that I would be restarting my life again from zero. Sometimes I was afraid that they would kill me because I was the head of the rural cadres, and they had found the v c and killed them." Were you surprised that the South lost the war? "No, but I was surprised by how quick it was. I realized the South would lose when the United States began to withdraw. Some people blame the U.S. government for letting down the Vietnamese government with no military support. I do not feel that way. I think that there was something wrong at the top level of the Vietnamese government, but I do not know what it was."

When Saigon fell to the North Vietnamese Army and v c on April 30, 1975, Bich, as former head of the Black Pajama Cadres, was, as he put it, one of their "number one enemies." After reporting for re-education Bich was held in a temporary camp near Saigon and then flown on a captured C-130, along with other high-ranking South Vietnamese officers, to North Vietnam. There he was to serve thirteen years as an inmate of several re-education camps.

Bich and his fellow prisoners were taken to a remote part of North Vietnam near the Chinese border. There they were forced to cut trees in the mountains and build their own prison camp. They had to pay for their scant rations and minimal clothing with hard labor. They did not know how long they would be imprisoned. For the first three years of his time in the camps Bich was not permitted to have contact with his family or to have any knowledge of the outside world. All he did was work, sleep, and struggle to survive and remain sane. There were 1,500 prisoners in the camp. Each month, the prisoners were rotated from building to building, and every year or two, to other camps. This continuous rotation, and the presence of many informers, kept the prisoners isolated from one another, afraid to share their innermost thoughts and feelings. As Bich described it, "Their intention was to brainwash you. The weapon they used was food, minimal rice and salt, and meat or fish only three times a year. Their goal was for you to talk and think the way they did. There was no torture or killing, but many people died of disease or went crazy. We had to work very hard. Instead of using buffalo to plow the fields, they used people."

Bich described the strategies he developed to survive.

In the first thirty days after my capture, I was very upset and angry because of our defeat. I thought only of how to fight back. My anger made me sick. I could not sleep or eat. I lost weight. I knew that if I did not do something, I would go crazy. So I tried to think of other things. I imagined ways I would avenge myself on them if I were in charge. I developed a breathing technique based on yoga, trying to increase the amount of oxygen I took in. It really helped, physically and mentally. Before using it I had to stop every 10 meters or so to rest when I carried heavy loads. With it I could go on all day. I also taught myself a trade. I learned to be a tailor. No one showed me; I just figured it out. I became the tailor for all the other prisoners in the camp. I took the threads from old shirts and used them to stitch up people's clothes and sew on buttons.

[My strategy for survival in the camps was] do not talk, do not hear, do not see, do not read. Whatever they said went in one ear and out the other. I did not let them brainwash me. They tried to brainwash everyone with the radio, magazines, newspapers, and meetings. I tried to avoid them. It worked!

Was he ever afraid in the camps? "I was afraid for the first two or three months. After that I developed my own tactics—'Do not think, try to do something'—like becoming the tailor for the whole camp. I did not do it for money. I did it to remain sane. My breathing exercises helped too." How did he feel in the camps? "I tried to avoid feeling. I tried to have a blank mind and not think." Did his experiences in the re-education camp change him?

No, I am still myself. There was no change at all. I struggled to stay myself. That kept me healthy. If I stop working, stop doing things, my life will be shortened. That is why I keep the same pace and do not slow down. I have nine years to go on this home to pay it off. It is funny. During the first three years I was here I had nine cars. The first one cost $500. After a few months I sold it and bought a $700 car. Then a $900 car, and so on. Finally, I got a brand new car. It is already paid off! I will not need another for at least ten years. My children help sometimes, but they have children and their own problems. In Vietnam we say that water flows down, not backward [meaning that help flows from parents to children, not the other way around].

What led to Bich's release from the re-education camp?

I was there for thirteen years, 1975 to 1988. Twelve of those years were in the North. Without the intervention of the U.S. government, I would have died there. An American general [John Vessey] came to Hanoi and set up some kind of exchange. An official from the [Vietnamese] State Department in Hanoi came and interviewed me. I was playing a game. [When he asked questions] I held my hand to my ear and asked, "What did you say?" I gained time to think of the correct answer. If they asked, "Are you well treated?" I would say, "I am not hungry." Finally, [the camp officials] asked, "Do you want to go home?" I said, "Look at me. I have a stomach disease." I had weighed 125 pounds when I went in, but by then I weighed only 85 pounds. I said, "I do not want to go home. If I go home, I will be a burden for my family. I will only survive another month. My family will have to pay to bury me. If I stay here, the camp will bury me."

Bich laughed, "So they decided to release me."

How did Bich feel about returning to his family after so many years?

It was a little strange. Initially, the children did not recognize me because I was so thin. I had trouble walking because of a nutrition problem. I was very weak. All but the youngest [child] had visited me in North Vietnam with my wife. For the first two years we were not even allowed to receive mail from our families, and for the first three years we could not receive visits. After that they could visit officially every six months, but my wife could not afford to come that often. She came every year or two.

How did she support herself during his absence? "She is bright and resourceful. She bought things and then resold them at a small profit. She was able to keep our house, although the government took it when we came here. When I got home she bought me a sewing machine. I worked as a tailor. My hobby in the camp became my main occupation at home."

What was it like in Vietnam after he was released?

It was chaos. The social organization [of the country] was completely different. The police were everywhere. People did whatever they could to survive. I stayed home and worked as a tailor. The children went to work for companies as accountants, clerks, and typists. They could not go to the university because of my status [in the old government and as a former prisoner], but they did not have any trouble finding jobs.

How did Bich get to the United States?

When I went home [from the re-education camps] there was a policeman across the street from my house every day. Whenever I opened the door he would be standing there. Every month a policeman came from Hanoi to see if I was still alive and to ask who came to visit and where I went. They did not believe me when I said that I just stayed at home. In 1990 he asked me, "Do you want to go to the United States?" I said, "No, I am too old. I have no occupation. I do not know how to support myself." I told him, "I will only go if the [Vietnamese] government pushes me out." [The Vietnamese government may have initiated his referral to the H.O. Program because it viewed him as a person who was potentially dangerous to the regime.] I had to play a game with him. Finally, the [government] let me go. Even on the plane I was afraid that they would tell the pilot to turn back. I did not relax until we got to Bangkok. By then I was no longer afraid the vc would take me back.

I came to the United States for the sake of my children. In Vietnam they had no future. They were not allowed to study beyond high school. During the time I was in prison my wife sent my eldest son to the United States. He was nineteen and escaped as a boat person. He started out as a laborer and eventually became a supervisor of thirty people. Then in 1985 there was an economic downturn here. He lost his job, his house, his car, and his fiancée. He went crazy. We lost contact with him. When we got here in 1991 I went looking for him. After several months I found him living in a Vietnamese pagoda. He was very sick. I took him to a mental health center for treatment. Now he is ok. He went to college and got a job as a mechanic. I pushed all [the children] to go to college. Four got graduate degrees in accounting and computer science. The youngest two are still undergraduates. For the first three years I had to work three jobs to support their college. All the jobs were related to tailoring. One was at home taking in extra work from a dry cleaner. The other two were at tailor shops. I worked sixteen hours a day, seven days a week. There was no day off on Sunday and no vacations, but I felt good. I was very happy to see the children finish their schooling, get jobs, and then get married.

What will he do when they no longer need his support?

I have to work until 2006 to get retirement credit. Then I will study computer science. I learned a bit about computers in 1996 attending a basic course at the Chinese cultural center. Since then I have read a lot of books. I want to get a degree and then go to [one of the big companies in the area] to volunteer my time in the laboratory. Then I can do what I want. If I finish a project successfully, they will pay me. But I will not take a salary. I will continue to work as a tailor.

I am sixty-nine [plus], but I still have to work very hard to support my family. The house and car do not pay for themselves! I have a full-time day job assisting other refugees, and in the evenings I work another eight hours as a tailor. I take in work from a dry cleaner and do alterations.

Does he ever think about the re-education camps?

In Saigon after I got released from prison I thought about them every night. I would hear a scratching at the door and wake up sweating all over. I dreamt of the Communists coming to take me away to prison. There is no more of that now. It stopped as soon as I got to Bangkok, when I was sure that they could not take me back. From then on I thought of the future, not the past. Others have PTSD [Post-Traumatic Stress Disorder], but I do not. I have no time to think about it. In prison I tried not to think of my misfortune. I thought of others, helping with my tailoring. I had 1,200 customers out of 1,500 detainees. I did it in my spare time.

Bich protects himself from depression by working hard, focusing on the present, and sublimating his feelings into charitable work with others. He is an outstanding example of the resilience—the ability to cope successfully with adversity—manifested by almost all of the former political prisoners I interviewed. Where does such resilience come from? Bich had a lifelong habit of keeping very busy and focusing on the task at hand rather than on his feelings about his present situation. Instead of seeking comfort or help for himself he has tried to comfort and help others. It is a trait that was strongly ingrained in his character from an early age, when circumstances required him to care for his brothers and sisters. I could not discover its roots in his earlier experience. Perhaps it is simply part of his biological makeup—a genetic endowment passed on from generation to generation until it is called forth by adversity. Or perhaps it is a result of the hard life of the people in Vietnam, where, as one former political prisoner told me, "We are taught from an early age to bear anything."

I asked Bich whether he had seen anyone killed or tortured in the camps.

Yes. Once, in Saigon, in the first camp, a detainee ran away. He was captured. They created a tribunal to try him, then shot him. I did not see it, [but] I heard it. The next day I saw the blood. I saw no killing in the other camps, but I heard about it. I did see people tortured. They beat them with anything they had. People's faces were swollen, but nothing was broken. They did it in front of others so that they would be afraid.

Does he ever get together with other former political prisoners?

There is an association of former political prisoners here. I have no time to go to their meetings. I work at my regular job eight hours a day, then spend two or three hours doing alterations at home, and another three or four hours working on the Vietnamese magazine [a magazine of advice and community events]. It makes me healthy because I am always busy inside here [pointing to his head].

Has he had any problems adjusting to life in the United States?

This is my third time in the United States. The first was in 1960, at the Fort Monmouth Signal School. The second was in 1964 to 1966, at Fort Leavenworth and Fort Bragg. I already knew something about life here. You cannot depend on welfare and Social Security. I had to support my children to go to school before I retire. I knew beforehand that to survive here you have to do something. You cannot sit down and relax.

Are there things he does not like about the United States?

People with lots of money set up a path for other people to follow. There is freedom and democracy here, but the country is under the control of the people with money. Fortunately, I do not follow their path. I try to be self-sufficient. My [community] organization started with nothing. Now we have fifteen computers, furniture, and office supplies. If you ask for a grant, you are dependent on [others]. If you work on your own, you depend on yourself. In this country, the only thing you have to fight is the Internal Revenue Service.

How are his children doing? "They are very happy. They have learned from my experience—how to be yourself, how to behave, how to deal with people, mostly how to get an education. My son with the [mental health] problems went to Vietnam to get married. He went to get a wife. He made the selection himself. He set up a schedule and interviewed a lot of young girls there." Is he fully recovered from his illness? "Sometimes he backslides. Right now he is waiting for his wife to come from Vietnam." What does Bich's wife do? "My wife spends her time gardening. She grows all her own vegetables, so we do not have to buy any. At the vegetable market they sell vegetables grown with chemical fertilizer. There is a 100 percent risk of getting cancer. We eat like we used to eat in Vietnam." What does he enjoy doing the most? "I need sleep. There is not enough time to sleep. I only sleep from 10 to 3, and then I get up and work on the magazine. I am never completely rested."

What lessons has Bich learned from his experiences in the re-education camps? "Under Communist detention they try to force you to tell them what you did. They tell you, 'We know everything, write it down.' But it is not true. I kept saying that I did not do anything. Finally, they had to release me. If you wrote it all down, you were signing your own death warrant. That is why I played games with them. They thought that I was at the end of my rope."

The preservation of one's dignity as a human being by not betraying oneself or one's friends was one of the themes touched on by almost all the former prisoners I interviewed. The Communists stressed to the prisoners that their cooperation with, and full participation in, the re-education program would hasten their passage through re-education and their eventual "transformation" into "new people." They were asked to recount in detail not only what they had done, but also the deeds of their fathers, grandfathers, and great-grandfathers, "Back five generations if you could," as one of the former prisoners told me. Those who did cooperate as instructed found that they had made a grave mistake. Now the Communists had that many more "crimes" of which to accuse them, and their stay in the camps became that much longer. Similarly, the "antennas," who betrayed not only themselves, but also their fellow prisoners in the hope that they would be released earlier, found that their behavior only extended their incarceration. Once the Communists learned that they could use them, they kept them on, year after year, rotating them from one camp to the next. Although I did not encounter any prisoners who acknowledged that they had functioned as antennas, it is not hard to imagine that such men, in addition to losing the respect of their fellow detainees, also lost respect for themselves.

5 / The Spy

S ang spent the war as an intelligence officer in the Central Intelligence
Organization (CIO), the South Vietnamese equivalent of the CIA. A
devout Roman Catholic, he had studied to become a priest, but was
asked to leave the seminary because his defiant, independent spirit was deemed
unsuitable for a religious life. After completing his baccalaureate exams he
entered Saigon University planning to become a lawyer, but his disenchantment
with Vietnamese politics prompted him to quit school and volunteer for service in
the South Vietnamese Navy. His father, who worked at the CIO, opposed this
move, fearing his son would be killed, and compelled him to become an intelligence officer. Sang continued his legal studies while working there, first in Saigon
and then in Hue. When Hue fell to the North Vietnamese Army in March
1975, he was captured briefly, but escaped and fled southward between the
warring armies toward Saigon and freedom. He arrived in the city late on the
evening of April 30, shortly after it too had fallen to the North Vietnamese Army
and the Viet Cong (VC). He then spent the next four and a half years in re-
education camps, escaping in 1980 with a group of his fellow prisoners, who
overpowered their guards, took their weapons, and fled into the jungle. Recaptured after a few days, he was sentenced to twenty years in a maximum-security
camp for "stealing socialist society property" (the guards' guns) and being anti-
Communist. He was finally released in 1996 after spending a total of twenty-one
years in the camps, one of the longest terms endured by any former political
prisoner. The deadline for application to the H.O. Program was already past,
but the intervention of his parents and a U.S. senator enabled Sang and his wife
to come to the United States in 1997. They now have two young children and are

working hard to adapt to life in their new homeland. Despite having spent almost half of his life in re-education camps, Sang remains strikingly optimistic and positive, happy to have the opportunity to work, to continue his education, and to rebuild his life here.

Sang is a short, sturdily built man with a sprightly walk, a friendly smile, and a healthy, youthful appearance that makes him look much younger than his forty-eight years. He prepared carefully for our interviews. Before we met he asked if I would submit my questions in advance so that he could study them and reflect on his responses. I sent him a list of the questions that I had used to guide my interviews with the other former political prisoners, and after he had reviewed them he agreed to meet with me. He began our first meeting by saying, "My story, like everyone else's story, is unique. How much depth are you interested in? Do you want to know my thoughts and feelings or just the details of what happened?" I told him that, while the details were very important, the former prisoners' thoughts and feelings helped to make their stories come alive and that I wanted to know as much about his inner experiences as he was prepared to share.

I was the oldest of nine children. My father had studied for the priesthood at a Roman Catholic seminary in Hue, but he failed to qualify and had to leave the seminary and return to a secular life. There were not many jobs then [in the Vietnam of the 1940s] for men with his qualifications—he had nine years of schooling and spoke French—and so he took a position with the Vietnamese government security service. My mother came from the same village as my father, but she had very little education, although she did know how to read and write. She was also a member of the Viet Minh. Almost everyone in her village was a member, and her uncle was a Viet Minh leader. My mother had been arrested and was being held and interrogated in a security office. My father bailed her out. They got married in 1950 or 1951.

I asked why a government security officer would bail out and marry a woman who belonged to the government's enemy, the Viet Minh.

My father's parents were large landowners, the wealthiest people in their village, and Roman Catholics. My mother's parents were also landowners, but they had only about 10 acres of farmland. My mother's mother did not want my mother going out into the jungle [with the Viet Minh] anymore and risking being captured again. So she met with my father's mother to discuss marriage arrangements. My father's mother agreed to the marriage and talked to my father.

I could understand why Sang's mother's family would want to have their daughter marry into a rich and well-connected family, but why would his father's family want their son to marry a woman in the Viet Minh who was under arrest?

I do not know. My parents just told me the story, and I never asked about it.

In 1954 [after the Geneva Accords] Vietnam was partitioned at the Ben Hai River [the 17th parallel]. The Communists took over the North. Since my father was a Catholic he moved his family south of the river, a distance of about 40 miles. His relatives were all Catholic, so they all moved to the South. My mother's family and their relatives were all Viet Minh, so they stayed in the North.

How did his mother, as a Viet Minh, feel about moving to the South? "It was not her decision. She had little to say [about it]."

I asked Sang what had happened to his father's family after their move to the South.

When my father's parents moved they lost all their land. In the North all the land belonged to the government. They were already old, and so they just retired.

After my parents' marriage they moved to the district capital, where my father was chief of the security service. In 1953, when I was one year old, my mother took me back to her village in the North to meet her relatives. The village leaders had a secret meeting. They decided to put me in a bag and drown me in the river. Some people who had been at the meeting told my mother about the plan. When she heard what they were going to do, she carried me away. They had wanted to kill me because my father's parents were wealthy landowners and he was the district security chief.

Sang's account of his parents' contrasting political and ideological backgrounds—wealthy, educated, pro-French Catholics and poorer, less educated followers of the Viet Minh—illustrates the sharp divide that often separated neighbors, and even family members, in the Vietnam of the early 1950s. It also highlights the intense class hatred that had developed out of decades of strife and oppression, a vindictive wrath that could lead one faction to murder the innocent child of the other. From the cauldron of these intense and highly personal animosities, seasoned by countless provocative incidents and simmered over many bitter years of war, the brutal re-education camps emerged as a final distillate of hatred and revenge.

I asked Sang to tell me about his life growing up.

My life was very peaceful and stable. I attended a Catholic elementary school until I was eleven years old. Then I went to Hue and attended the same seminary as my father. I too wanted to be a priest. I was in the seminary for five years. I had many outstanding teachers there, all of whom were priests. One of them was Nguyen Van Thuan. He was a nephew of [South Vietnamese President] Diem. Eventually, he became an archbishop and an emissary to the Vatican. Now he works in the Vatican as an official there. In the seminary we studied math, French, Latin, music, and theology. The regulations and discipline were very strict. They wanted us to learn to respect discipline and responsibility. I was a rebel against the regulations. There was a youth program, sort of like religious Boy Scouts. I did not like or agree with the group's leaders because even if I did better than they did in class, they were still in charge of me. My teacher gave me the option of either joining the group or forming a group of my own. I decided to form my own group and became its leader. There were four or five of us in my group compared to two or three hundred in the other group. When the other group had a meeting, we did too. After three or four months of this the teacher asked me again if I would like to join the other group. He asked two or three times, but I would not do it. Looking back [on my actions] I can see that my decision was not very mature, but at the time I stood firm.

Did he get in trouble for taking this independent stance?

A year and a half later the teacher asked to talk with me. He said that my actions were not appropriate for someone in a religious life and that I should go back to a secular life. I was one of the top students in my class, and he said that if I changed my views, I could come back, but I never did. I left the seminary and went back home to live with my family. By that time they had moved to Hue. I have always had a very clear sense of what is right and wrong. There is no in-between for me, and decisions are always clear cut. In my youth my friends used to call me a lawyer because I liked to act like a judge. That is why I later studied law.

What did he do after he returned home?

I continued with my high school education. I attended a French Catholic school, Providence High School. The teachers were priests. I graduated with a Baccalauréat II in 1970. After graduation my parents wanted me to attend college in Hue because it was less expensive, but I went to Saigon University instead. They wanted me to study medicine there, so I entered the science faculty, but I really wanted to study law. I spent a year at the university, but I became disillusioned with the political situation in the country and decided to quit school and go into the military. A lot of my friends were in the Navy, so I applied there too. When my uncle found out what I had done, he told my father. My father came down from Hue to Saigon and pulled my application to the Navy. He said, "If you do not want to go to school, you have to work." My father worked for the Central Intelligence Organization. He did not want me to go into combat and get killed. He wanted me to find a job in an office and be safe. A friend of his was a high official in the c I o, and he found me a place there. I joined in May 1971 and received my training as an intelligence officer in Saigon. It lasted five months. We were taught to follow people, to know if we were being followed, and to gather and protect information. After that, in January 1972, I was sent to the infantry officer training school in Thu Duc for basic military training. At that time people with my background and education were a valued national resource. When the country needed us it could use us in whatever capacity it wanted.

After military training I returned to Saigon in September 1972 and began to work as an intelligence officer [cán bộ tình báo]. I still wanted to go back to school and study law, so my father's friends created an opportunity for me to work at night so that I could attend school during the day. I was sent to the technical intelligence department, where we did coding, decoding, and listening [over the radio]. I did that for a year, then in October 1973 they sent me to Hue. By that time the [military] situation there was very intense. My family had already moved back to Saigon. A lot of my coworkers were married and had families and did not want to go. I was single, so I accepted the assignment. Also there was less work to do there, so I thought I would have more time to study law.

Hue fell in March 1975. We had asked Saigon for permission to pull out, but we were told to wait until the military pulled out and to go with them. We waited too long. In the end 80 percent of the military and all of my group were captured.

What happened after his capture?

I had papers saying that I was a student, but they did not believe me. I also had papers saying that I was an army officer. I did not show them the papers that said I was an intelligence officer, so they put me in with A R V N [Army of the Republic of Vietnam] infantry officers, in what had been a resettlement camp. The Communists had pushed the civilians out of the camp and made it a temporary camp for military prisoners. There were about 10,000 of us there. Each day they picked 700 to 1,000 prisoners and sent them to re-education camps in the North. I did not want to be sent there. I thought of the North as a place of no hope, like receiving a death sentence. Security in the camp was not very tight because the war was still going on, the situation was fluid, and there were so many prisoners. Most of the prisoners stayed in the camp, not because they could not get out, but because they did not know what was going to happen and they were scared. A few friends and I decided to escape and set out for Saigon [which was still under South Vietnamese control]. I walked all the way to Da Nang. It was about 70 miles and took four days. By that time the Communists had already taken over the region and no one checked my papers, so I just walked along normally in street clothes. Most of the time I walked along Route One.[1] When I got to the Hai Van Pass [a pass through a mountainous region north of Da Nang that cuts across Vietnam to the sea] I walked along the railroad tracks. I had some money with me to buy food. I did not sleep a lot. When I got tired I just lay down by the side of the road and slept. The only thing that really bothered me was the flies.

From Da Nang I was able to get bus transportation to Tuy Hoa. Then from there to Nha Trang I had to walk again. Nha Trang fell to the Communists one day before I got there. I went to visit Nguyen Van Thuan [the former seminary teacher mentioned earlier], who by then was bishop of Nha Trang. I asked him if he could help me find a boat to take me to Saigon. He said no, that it was too dangerous and that Saigon would soon fall anyway. He advised me to stay in Nha Trang, wait for the fall of Saigon, and then go when it was safer.

Did Sang take his advice?

No. I wanted to keep going and try to find freedom until I could not go any further. I also did not believe that Saigon would fall.

At Phan Rang, about 230 miles from Saigon, two generals, one from the air force and one from the army, had built fortifications around the city to block the enemy's advance toward Saigon. When Phan Rang fell on April 22nd or 23rd, they were captured. One was sentenced to eighteen years and the other to twenty years. At the time Phan Rang fell I was at Cam Ranh Bay. The military had fallen back from Phan Rang to Long Khanh and again built fortifications. I was able to join the flood of refugees who had begun to return to their homes after the fall of Phan Rang. There was still a lot of fighting around Long Khanh, so I could not get any transportation there and again had to walk. I arrived there on April 27th. I decided to try to pass through the fighting and keep heading south [toward Saigon]. All the civilians had moved out of the area [because of the heavy fighting]. There were only the Communists and the South Vietnamese Army. It was very dangerous. If the Communists saw me, they would shoot me. If the South Vietnamese saw me, they would shoot me. I wore black clothing and moved only at night. I did not want anyone to see me. There were dead bodies and guns everywhere. I did not carry a gun because I did not know who was who or who to fight against. I finally came upon an abandoned house, went in, and found some rice and peanuts there. I cooked the peanuts and carried them in my pockets along with some water. I applied the survival skills I had learned during my training.

How did he feel during that time?

I have never been afraid of dying. If I had to die tomorrow, I would die peacefully. Living meaningfully is more of a struggle than dying. If I am alive, I want to be doing something of value. Dying is better than living a meaningless life.

When I got to the fortifications around Long Khanh, [I could see that] the only way through them was along Route One. This meant passing between the two armies, which were still fighting. There was no safe way through. Anyone trying to pass was shot. So I stayed outside of the fortifications the night of April 29th. Then on the 30th [the day Saigon fell] people on the inside of the fortifications began to come out, so I went in. When I got inside I heard Duong Van Minh's [the last president of South Vietnam] announcement on the radio that we should surrender. But not everyone stopped fighting. Some continued to fight. It happened all over the country.

How did Sang feel when he heard the announcement that the South Vietnamese military should surrender?

I felt depressed and hopeless, but I kept on walking toward Saigon. There were a lot of people moving around and there was no transportation. It took me eleven hours to walk there, and it was about 11 P.M. when I arrived. I tried to find my family, but when I got to the house no one was home. They had all gone to Go Cong [a city south of Saigon in the Mekong Delta]. Many people had gone there hoping to find a way out of Vietnam. They hoped that foreigners [such as the Americans or the French] would come and rescue them as they had done in 1954 when Vietnam was partitioned.

I was really depressed that day. All my hope was gone. That night I walked around Saigon. I saw a group of people wearing red armbands. They were not Communists, but a "third force" [*thành phần thứ ba*]. They thought that they would join the Communists [after their victory], so they went around destroying buildings and the U.S. Embassy. They killed two foreign journalists. I saw them beat one of them to death. It was on May 1st in Hai Ba Trung Street.

On May 2nd there was an announcement on the radio saying that all officers and officials of the old government must present themselves to the new government. A very small number of people did so on the 2nd. Then on the 3rd and 4th many more came out and presented themselves, perhaps 60 to 70 percent of the total. Twenty to 25 percent did not come out. I presented myself on the 4th. By that time my family had come back to Saigon from Go Cong, and my parents said to me, "You have reached the end of the road, the fall of Saigon. You should go and present yourself." I went to the CIO building at number 3 Bach Dang Street. The Communists had already taken it over. Initially, I was afraid and nervous, but after I arrived I saw that there were a lot of people there, so I was less frightened. I signed in by giving my name and position in the government and was given a piece of paper with my name on it and the date I had signed in. The person who had taken my information signed the paper. Then I went home.

On the 10th of May I heard a radio announcement saying that former officers and officials of the old government should prepare for re-education by gathering together enough supplies for twelve days and bringing along twenty to twenty-five thousand *đồng* [about U.S. $70] for spending money. It did not say where to go, but the meeting places were usually old prisons or large abandoned buildings like schools. There was nothing for me to do in Saigon. There were no jobs for people like my father and me because we had been officials in the old government. I had a friend in Binh Tuy. My father and I decided to move there and become farmers. When I arrived I presented myself to the local security office. This time they took my information more carefully. They asked about my background and what sort of work I had done.

Did Sang tell them the truth?

A lot of people, including myself, felt that there were many people who knew about our activities, so I told the truth. If I had thought that there were activities that were not well known, then I would not have talked about them.

After my interrogation they let me go home. Then they began to assemble the local population for meetings every night between 8 and 10. Similar meetings were held all over the country, except in Saigon. The purpose of them was to read aloud to the local people the histories the Communists had collected from former officers and officials like me to see if we had told them everything and told the truth. If something was left out or was wrong, the people from the local area who knew you would tell the authorities. The investigators had told us that if we told them everything and told the truth, we would get less prison time. But we did not believe them and left things out if we thought that they were not well known and would not be found out.

When the investigations were complete I went home and began to work the land. My family had a house in the forest. We burned down trees to clear a space for farming. Each day I went out and worked the fields. One Sunday, after church, I took my hoe and went out into the forest to farm. I had brought along a bag to carry ashes from the burned trees for use as fertilizer in our vegetable garden. When I arrived at our land I saw three men there, two soldiers and the village chief. They asked me to come to the village chief's house for a talk. I put some ashes into my bag to drop off at home. They let me carry it, but they did not let me take it to our house. Instead they led me to the village chief's home. When I got there I saw that my father was already there, along with a jeep carrying seven district security officers. They told us that they wanted us to go with them to the provincial security office to discuss the histories we had given describing our backgrounds and activities. I asked if we would need blankets or extra clothing. They said no.

When we got to the provincial security office they separated my father and me and put us into two small cells. In a larger cell they had crowded together twenty or thirty other people. Each day at 11 A.M. and 5 P.M. they gave me a bowl of rice, salt, and a glass of water. I did not drink the water because there was not a proper toilet in the cell, only a bucket.

What did Sang think was going on?

I was really surprised. I had expected to be taken to a re-education camp, but instead they took me to a prison. I felt hopeless. Later I found out that they kept higher-ranking officers in that prison. I had been in the same small cell for ten days when they called all the prisoners together for a meeting. They told us to rewrite our histories. I did so and presented it to the security officers. They said, "No, this is not right. Rewrite it." We had to write it over five or six times. When it was done they took me from the small cell and put me into the large cell with the others.

There was nothing else to do in the large cell but talk to one another. We just lay around all day. They let us out once a week to bathe. I was there for a month and spent a lot of time talking with the other prisoners, listening to their stories and learning how they had been caught. One man had been chief of a provincial youth department. There was an announcement telling the chiefs to prepare enough supplies for three days of re-education. All the other chiefs were called and went [to re-education camps], but his name was never called. So he went to the local security office and complained. He kept on complaining until they finally sent him to the re-education camp. He stayed there for five or six years. If he had kept his mouth shut, they probably would not have sent him at all! They did not consider his position that important.

After a month in jail they announced that they would be sending us to re-education camp for three years, but that if we behaved well and worked hard, our time would be reduced to from one and a half to two years. The prisoners reacted to this announcement in a variety of ways. One group, usually young single men, could not accept it. All they thought about was escape. They were prepared to do anything. A second group did not know what to think, but they kept calm. A third group accepted what they had been told. Their thinking was, "What can I learn in the re-education camp that will help me when I get out? Can I learn to weave baskets or do carpentry? Then when I get out I will have a skill and can support myself."

After a month in the cell they started sending us out to work cleaning up buildings the Communists had taken over from the old government. When we returned from work they searched us. If you went out to work, you got to take a shower. People who did not work were not permitted to take a shower. Once a month they allowed us to send a message to our relatives to let them know where we were and to send them a permit so that they could visit us and bring supplies. They were allowed to bring us 10 pounds of supplies, but no tea, coffee, or alcohol. Before we got the supplies they were carefully searched. During our visits, which only lasted for five minutes, we had to stand 7 or 8 meters apart from our relatives. Because of the distance we had to talk very loudly [and the guards could overhear everything we said].

I was in the jail for a total of three months. After that they divided us up. They screened a group of ten prisoners every five to seven days and sent them to re-education camps. My father and I were sent to a camp about 150 miles north of Saigon in a mountainous region. In the camp there were Roman Catholic priests, Protestant pastors, Buddhist nuns and monks, and officials and officers of the old government. There were also people who, after the Communists took over, had protested against them. They were taken to court and sentenced either to execution or to life in a re-education camp. There were also South Vietnamese soldiers there who had not surrendered at the end of the war, but had hidden in the jungles and kept on fighting. These soldiers and the protestors were handcuffed in pairs by their wrists and ankles and put in a cell. Everyone else in the camp was forced to do physical labor. We were sent out in groups of twenty-five or thirty along with two guards. We would go out in the morning to work, return for lunch and a rest, then go out again in the afternoon to work until dinner. We had dinner about 6:30 P.M. and then went back to our barracks until 7 P.M. Then from 7 P.M. until 10:30 P.M. every night we had to go to a meeting, where we learned to sing Communist songs. The point of all this was to make us tired, too tired to think about anything except going to sleep.

We also had self-criticism sessions every night. We had to tell them what we had done that day and especially what we had done wrong. If you did not criticize yourself, then they asked some other prisoner to do it for you. Each week the prisoners had a meeting to conduct a review of our work. We divided ourselves into three groups—good, average, and bad—based on our performance. The guards cut down the rice allotment for those in the bad group and gave it to those in the good group. They also cut down the bad group's monthly supplies from their relatives to 3 or 4 pounds.

Who got put in the bad group?

People who did not work as hard as they should have, or read books or newspapers instead of working, or thought about something they should not have thought about. We based our judgments on people's self-criticism and on our own observations of them. There were also "antennas," a small group of prisoners, maybe 10 percent, who reported to the guards if they learned anything of interest. The antennas [betrayed their fellow prisoners], hoping that they would get out of the camp earlier, have longer family visits, or get to have their wives stay overnight. In reality, however, that is not what happened [to them]. Once the Communists learned that they could use them, they kept them longer to keep them working for them.

You were not allowed to read books or newspapers in the camp. And if you wore glasses, you had to take them off when speaking to the guards; otherwise it was a sign of disrespect. They hated people with glasses; it showed that you were educated. If you spoke a foreign language to one of the other prisoners and they heard you, they handcuffed you for a week. They were very strict about foreign languages, but we still wanted to learn either French or English so we could use the language when we got out of the camp. Those who knew French and English well taught the others. We would write down five new words on a very small piece of paper, hide it in our *nón lá* [the conical straw hat worn by the Vietnamese], and study the words when we were out working in the fields. The first time you were caught doing this they would handcuff you for seven to ten days and give you porridge to eat instead of rice. The second time you were caught it was considered a systematic violation of the camp regulations and you were handcuffed for three to six months, put in a small cell, and given less to eat.

Why were the Communists so opposed to the prisoners learning foreign languages? "Most of the Communists were uneducated. They did not like people with education. Also, if the prisoners learned a foreign language, they might be able to communicate with one another without the guards knowing what they were saying." Where did the prisoners get the paper to write down the foreign language words?

Their relatives would hide the paper in their supplies or bribe the guards not to check too carefully. They were often even able to sneak in a small dictionary or a newspaper. We had to be careful not to get caught using a dictionary. If you were caught, the dictionary was taken away and you were handcuffed. Later you could bribe the guard to get the dictionary back, but if another prisoner saw the guard taking the dictionary away from you, he might bribe him to get it for his own use.

Let me give you another example of life in the camp: The fence around the perimeter was built of live bamboo. During the rainy season the bamboo grew shoots. We cut them off, boiled them, and ate them. However, if we were caught doing this, they accused us of destroying the fence around the camp so that we could escape and we were given a longer sentence.

Every two or three months a group of prisoners would make plans to escape, either by jumping over the fence or by running away from work. Some prisoners did escape, and others were shot trying. Some got away for fifteen to twenty days and were then recaptured. They were handcuffed and placed in a small cell for three to six months. After that they became regular prisoners again, but they were kept in the camp longer. I knew one prisoner who decided he would either be free or die. When he was captured he fought back. I saw them bayonet him right through the mouth to the back of his head.

What sort of work did Sang do in the camps? "We grew corn, beans, rice, and sesame seeds. We did carpentry, making desks and chairs. We made bricks and used them to build huts." Was the work hard?

The guards wanted us to work hard, but we knew we would be there for a long time, not just three years. We did not want to use up all our strength. We worked at a moderate rate and learned English or French at the same time. For the first five years there were no protests about the physical labor in the re-education camps. But then in 1980 there was a big one at the central re-education camp, Trai Ham Tan. The prisoners took over the camp for three or four days. During that time the prisoners sentenced the antennas and trustees and beat them up. Then tanks surrounded the camp and the military negotiated with the prisoners. Finally, the leaders of the uprising were taken away to Chi Hoa prison in Saigon and the other prisoners were sent to a disciplinary camp.

After four and a half years in the camp eleven other prisoners and I decided to escape. Some of the prisoners' relatives had made contact with people who had bases in the jungle and who were still struggling against the Communist government. Between 1976 and 1980 there were about eighty such groups. They published newspapers, made radio transmissions, and even printed their own money. Their goal was to destroy the Communist government. They saw us prisoners as potential allies. They helped us make a plan to escape. One day we went out to work in a group of forty prisoners with one political officer and two soldiers. The twelve of us overcame the guards and took their weapons. We had two M-16s and a K-54 [a pistol carried by North Vietnamese officers]. We went into the jungle to a place where one of the dissident groups had built a base for us. The Communists sent out two regiments of soldiers, and police spread out over two provinces, Thuan Hai and Dong Nai, to search for us. After six days I was the first one captured. Four days later nine more were caught and two were shot dead. They took us back to the re-education camp and locked each of us into a small, dark cell. The cells were very dirty, smelled bad, and the floor was wet. The first night lice and bedbugs crawled all over me. There was no light at all except when they opened the door. My hands were bound behind my back and my feet were tied. They beat me twice a day with their bare feet and hands. They kicked me in the head. They beat me until I could not move anymore. They did this before each meal for seven days. After that they only bound my feet. I was fed dry manioc with salt and a small glass of water. They put a bucket in the cell for waste. During each meal someone came and emptied it. Once a week they let me out of the cell so I could wash myself.

When you were put in a re-education camp all your hope for life was gone. That is why we had no fear of dying. We did not want to kill ourselves because of our religious beliefs. [Our hopelessness] gave us the courage to escape and join the groups that wanted to overthrow the government. We wanted to do something for our country. After we were recaptured, there was no hope at all; we had no control over our lives. We had to accept whatever happened to us.

After four and a half months in isolation they had a trial to sentence us as examples for the other prisoners. The judges came to the re-education camp. I was charged with two crimes. The first was for being anti-Communist and trying to escape from the camp. The second was for stealing three weapons that belonged to the socialist society. The charges were worded in such a way that they could sentence me for robbery. They sentenced one man, the leader of our group, to life in prison. Another man and I were sentenced to twenty years. The others were sentenced to ten to eighteen years. After our sentencing they sent us to another re-education camp to wait for fifteen days to see if either the prisoners or the prosecutors would appeal. After fifteen days the sentence was final. We were then sent to another re-education camp run by the Ministry of Internal Affairs. In Vietnam there were more re-education camps than schools! There were over 600 district re-education camps, one or two per district. Then there were more than 100 provincial camps and more than 20 national camps. Each camp had between 500 and 800 prisoners. I was sentenced to one of the national camps, camp A-20. It was a maximum security camp with harsh discipline. It was where the prisoners were sent who could not be controlled in the other camps. The main camp had five sub-camps, separated by 3 to 4 miles. Each sub-camp had 500 to 600 prisoners. One of the sub-camps was for people who, after the fall of Saigon, had gotten on a ship and sailed to Guam. There were about 2,000 people on the ship, which belonged to the Vietnam Commercial Bank [Việt Nam Thương Tín]. They stayed in Guam for two or three months. Then the Communists sent them a radio message saying that it was all right to come back. They returned to Nha Trang and were captured. The men were separated from the women. They kept the women for a week and then released them. They kept the men in sub-camp A. They were considered especially dangerous because they had tried to escape. The Communists also believed that they might have been trained as spies or intelligence agents in Guam.

When I got to the sub-camp it was divided into three sections: criminals, officers of the old government, and anti-Communists. The officers did not have sentences [they were there indefinitely], but the anti-Communists did. I was placed in with the anti-Communists. I stayed there from 1979 to 1989. Usually, they kept a person in the same camp for ten years and then sent him to another camp. In 1989 they sent me to camp Z-30-A. I was there from 1989 until I was released in 1996.

During my stay in camp A-20 I learned that there were prisoners there from more than seventy different antigovernment political groups. The groups were of three types. One was made up of anti-Communists. A second was made up of people who had joined fake groups the Communists had set up to trap counterrevolutionaries. There were also people there who had known about these fake groups, did not join, but also did not tell the Communists about them. They had been faced with a terrible choice. Join the group and go to jail. Do not join the group, but do not tell and still go to jail. Tell the Communists about the group and betray your friends. Whoever the Communists had their eye on had no escape. The third group was made up of religious people who had tried to practice their religion as they saw fit and not as the Communists wanted them to. The Communists created approved religious groups that were to follow the Communist concept of religion. People who did not follow their rules were put in the camps for being anti-Communist. There was a Roman Catholic priest who loved young children. One day after services the Communists had the five-year-old daughter of a Communist go to him, ostensibly to learn about the Bible. She followed him to his room. They sentenced him to four years in the criminal section of the re-education camp for molestation and took away the church's property. Then there was a Vietnamese Roman Catholic order, Dong Cong, half of whose members came to the United States after 1975. [Those in the United States] sent back money to those members who had remained behind in Vietnam so that they could run the church. The Communists set a trap for them by hiding guns in the church. Then they arrested eleven priests, two of whom are still in prison.

What was daily life like in camp A-20?

The officers' group got 20 grams of meat once a month. The other groups, criminals and anti-Communists, only got a meatless broth. This was done to create tension between the groups. A small piece of meat was a big deal, and because of their starvation state people did not always behave properly. Each person got a 2-feet-wide space in the barracks for sleeping. Each barracks had over 100 people. The toilets for use at night were inside the barracks. They were just big buckets, and there were four of them per barracks. New prisoners were forced to sleep closest to the buckets, and it was very hard for them to sleep at night with 100 other people always going to the toilet. The barracks smelled bad and were very crowded. Outside there was a well for drinking and washing. The latrine was only about 40 feet away from the well. It was very unsanitary. During the rainy season the water in the well was plentiful. In the dry season the water level was very low. We had to climb down by rope into the well while carrying small buckets for the water. In a half-hour we were only able to fill seven buckets.

We [usually] did physical labor six days a week. [However,] every other week we were also forced to work on Sunday morning. They called it "socialist labor" [*lao động xã hội chủ nghĩa*]. There were two work periods, one from 6:30 A.M. to 10:30 A.M. and the other from 1:00 P.M. to 4:30 P.M. As we worked they had us count off every fifteen minutes to be sure that no one had escaped. We had to work out in the fields in our bare feet. They said that this was done to prevent us from escaping, but the real reason was to humiliate us. After the first work period we went back to the barracks to rest and eat. After the second work period we went back to the camp, ate dinner, and returned to our barracks. We did not have self-criticism sessions in the evening as in the other camps. Our work consisted of farming, carpentry, and metalwork (making tools). The criminal prisoners had a different attitude toward work than the others. They worked very hard and did their best. The political prisoners did not care; they had lost hope. Their lives were at a dead end, and they did not work hard.

Once a month the prisoners had a meeting to decide who among us was a good, average, or bad worker. We would select whoever needed a relative visit as a good worker. Sometimes the guards disagreed with our choices. In this camp the guards had a system. They picked two prisoners to function as trustees and to oversee the other prisoners at night. These trustees did not have to do any physical labor and slept during the day. The Communists were cruel in their choice of who got to be a trustee. They always picked former high-ranking officers or officials to dishonor them by forcing them to betray their fellow prisoners. If they refused to accept the job, they would be kept in the camp longer. If they accepted it, then it was even worse than being an antenna because they were publicly acknowledging that they worked for the Communists. Their job was to watch the other prisoners to make sure that they did not talk to one another or make plans to escape.

If a prisoner felt sick, there was a small clinic run by a Communist nurse. He was the boss of two doctors who had worked for the old government. They examined the prisoners, wrote out a prescription, and then had to have the prescription approved by the nurse. If the nurse did not approve of what they had written, the prisoner had to return to work. A couple of times prisoners were sent back to work and died. Most of the prisoners had tuberculosis because of their malnutrition and poor living conditions. There was only one medicine available in the camp, and it was used to treat every illness from headaches to stomachaches. It was an herbal medicine from a grasslike plant called *xuyên tâm liên*. For those who had worms there was no medicine at all, so they had to find alternative treatments. Some of the prisoners tried using the roots of the Japanese lilac tree [*cây soan*]. It did not work, and several prisoners died of poisoning from it.

Did Sang see people killed in the camps?

They did not kill prisoners directly. I heard rumors that if the guards wanted to kill someone, they held them in an isolation cell and killed them slowly by making them drink detergent. There were four priests killed in the camp between 1981 and 1985. They were held in isolation cells away from the other prisoners. Within a year and a half after they were placed in the cells, they were all dead. The guards believed that these priests had a bad influence on the prisoners and that they were the leaders of anti-Communist groups. The security guards could do whatever they wanted to the prisoners. They had little training in how to re-educate people, but they had a lot of training in interrogation and torture.

How did they torture people?

For example, the prisoners used to catch frogs, grasshoppers, and crickets and keep them until they could cook and eat them. The prisoners would do anything to catch this protein supplement. If the guards caught them, they forced them to eat the frogs and insects alive. The reason they gave for this was that it was unsanitary to eat frogs, grasshoppers, and crickets. Another example is that of a sixty-year-old prisoner. They made him lie down on the floor so they could beat him. If he refused, they hit him in the face. The guards were only in their twenties, and this was a way to show [an older prisoner] disrespect. Prisoners sometimes tried to steal some of the produce we farmed. We tied it around our knees beneath our clothing. One prisoner was caught. The guard kicked him in the spleen and he died instantly. The guards did not view the prisoners as human beings, and their superiors approved of their attitude.

Where did the guards come from? "Eighty to 90 percent came from Nghe Tinh Province. It is north of the central region of Vietnam, just above the 17th parallel. It is where Ho Chi Minh was born. Many ardent Communists came from there and people from that region were very loyal Communists." Were there any guards with whom Sang could develop a relationship?

There were a few humane guards, but they were not nice to all the prisoners. They were selective. They would be nice to one prisoner, but not all of us. If a guard was caught being nice to a prisoner, he could lose his job. That would be going against Communist principles.

Every three or four months we had a learning session that lasted two days. The prisoners had to participate and afterwards had to write a report that was divided into five parts. In the first part, Viewpoint [*tư tưởng*], we had to state that we accepted the re-education camp, trusted in the Communist principles, and admitted that we were guilty of crimes against the Vietnamese people. In the second, Labor [*lao động*], we had to describe the highest standard of physical labor, tell whether we had achieved it, and if not, why we had not. In the third, Regulations [*nội qui*], we had to write down the camp's thirty regulations and the twenty principles of the "new civilized way of life." Then we had to say which of the regulations we had violated during the past three or four months. In the fourth, Re-education [*học tập*], we had to describe what we had done to get involved in re-education, like going to meetings, reading the Communist newspaper (*Nhân Dân*), learning the principles of Marxism-Leninism, viewing movies from Hanoi, and singing Communist songs. If a prisoner did not go to see the movies or participate in the singing, he would get diluted porridge instead of rice to eat. Finally, in the fifth, Future Plans [*phương hướng*], we had to write down what we would do in the future, how we would change, and how we would become good laborers.

What were the songs about?

They are still sung in Vietnam on the radio. Most prisoners did not want to sing them because after working all day we just wanted to rest. The criminal prisoners sang the songs and clapped their hands along with the music. The political prisoners did not sing; it would have been a betrayal of themselves and the other political prisoners. Here is an example of one of the songs. It was written in 1975, the year of the Communist victory. It is dedicated to Ho Chi Minh, who died in 1969. "It seems like Uncle Ho is here to enjoy the victory day. Uncle's words have come true in a splendid victory after a thirty-year struggle for independence and freedom. Vietnam, Ho Chi Minh. Vietnam, Ho Chi Minh. Vietnam, Ho Chi Minh."

So many of the things the prisoners were forced to learn, recite, and sing seem so silly and banal. Did the prisoners ever talk about the mindless, inane quality of it?

We thought that none of it made sense and that there was nothing good about it. We used to make a lot of jokes about Ho Chi Minh, referring to him as a prisoner named Tám Keo. Essentially, it means "Ho the pervert" [*Tám* = eight, the eighth figure of the Zodiac is the goat, a goat is a Vietnamese slang word for a pervert; *Keo* = *Hồ*]. He never had a wife, but it was rumored that he had women everywhere and that he fooled around a lot. It is also rumored that the present head of the Vietnamese Congress is a son of his. The man's mother came from a minority group in the region [Bắc Bộ] where Ho hid during the French time. When the prisoners mentioned Tám Keo to one another the guards did not know what they were talking about.

Were there any women prisoners in your camp?

There were some in other re-education camps, but very few. Some were political prisoners and others were people who had tried to escape from Vietnam. Most of the political prisoners did not want to get involved with them [sexually] to preserve their own dignity. The few who did were people who were considered to have a low standard of dignity.

In our camp the prisoners believed that the Communist government would not last long and would soon be overthrown. Between 1975 and 1985 the Communists were very extreme in their beliefs, and the prisoners in the re-education camps suffered a lot. Then in 1985, when the prisoners learned that [U.S. General] John Vessey was in Hanoi discussing the possibility of the prisoners emigrating to the United States, they began to have some hope. There was no change in the camp's policy, but the attitude of the guards toward the prisoners became more open-minded and lenient. When Nguyen Van Linh became the president of the Communist Party in 1986 or 1987, he wanted the prisoners to be folded into the new economic policy [đổi mới, or renovation] and be used to benefit the Vietnamese economy. From then on the prisoners had the option of being self-sufficient. If they could provide their own supplies, like food and clothing, and give the camp between twenty and forty thousand đồng [about U.S. $5 to $10] a month, then they did not have to do physical labor. They were also allowed to go outside the camp during the day to a few selected locations where they could earn the money that would allow them to be self-sufficient. The idea was that the camp would not have to support the prisoners anymore; they would support themselves. Most prisoners did not do it. The majority did not have enough money to pay to be self-sufficient, and they found that they had to work harder outside the camp to get the money than they worked inside the camp. Also, the prisoners who remained behind had to work that much harder to cover the work of those who had left, so it was like those who chose to be self-sufficient had betrayed their fellow prisoners. Only about 10 percent of the prisoners did it. They accepted the fact that the others saw them as betrayers, but they had a different intention. They took advantage of working outside the camp so that they could escape. In one year, twenty-seven prisoners escaped from our camp. Some even got away to the United States and Canada. Because of these escapes the head of the camp himself was put in a re-education camp. The Communists thought that the prisoners must have bribed him to let them escape. He had a long history in the party, connections, and a high rank, so they gave him a sentence that said he had a mental disorder and only put him in the camp for three years.

Between 1975 and 1987 former officers and officials of the old government were released so that they could leave the country. The Communists kept 127 prisoners who were considered the most dangerous because they thought that they had worked for the CIA. They were finally released in 1993. They were not sentenced to a fixed term like I was. After that there were only forty or fifty former officers sentenced as political prisoners who were still being held. I was finally released in January 1996. I had been sentenced to twenty years, but they reduced the sentence to sixteen years, six months. It was their policy to reduce sentences each Independence Day [September 2nd, the day on which Ho Chi Minh proclaimed Vietnamese independence from France and Japan]. Over a ten-year period I received ten separate sentence reductions, totaling three years, six months. The prisoners had mixed feelings about the sentence reductions. They were happy to go home, but they felt ashamed, as if they had betrayed the other prisoners. Also, in the year before they were released the prisoners began to think and worry more because they had to deal with the reality of leaving. The wives of some of them had left and the children of others were working as maids. If you still had seven years left on your sentence, you did not have to worry about things like that or to make plans for your future.

Political prisoners like me who had served the old government and been put in the camps for at least three years after the end of the war were qualified to immigrate to the United States under the H.O. Program. [The H.O. program enabled former officers and officials of the South Vietnamese government who had been in re-education camps to immigrate to the United States.] Those people who were put in the camps not because they had worked for the old government but for taking part in anti-Communist activities after 1975 were not qualified. We had some hope, but they had none. When they got out of the camps they had nothing—not even a little land to farm. When they got home their friends and neighbors did not want to associate with them because that might make them appear to be anti-Communist. They could not get jobs because no company would hire them. Each week they had to report to their local and district security office. Security wanted to keep an eye on them. They had little hope and their lives were very difficult.

I did not have to face those problems. My parents were in the United States, and my brother and sister in Vietnam were pretty well off. The only work I had to do was to help them and to apply for the H.O. Program. Think of those poor former government officers and officials who were released early from the camps after only being there for one or two years instead of the three years that are required to qualify for the H.O. Program. They are not considered normal Vietnamese citizens. They cannot own their own businesses. They are still in Vietnam and they have no chance of getting out. The security service still keeps an eye on them. The Communists have said that their families will have to be monitored for three generations to clear their record. So if a father was in the camps, it would have an effect on his children and grandchildren!

What was it like for Sang after his release?

When I returned home some people were afraid of me and did not want to associate with me. Others were sympathetic, but I did not want to get them into trouble by spending time with them, so I lived a very isolated life. After coming home many of the former prisoners led isolated lives. Their wives had left some of them while they were still in the camps. Others came home so mentally disordered that a short time after their return they would divorce. Most did not have jobs. Those who had been in the camps for many years had children who were grown up and who hardly knew them. The children were independent, and there was no closeness between them and the prisoners. When the prisoners and their wives got divorced, the children felt disappointed and hopeless. While their fathers were in the re-education camps the children usually could not attend school. Before 1985 children of prisoners were not allowed to attend high school except for those who lived in Saigon, who could do so only with special permission from the government. Because of their fathers' records the children had very difficult lives. If the children's thinking was immature, they blamed all their troubles on their fathers.

Most people who had been prisoners in the re-education camps hoped to become refugees in another country. The Communists kept following them and checking up on them. They wanted to be free of that and were prepared to go to any country that would accept them. A small proportion of former prisoners—perhaps 5 to 10 percent—wanted to stay in Vietnam. They were especially high-minded and idealistic. They hoped to stay and help overthrow the Communist government or at least share in the suffering of the Vietnamese people. Most former prisoners, however, wanted to go, and I was one of them. All I thought about was how to leave Vietnam and come to the United States. It only took one year and four months after my release for me to get here.

How did he first learn about the H.O. Program?

When [General] Vessey came to Vietnam everyone in the camps knew about it. There were a number of ways to get news there. Some people had very small Chinese radios, about the size of the palm of your hand, which had been smuggled in by their relatives during visits. We listened to them at night and hid them during the day in Guigoz powdered milk containers. [This was a popular French powdered milk preparation.] Those cans were very prized in the re-education camps. They were made of aluminum, so they did not rust. Before 1975 the children of wealthy families drank that kind of milk. Our families used them as containers to bring things to us in the camps. After we got them we cut the cans into two parts. We hid the radio in the bottom part and covered it with supplies in the top part so the guards would not suspect there was anything there. If the guards caught you listening to the radio, you were executed or sentenced to twenty years to life. We listened to the BBC or the Voice of America. Another way to get news was from your relatives. In the camp, if one person got news, everyone got it. We followed the news very carefully.

How did he apply for the H.O. Program?

The final deadline for the program was September 30, 1994. I got out of the camp on January 29, 1996. After I got out I wrote a letter to the ODP [Orderly Departure Program] office at the U.S. Embassy in Bangkok. I waited for about two months, but did not hear anything. My parents and some of my relatives were already in the United States. One of my cousins called the office in Bangkok. They asked him to fax my material and said that they would review it right away. My father went and talked to [a U.S. Senator from the state where Sang now lives]. He called Bangkok on my behalf. One month later I received a letter from the U.S. Embassy with an identification number and a letter of introduction to the Vietnamese government saying that my file with the ODP program was open. I had to take it to the Department of Entry and Exit Management in Saigon. It should have taken only three months to process an application. However, the workers in the department wanted to make things more complicated and delay the process. The reason they did this was to get bribes. When I went for my interview for the ODP program I told the interviewers that my paperwork still was not done. They said that they would give me another letter of introduction to speed things up. When I told this to the people at the Department of Entry and Exit Management, they said, "If they dare, they can come and talk to us!" Then they talked straight to me: "If you want this process to go fast, you have to give us money!" When you deal with paperwork in Vietnam there is always money involved. If you want something to move faster, you have to give more money. The bureaucrats made it difficult for qualified people, but for unqualified people, no amount of money would do. I gave them U.S.$2,000 that my parents had sent me. Then the bureaucrats divided it up among themselves. My paperwork was done in March 1997. By then I had been married for a year. I applied for my wife to go to the United States with me.

How did Sang meet his wife?

After I got out of the re-education camp I was qualified to go to the United States, so I did not have any trouble finding a wife. Anyone would have married me—a doctor, a teacher, anyone—because they all wanted to get out of Vietnam. I chose a woman who was right for me, someone with whom I could live all my life. My parents arranged the marriage. The woman was from the same village as my parents. She was thirty-six years old. In Vietnam she was considered old, but I was already at an advanced age. My parents told me about her and I met and liked her.

Did he fall in love? "No, I got married to establish my future." What made her the right woman for him? "She came from a religious family and her brother is a priest. She was well educated and was a teacher. When we went for our ODP interview she was already four or five months pregnant. After everything was approved we asked if we could leave before she gave birth. Ten days later they told us to go register for the flight. We left Vietnam on May 13, 1997, and arrived here on the same day."

How did he feel about leaving Vietnam?

I had mixed feelings. I was sad to leave my friends and relatives, but I had no way to make a future for myself in Vietnam. Since I had been in the camps I had no future, no hope. Also, my neighbors looked down on me because I had been in the camps. I knew inside that I had to go. None of my wife's relatives came to see us off. She was the first person in her family to leave, and they were too sad to come and say good-bye. My relatives all came because they were going to be leaving themselves in a month.

How did his wife feel about leaving? "She agreed to go because of the chance for a better future and the opportunity to be able to help her family in Vietnam. She also has an uncle who has lived in the United States for twenty years."

Was the reality of life in the United States different than he had imagined? "I was very familiar with life in the United States because I had friends and relatives here. I knew our life would be better materialistically. I expected that there would be cultural differences and that I would feel lonely. However, once I made a decision to come here I stopped worrying."

Did the experience in the re-education camps change him in any fundamental way?

I was very young and ambitious before I went into the re-education camps. I thought that I could do anything! In the camps I got to know all kinds of people—very educated and uneducated people, religious people, and malicious people. I learned a lot from them, both the good ones and the bad ones. Observing their actions caused me to reflect on my own behavior and myself. When I got out of the camps I was a stronger and more mature person. I learned a lot there about people. Now after talking to a person for ten or fifteen minutes I can tell what kind of a person I am dealing with.

Did the experience in the camps change his outlook on life?

Before 1975, the Vietnamese people had different values, attitudes, and beliefs about life. They believed in education and humanitarian values. After 1975 the Communists taught them to judge people by their material status, by the clothes they wear and the possessions they have. After I got out of the camp I could see how the country had changed. I could sense the hatred in it. I was very disappointed that the Vietnamese people had lost their old values.

What are Sang's goals for himself here in the United States?

When I got here the International Refugee Commission helped me find a job and learn English. I thought I would be able to learn English in six months, but because of my age it has taken me a lot longer. If I were twenty-five, I think I would improve faster. It is very hard to talk on the telephone. I feel nervous and afraid. Since I have a family with two young children I had to go to work right away. I worked for two years in a factory that produced vitamins. Then the company closed, but the severance package made it possible for me to go back to school. Now I am studying office applications for non-native speakers. I have had a lot of office experience, and I hope that I will be able to work in an office someday. In America there are many opportunities to go to school. In Vietnam there are only limited educational opportunities, and you have to be wealthy to take advantage of them.

Does he ever think of the camp or have flashbacks to his experiences there?

Once every two or three months I will have a nightmare in which I am back in the camp. I am planning to escape, but they arrest me. Or I dream that I have the papers to leave, but they will not let me go. I wake up from those dreams sweating, but then I realize that I am in the United States and not in Vietnam. Yet I still feel afraid for the next hour or two. When my friends write to me from Vietnam I can sense the pain of their situation. I write back and send them money.

Is there anything else he would like me to convey in this book?

Other former political prisoners and I are concerned about the young people of Vietnam, especially those with little education. They look down on the old government. They do not see the right and the wrong of it or of the Communists. Their education is biased. The Communists have distorted their view of history. They have been taught to hate the old government and to think that the Communist government is all good. They have even been taught to look down on their own fathers. They are not able to understand the problems the Vietnamese people have had to go through. We are also concerned about those former political prisoners who are still in Vietnam and want to leave, but who are not able to qualify for the H.O. Program [those who served less than three years in the camps or were sentenced for political crimes after 1975].

At the end of the last of our four interviews, I asked Sang if it might be possible for me to interview his father and mother for the book. "They are afraid. They fear that if the Communists read this book and figure out who they are, they will not be able to go back to Vietnam again. But I am not afraid. What I have said is the truth. If the Communists read the book, they will see their own lives reflected in it."

PART II

Former Political Prisoners
and Their Families

6 / The Pilot

T

he life histories in the following three chapters are those of a family— a husband, a wife, and their eldest daughter. Tra, the husband, came from a wealthy and privileged background in North Vietnam. His family's wealth was stripped away in 1954 after the Communist takeover of North Vietnam and the resulting campaign to rid the newly formed Democratic Republic of Vietnam (DRV) of those perceived to be exploiters of the people, such as capitalists and large landowners. Tra fled to South Vietnam to escape Communist retribution, became a pilot in the South Vietnamese Air Force, and started a family. After the war he was put in re-education camps for seven years. During his incarceration his wife and children fled from Vietnam as boat people and resettled in the United States. He was finally reunited with them after a fifteen-year separation. Together, he and his wife have endured a painful and difficult process of readjusting to one another and to new roles in their relationship.

Tra was born in 1935 in a village not far from Hanoi's Nội Bài airport. He spent the first ten years of his life there and attended the local public school. He was the oldest child and had a younger brother and three younger sisters. His family owned enough paddy land both to provide for his family's needs and to hire out land to local farmers. "We were large landowners and our family was one of the wealthiest in the region. I was the oldest son and so I enjoyed a favored position in the family. I was spoiled and could get anything I wanted." Tra has few memories of his early years. "I can remember fishing in the river. And I remember an air strike [during World War II]. The allies were dropping bombs on the bridge in our village to prevent the Japanese from going to Hanoi. It was terrifying."

Tra's father was a career soldier. Prior to and during World War II he was a noncommissioned intelligence officer in the French army. When the Japanese disarmed the French forces in March 1945, he left the military and for the next four years worked as a farmer and businessman in his native village. Those four years following the end of World War II were a very unstable period in Vietnamese history. "The French and the Viet Minh were fighting for control of Vietnam. The Viet Minh were masters of the countryside, where we lived, and it was a very dangerous place. There was fighting all the time." To protect his children, Tra's father evacuated them to safer places several times when the fighting around their home became too intense. "He left my mother and grandmother behind to manage our land. We moved to four or five different places during those years. Often the local school moved with us, so we could continue with our lessons." His memories of this period of his life, from the ages of ten to fourteen, "are of moving a lot and of the French and Viet Minh fighting. It was a scary time."

In 1949 Tra's father rejoined the army, this time as a warrant officer in the Régiment Infantrie Colonial, a Vietnamese military unit formed by the French to defend their newly created Associated State of Vietnam against the Viet Minh. He was stationed in Hanoi and shortly thereafter placed Tra, now fifteen, at a boarding school there to continue his education. "I remember my father coming to visit the school and taking me out to eat at nearby restaurants. There was one that had especially delicious food. I wanted to go back there when I was older so that I could eat the food again. I also remember my father's girlfriend [he was still married to Tra's mother] giving me money to go to the movies so that she could be alone with my father."

In 1951 Tra's father bought a house in the city and moved his entire family there except for his wife and mother, who remained behind in the village. In addition to the girlfriend mentioned above, Tra's father had also acquired a second wife, with whom he had two children, and who lived with him and Tra in Hanoi.

He had told my mother to ask a girl in the village if she would marry him. After he got married he was not around much and only came to visit my mother to drop off money. In Vietnam in those days a man could have as many wives as he could afford. Then in 1956 or 1957 they passed a law saying that you could have only one wife. My father's second wife was afraid of me. I was the oldest son and I had a lot of power over her. If my father was not at home, I decided everything. If she wanted something, she had to ask me.

Between 1950 and 1954 Tra completed middle school (grades six through nine in Vietnam) and the first two years of high school (grades ten and eleven). He had a lot of memories from this period. "I joined the Boy Scouts when I was seventeen. We used to go on weekend camping trips. I learned a lot from the Boy Scouts—how to take care of myself, how to solve problems, how to deal with difficult situations, how to take care of and help others. I am still in touch with old friends from my Boy Scout days." He also remembers a painful incident with his father:

I respected my father. He treated me well, but I always obeyed him and was afraid of him. One day a teacher at school thought I had thrown some bread out a window at a girl to attract her attention. It was really an older boy who had done it, but when she looked up he had moved away and she only saw me. In those days boys used to do things like that hoping girls would notice them and eventually become their girlfriends. Of course, back then in Vietnam a girlfriend meant something very different than it does here in the United States. There was no sex, no living together. You could talk or write to each other about love, and love with your eyes, but you were not even allowed to hold hands. Anyway, the teacher thought that I had thrown the bread at the girl and wrote a letter about the incident to my father. As soon as my father saw me after I got home he slapped me across the face. Then he asked me why I had done it. I explained to him that I had not, that it had all been a misunderstanding.

In March 1954, shortly before the Battle of Dien Bien Phu (in which the Viet Minh defeated the French) and the subsequent Geneva Accords that ended the war, Tra's father was killed when the Viet Minh overran his military post. Tra remembers his family receiving a letter informing them of his death.

I felt very sad and lost. I did not know what my future would be. Would I be able to continue my studies and complete high school? I was still living in Hanoi when he was killed. Shortly thereafter Vietnam was partitioned by the Geneva Accords. The Viet Minh were leading a campaign against the land-owners in the countryside. They would set up people's courts in the villages and invite the peasants to denounce [đấu tố] the landowners who had ex-ploited them. Then they pronounced a verdict—it was usually death—and buried the landowners alive so that they would not have to waste a bullet. They had come to our house in the village and told my mother to go get me so that I could be put on trial in place of my dead father. She sent my uncle to Hanoi to warn me not to come home. If I had gone home, they would have killed me. My mother had sent me some money and gold, and I decided to run away. I was afraid and sad because I did not know what I was going to do about completing my schooling, but I knew I had to go or the Communists would put me in jail or kill me. I had no choice. My uncle, who had recently deserted from his unit in the Vietnamese army, came with me. That was a very chaotic time in Vietnam. The Communists had not gotten things organized yet, and the government was not in control of people's movements. We took the train to Hai Phong [a port city on the South China Sea], which still belonged to the French. When we got there my uncle rejoined his army unit. I bumped into an old friend from the Boy Scouts who was helping to organize those students who had no relatives and who wanted to be evacuated to the South. He helped me to get a plane ticket, and two days later I flew to Saigon.

I arrived at Tan Son Nhut Airport [the main airport in Saigon] alone. A family friend from the Boy Scouts picked me up and took me to his house. I stayed with his family for about a month. Then I went to a camp for students who had been evacuated from the North. I stayed there for another three or four months until I could re-establish contact with my uncle, whose army unit had come down from the North and was now stationed in Saigon. I went to live with him and his wife in Gia Dinh [a part of Saigon]. I finished my last year of school at the Chu Văn An High School, which had moved from Hanoi to Saigon at about the same time I had. The school shared space in the Pétrus Ký High School, the most famous high school in Vietnam.

After graduating from high school with my baccalaureate degree [in 1955] I was not sure what to do. I did not have any more money, and so I considered attending a training school for army officers in Saigon, but I finally decided that I would rather join the [South Vietnamese] air force. I had been told that my thyroid was enlarged and that I needed an operation. The doctor recommended that I go to France and have it done. In those days the Vietnamese Air Force sent all of its officers and noncommissioned officers to France for training. So I decided to volunteer for the air force in order to get the operation. When I went in for my physical exam I had to be careful to keep my chin down so that they would not see my enlarged thyroid. I was sent to a seacoast town in France, where I began my training. A month after I arrived there my thyroid problem went away.[1] Maybe I had developed the problem in Vietnam because I was so depressed about my future. I was very sad back then. I had no money, I was lonely, and almost all my family was living in the North. Once I got to France I felt very happy. I was twenty years old, I had money and a career, and I got to travel a lot. I was there until June 1957. After that I returned to Vietnam as a sergeant first class and was sent to the Bien Hoa Air Force Base [an air base near Saigon that later became a major air base for the United States]. They put me to work in an office, partly because I had done very well in [the training] school and partly because I had no experience. At night I took courses in Saigon. I had only completed my first *baccalauréat* in high school and wanted to complete the second so that I could go on to the university. Once I got the second *baccalauréat* I spent the next two years studying law, but there was not enough time to do my job, attend courses, and pass all the tests. So I volunteered to train as a pilot. I did it mainly because I wanted to become an officer. In the lower ranks it was harder to find a girl, and I wanted to get married. I tried to pass the flight physical several times, but kept failing until 1961 when they decided they needed a lot more pilots and lowered the standard.

Tra was first sent to Nha Trang, a major seacoast town and military base, for his pilot training. He completed training there in January 1963 and then commuted between Tan Son Nhut, Can Tho (a major city in the Mekong Delta), and Nha Trang until 1965. During this time he worked as a forward air controller, directing air strikes against military targets. He met his wife Oanh in Can Tho in 1964, when he was twenty-nine and she was twenty-two.

I saw her walking along the street. I thought she was cute and wanted to meet her. A friend of mine knew where she lived. He and I went to her house to visit. Her parents let us come inside and talk. After that I went back every night. My unit was stationed at Tan Son Nhut Air Base in Saigon, but there was always a seven-plane detail assigned to Can Tho. Usually, you were sent there for just a few weeks, but once I met her I volunteered to stay indefinitely. After I had been seeing her for six or seven months I asked her to marry me. She already had a boyfriend, but he was in a different city. She said, "If you are serious, tell your family to come and see my parents." The only family I had was my uncle in Saigon. He is not really my uncle; he is my second cousin and is only a couple of years older than I am. Her parents asked him why I was twenty-nine and still single. They wondered if maybe I had another wife. They were also bothered by the fact that my uncle was very young too. People in the South just do not trust people from the North. Her parents gave me a hard time. They asked me to get a document from the Defense Ministry giving me permission to get married. Paperwork like that takes a long time. We got engaged and the wedding was announced, but the paperwork still had not arrived. Her father said that without the paperwork, we could not get married.

My wife talked to her mother. She told her that she really wanted to get married and proposed another solution. She had a relative in military intelligence. She should not have done it, but she asked him to check to see if I was still single. He looked through my personnel folder, confirmed that I was, and the wedding took place. We had to wait another month for the paperwork to come through so that we could do the official civil ceremony. In those days officers had to get authorization from the Defense Ministry to get married. The government was trying to be sure that people were not marrying Viet Cong [v c].

After their marriage Tra and Oanh were stationed initially in Can Tho, where their first daughter (whose story appears in "The Pilot's Daughter") was born in 1965. Shortly thereafter they were transferred to Nha Trang, where their three other daughters were born, in 1966, 1970, and 1972. In 1970 Tra was sent to the United States for further training at the U.S. Air Force Command and Staff College. After completing the program he returned to Nha Trang and was assigned to the South Vietnamese Command and Staff School. In 1973 he was named chief of the Office of Research and Evaluation there. He stayed in this position until the end of the war, in April 1975.

I asked Tra when he had begun to sense that the South might lose the war.

In 1971 when Kissinger went to China. The United States sacrificed my country to get good relations with China. After Kissinger's meeting with the Chinese the United States began to cut its aid to Vietnam, even things like heating and cooking oil. Those things were being sent to China, not to us. The United States figured that if they had good relations with China, they did not need seato [the Southeast Asia Treaty Organization, of which the United States and Vietnam were members] and us anymore. If the Americans had continued to support us, we could have won the war. It was a big mistake to send U.S. forces to Vietnam in the first place. It became America's war, not ours. We were only collaborators. We were not fighting for our people, but for the Americans. We lost the spirit and meaning of nationalism. When you make war you have to justify it, you have to have a righteous cause [*chánh nghĩa*], [such as] independence, liberation, and nationalism. We gave that cause to the Viet Cong. They were able to say that they were freeing Vietnam from the Americans.

Former political prisoners explained their country's defeat in several ways. Some believed that the United States had let them down, reducing its military assistance to the point where it was inevitable that the South would lose. Others thought that it was corruption at the top of the South Vietnamese government that had led to defeat. Several, like Tra, also mentioned the lack of a "righteous cause" as a key factor underlying their low morale and the Communists' victory. The Viet Minh and later the Communists were skillful at exploiting the Vietnamese desire to rid their nation of foreigners and unify a divided Vietnam. The South Vietnamese came to appear as lackeys of French and American colonialism, whose goals were ultimately selfish and not those of the Vietnamese people. The rabid anti-Communism of the 1950s and 1960s in the United States helped to blind Americans to the nationalistic strivings of the Vietnamese. The United States was drawn into a struggle in which it and its allies came to symbolize the colonial past, not an independent future. America's enemies, on the other hand, fought under the nationalist motto inscribed on Ho Chi Minh's tomb in Hanoi: *Không có gì quí hơn độc lập tự do* (There is nothing more important than independence and freedom).

Tra continued to present his views on why South Vietnam had lost the war:

We also used the wrong weapons. We needed Skyraiders [a propeller-driven aircraft used in ground support operations], not AT-37s. Their flying time was too limited. We needed planes that could stay up longer and provide close air support for the ground forces. I discussed this a lot with my classmates in the United States [during my time as a student at the U.S. Air Force

Command and Staff College in 1970]. As a result my teacher there wrote on my evaluation, "Anti-Communist, but also anti-American." That was not true. I was just saying what I thought, but with the Americans you have to agree with everything they say and do or you are against them. The United States needs to change the way it works in the world, the way it behaves. In France I once saw a convoy of U.S. troops going through the streets. They threw empty soda cans at people standing by the road. I saw a lot of that kind of behavior in Vietnam too.

I did not think that we would lose the war so fast. We had a lot of weapons at Pleiku.[2] Who decided to withdraw from there? Why did they not destroy the weapons? There is something fishy about the whole thing. Vietnamization was a good idea, but what it really meant was that the United States was leaving. They did not give us enough support. I do not think the United States wanted to win the war. When I was training at the Command and Staff School I saw a film about a C-130 with a 105 mm howitzer on board shooting Viet Cong at night. A weapon like that could have kept the North Vietnamese tanks from coming in 1972.[3] They trained us to use the C-130 with the 105, but then they never gave us any. We made flights along the Ho Chi Minh Trail every night in 1972 and could see the tanks, but we could not do anything about it. The Americans just did not want to win the war.

Did you try to escape at the end of the war? "I discussed it with my wife, but she did not want to leave without me." Tra and Oanh decided to wait until the last moment to escape so that he would not have to abandon his men and so that he and she would not be separated. Unfortunately, they waited too long, and in the end they were unable to find a way out of South Vietnam. While defeat seemed inevitable to many South Vietnamese, few anticipated how quickly it would come and most, like Tra and Oanh, waited until it was too late to leave. As the former South Vietnamese General Cao Van Vien remarks, "The rapidity and relative ease with which the Communists took over South Vietnam struck many people, the enemy included, as something unbelievable. How could it be possible? they asked. Why did South Vietnam go under so readily? What happened to the Vietnamese armed forces and the same army that had withstood so gallantly the two ferocious Communist onslaughts of 1968 and 1972?"[4] In the chaos following the Communist victory only those who were well placed and acted very quickly were able to get away. Most South Vietnamese who did escape made the decision to flee within twenty-four hours. They grabbed whatever they could carry, usually gold and some clothing, and rushed to airports and harbors, or commandeered their own transportation, in a headlong flight toward the American fleet lying offshore.

I asked Tra what he had done on that last day, April 30, 1975, when Saigon fell.

It was a terrible day. We lost everything. We did not know what to do. Some units fought until the end; others did not obey the orders of the [South Vietnamese] president [Duong Van Minh to surrender]. I did not know if our neighbors were Communist or not and did not know what they would do, so I decided to stay with a friend for a couple of days before coming home just to see what was going to happen. I told my wife where I would be so she would not worry. The night of the 30th was very quiet—it was scary. The night before there had been lots of rockets and noise, but on that night there were no rockets. The quiet was frightening because we did not know what was happening. After two days my wife encouraged me to come home. Nothing had happened. I did not know what to do. I had no idea how I would support my family.

Tra then described the events leading up to his entry into re-education camp:

There was an announcement [on the radio and over loudspeakers] that all soldiers of the old regime had to undergo re-education. You were told to go to a government office or school and write down everything in your past, a sort of curriculum vitae. Then you went home and waited. After a month there was another announcement telling you to present yourself for re-education. Warrant officers, noncommissioned officers, and lower ranks were told that their re-education would last three days and that they would be able to go home each night. Higher-ranking officers, majors through generals, and higher-level government officials were told that their re-education would last longer and that they should present themselves at a nearby high school or university with enough food and clothing for thirty days. You were given a three-day period during which you had to report. For me it was the 13th through the 15th of June. I did not go the first day, so somebody came to my house to remind me. The first day or two at the school the food was good. An excellent restaurant catered it. Then after a couple of days they moved us to the re-education camp. We did not know then that they were lying about the thirty days. Once I asked them, "Why did you say the camp would last only thirty days?" They said "We never said anything about a camp or how long it would last. We just said, 'Prepare for thirty days.' "

Looking back, a number of the former political prisoners I interviewed speculated that the Communists' rationale for engaging in this deceitful word game was to prevent a general uprising among the South Vietnamese population. Such an uprising might have occurred had their true intentions been known from the beginning.

On June 15th they came to the school with a big covered truck. They moved us at night. The truck drove for four or five hours. I did not know where we were going or why the truck was covered. I was frightened. I thought that maybe they were going to kill us. Finally, we got to where we were going. All around us there were big dogs and men with rifles. It was Hoc Mon [an area just outside of Saigon]. We stayed there for four or five months. They gave us lectures about politics, Communism, capitalism, why they had won, and why the United States had lost. Then they moved us to Bien Hoa for continued indoctrination. But after about ten classes they ran out of things for us to do. Once or twice a week they let us out to do some work, but there was not enough land for all of us.

In July 1976 they moved us again. We did not know where they were taking us. They moved us to the seaport in Saigon and we got on a ship, the *Sông Hương* [Perfume River, the river that flows through Hue]. I saw one guy jump into the water and drown himself rather than get on that ship. It was terrible! It was hot and there were no toilets. You had to go to the bathroom right where you were sitting. After a couple of days it smelled awful. You could not move. You could not lie down. You just sat there. We were given dried food, a Viet Cong battle meal. I did not eat it because I was afraid I would get diarrhea and there were no toilets. Later on when I was in the re-education camp and I thought back on that ship I said, "If I had a choice of either being released and going back to Saigon on that ship or staying here, I would stay here." We thought they would kill us on the ship, perhaps by pushing us into the sea. We were in the hold and could not see anything.

We were at sea for four days. Then we arrived in Hai Phong, in North Vietnam. People from the ship were divided up and sent to different places. Half of us spent the first night in a warehouse at the seaport, then we were moved the next day by train to Yen Bai. From there we walked the 30 kilometers to the forest where the camp was. They left us in the forest with next to nothing, only a machete and no other tools. They gave us a little raw corn mixed with rice to eat. They told us to build houses for us and for them. We had to build their house first, then ours. We worked in the forest cutting bamboo for the houses. Then we burned the forest to make a space for fields to plant crops. We raised manioc [a tuber similar to tapioca] for eating. That was our primary food. We did not get any rice [the staple food of any Vietnamese meal]. They took a lot of the food we raised and sold it.

We changed camps frequently. Usually we stayed in a camp for about two years, and then they moved us. Each camp was divided up into seven to ten sub-camps. There were about 500 people in each sub-camp, with five to ten barracks to hold them all. Each person had a small space, about 2 feet wide, to sleep in. We had to sleep end-to-end so that there would be enough space for everybody. The living conditions were very bad. There were 80 to 100 people in each barracks. The toilet was inside. It consisted of one or two buckets for everybody to use. We were locked in at night. It was terrible for those people who slept next to the toilet. There were people coming and going all night.

We did not have any Western medicine, only herbal medicine. After the first couple of years we were allowed to get one parcel from home every two months. My wife and mother would send things I needed, like dried food and medicine. It was not enough—the parcel could only weigh one kilogram [2.2 pounds]. A lot of people died. After three years in the camp they let your family visit every three months and bring food.

In one respect I was lucky. My father had a brother. He was a district chief in North Vietnam under the Vietnamese government that the French had set up with the old emperor, Bao Dai, as its head. Back then the French and the emperor controlled Hanoi and the Viet Minh controlled the countryside. When the Viet Minh took over in 1954 my uncle was put in a re-education camp and stayed there for three or four years. He had a daughter who was killed in an American bombing raid while working as a nurse. This made her a "martyr of the resistance" and her mother, my aunt, a "hero's mother." As a result my aunt was allowed to visit me in the camp in late 1977 [after I had been there for two years]. She brought along my mother. I was the only one in the camp to get a visit. When she came there they read out her name, but I did not recognize it because it was her married name. I said to the guards, "I do not know her." They said, "You may not know her, but she is here to visit you. She is from your village." I had to walk two hours from my sub-camp to the camp headquarters for the meeting. When I got there I waited another hour before they called me in. In the room I saw two old ladies. One of them was my mother, but I did not recognize the other one, who was my aunt. I visited with them for about half an hour. We talked about our relatives, and they told me to behave well in the camp. The cadre had asked them to encourage me to believe in the new government and in the goals of the re-education camp. We were not able to talk about anything else because we were in a small room with an open window and someone was listening beside it.

My wife left for the United States in 1978. We were separated for fifteen years! I entered the re-education camps on June 14, 1975, and was reunited with her on July 17, 1990—fifteen years, one month and three days! We kept in touch through letters. Each month we were allowed to write one letter, which was censored by the guards. But I also wrote "unofficial" letters.

Sometimes I would sneak them out during family visits with my mother and aunt. I would hide the letter down here [as he said this he pointed to his crotch] and give it to them at the end of the visit. I also made a drinking cup with a false bottom. I hid the letter in the false bottom and brought the cup to the family visits, leaving it on the table for my aunt and mother to take. I had to keep changing methods so that the guards would not find out what I was doing. In the camps, criminal prisoners supervised the political prisoners. Another way I could write a letter to my wife was to give my [criminal] supervisor a bribe of some food or clothing and he would mail it. Sometimes, though, he would take the bribe and just throw the letter away.

Did Tra see anyone killed in the camps?

Twice. The first time was in the South at Bien Hoa. A guy tried to escape from the camp at night but was captured. The next day they had a trial for him. They forced us to listen to it over a loudspeaker. An hour after it ended they shot him. The second time was in North Vietnam. Three or four people escaped from the camp. After a few days they were recaptured and brought back to the camp. They beat one of them to death. The others were taken to another camp.

Did he witness or experience any torture?

I did not see any. Other people have talked about it, but there was not any at our camp. Their policy was not to touch us, but they did use harsh disciplinary measures. They put you in a "tiger cage" [a small corrugated tin box like a shipping container], placed it out in the middle of an open field in the hot sun, and gave you only a little food—two mugs of water and a bowl of manioc twice a day. Or they handcuffed you to the wall by your wrists and ankles. It was really uncomfortable! I remember one guy who was probably crazy complaining to the guard that he was so hungry that he did not have enough energy to work. The guard probably thought that he was criticizing the government by saying it made him work too hard and did not give him enough food. The prisoner said to the guard, "If you want to kill me, go ahead." Then he opened his shirt and dared the guard to shoot him, but he did not. You could tell the guard was angry, but he only shot in the air. Then the other guards came and took the guy away. The next day the chief of the camp came and talked to us. He said, "That guy is very bad. He will be the last to be released." Their philosophy was that the government is always right. They saw re-education as a measure of clemency. They used to say, "All the government is asking you to do is to work. If you complain about the food or the work, then you are defaming [*bôi bát*] the government."

How was the food in the camps?

During the first year in the South we got rice mixed with sorghum [*bo bo*]. It was not ground sorghum, just the raw grain. We tried to cook it to make it soft, but it was not very good. The second year in the North we got rice mixed with ground corn. The third year we got dried manioc and sometimes rice on major holidays like Tet. The worst years were 1978 and 1979. There was a shortage of food in the entire country and a lot of people died. As a result of the food shortages they started letting families come to visit us in the camps so that they could supplement our rations. They brought rice, dried food, and medicines.

In evaluating the conditions in the re-education camps, it is important to keep in mind what living conditions were like in Vietnam as a whole during the decade following the war. Between 1975 and 1986 Vietnam was desperately poor. Most people in the country did not have enough to eat, and meat and other sources of protein were in especially short supply. In 1976 the monthly food ration was only 14 kilograms of rice, four cans of condensed milk, and 2 kilograms of sugar per person. This was even less than was fed to the starving guerrilla fighters in Vietnam's jungles during the war. They received a ration of 20 kilograms of rice per month.[5] Even in 1990, when I first returned to Vietnam fifteen years after the war's end, I was struck by how little food was available and by its generally poor quality, at least by Western standards. During the month I was there I always felt hungry, even though I had far more to eat than the average Vietnamese. Life in postwar Vietnam was very, very hard, and people had to exert all their energy just to stay alive. Despite this, however, I believe that most Vietnamese would have viewed the former political prisoners' circumstances as markedly worse than their own. Family members who visited the camps were shocked and appalled at the physical and mental condition of their relatives there. They had little to eat, especially considering the strenuous physical labor that they were compelled to perform, and few if any received adequate medical care. While Western medicines were hard to come by even for the civilian population, the prisoners had none at all. Despite the efficacy of some of the herbal preparations that were available, they were of little use against diseases like malaria, a common ailment in the more remote regions of the country where many of the camps were located.

In the camps we were divided up into groups [đội] of twenty to thirty people. The men in each group ate, worked, and lived together. There were two or three đội in each barracks. They were your friends, but you had to be careful to talk openly only with those you knew very well because there were spies. Once a spy betrayed me by telling the guards that I had a book of Buddhist sutras hidden under the roof of the barracks. It had my name in it, so when they found it I could not deny that it was mine. As a punishment I was forbidden to send or receive letters for two or three months.

How did Tra cope with life in the camps?

I could not change the situation, so I accepted it. I was sad, but I tried to be happy. For example, when I would go into the jungle to work, I would think "This is a beautiful day." I tried to enjoy the beautiful day and the pretty scenery. It was a spiritual acceptance of the situation. Sometimes I thought that I would die in the camps, but I accepted it. When I was young I read Dale Carnegie's book *How to Stop Worrying*. It was very popular in Vietnam and had been translated into Vietnamese. I reread it several times. What I learned from that book helped me to survive! Also, when I was in the United States in 1970 I studied problem solving. That helped too. I never had any periods of real depression. And after my wife and children got to the United States I was very happy. Before she left my wife had written a number of times saying that she was going to try to escape. Of course, she had to disguise her true intentions because the guards read our letters. She had a nephew in the United States. She wrote to me that she was going to move to the New Economic Zones to be with her nephew. [The New Economic Zones were sparsely populated areas into which the South's surplus population was to be resettled.] The Communists wanted people to move there, so they thought that was a good thing to do. But when she mentioned her nephew I knew that she meant she was going to the United States.

In 1982, after I had been in the camp in the North for six years, they decided to send us to the South. I am not sure why they did it. They had closed a lot of camps in the North. Maybe it had something to do with their discussions with the United States. They sent us by train. When we stopped in Hue the guards said to us, "Do not look out, the people are mad at you. If they see you they will throw rocks." But when the people saw us they gave us candy and cigarettes even though they were very poor! They called out, "If you want to send a letter to anybody, just throw it out to us!" Their reaction made us feel very happy. Let me give you another example of how the people really felt about us: Once I got settled in the camp in the South, I wanted to let my relatives know where I was. I wrote down the information on a small scrap of paper and gave it to a friend, who was being visited by one of his relatives. My friend's relative was going to send the paper to my relatives, but by mistake he left it on the seat of a *cyclo*. The *cyclo* driver found the paper, read it, and took it to my relatives. They offered to pay him, but he refused, saying that he knew the information was from a political prisoner and that he understood how it must feel not to know where your loved ones were.

When was he finally released from the camp?

In 1984, a couple of days before Tet. We went out to work, just like all the other days. Then they read a list of names of those who were going to be released. I could not believe it! I checked with my friends to see if they had really read my name. I just could not believe that I would be released so soon. But they let me go. They gave me the bus fare to get to Saigon. I walked out from the camp to the highway and got on a bus. When the bus driver realized that I was a prisoner, he did not ask for any payment.

After I got to Saigon I went to live at my uncle's house. [I had only intended to stay there for a short time, but] I was on probation and had to stay where I had been sent, so I stayed for a year. Once a week I had to present myself to the local ward [*phường*] administrative office. After a year I was able to move in with a friend. I was not able to work. There were not enough jobs to go around and former political prisoners like me were last on the list. My wife, who was already resettled and working in the United States by then, supported me. She sent me money and gifts. I tried to escape by boat several times, but the guides tricked me, leaving me behind. The last time I tried to escape a couple of my friends and I bought a boat. The plan was for us to have the boat anchored offshore. We would get out to it in sampans. But my sampan driver got lost, and we never made it. The other two guys did make it and sailed to Malaysia. I finally got out in 1990. The Communists had put me on the H.O. Program [a program that enabled former political prisoners to immigrate to the United States] list, but since my wife and children were already United States citizens I was transferred to the ODP [Orderly Departure Program; a program to allow the safe immigration to the United States of Vietnamese wanting to leave Vietnam]. My wife had to buy my plane ticket. The American ODP interviewers told me that how soon I got out depended on when she gave me the money for the ticket.

I asked Tra about his reunion with his wife in the United States and how their fifteen-year separation had affected them as a couple. Tra turned to me with tears in his eyes and said, "My wife is a wonderful woman. She raised four children without me, and they have done very well." He then played for me the videotape of a local television news report about their reunion that had been broadcast nine years before. The camera showed Oanh and their four daughters waiting excitedly at the airport gate for the husband and father they had not seen in fifteen years. They watched as the passengers and then the pilots and the crew disembarked from the plane. Tra was not on board! The eager excitement in their faces turned to anxiety and frustration as they, a resettlement worker, and the news crew tried to find out where he was. After a few phone calls the airline determined that he was coming in on a later flight. Three hours later, when the door of the boarding gate opened, they were not disappointed. There was Tra, clad in a new suit that was a little too large for him, beaming as his family rushed to embrace him. After an ecstatic reunion in which Tra unsuccessfully fought back tears ("I had not cried in fifteen years"), the camera showed the backs of the newly reunited couple as they walked arm in arm down the long airport corridor as if into a bright new future. However, as I was to learn from Oanh and Tra, the years following their reunion were a painful and difficult time. He, as a former political prisoner, and she, as a single mother who had raised and supported four children by herself for fifteen years, had to work hard to accustom themselves to new roles in their relationship.

Tra acknowledged that their reunion "was a big adjustment":

We had a lot of problems. Sometimes I thought we would not make it. After we had been back together for a few years she said to me, "You know, we are still adjusting. There is still a distance between us." In Vietnam, as the husband, I took care of everything. Here I had nothing, no job and no money. She gave me everything. I felt belittled. She said, "Stay home and rest." I said, "No, I want to go to work as soon as possible." So she went and talked to the manager of the factory where she works. He offered me a job as an electronics assembler in 1991, and I have been doing it ever since.

At the end of my interview with Tra, I asked him whether he ever dreams of the re-education camp.

7 / The Pilot's Wife

*T*ra's wife Oanh was born in South Vietnam and enjoyed a comfortable lifestyle as the child of wealthy parents. She met her husband
when he was stationed at an air base in her hometown. After their
*marriage they had four daughters, the youngest of whom was only two years old
when Tra left for re-education camp. After her husband's incarceration Oanh
struggled to support their young children, finally fleeing Vietnam with them as a
boat person in 1978. Resettled in the upper Midwest of the United States, she
searched for ways to survive as a single mother. The town in which she first lived
did not offer enough employment opportunities, and so she and the girls moved to
a much larger city, where she could work two jobs to support both them and her
husband in Vietnam. The transition from a life of privilege and affluence to one
of poverty in postwar Vietnam and in the United States transformed Oanh from
a traditional Vietnamese woman into a strong-willed and independent person
capable of surviving on her own without a husband. When she and Tra were
finally reunited in the United States after a fifteen-year separation, they began a
lengthy and ongoing process of adjusting to new roles in their relationship.*

Tra's wife Oanh was born in Can Tho in the Mekong Delta region of
South Vietnam. Her father, although the youngest son in his family,
received more education than his older brothers and graduated from an
accounting school in Saigon. After graduation he took a job with the
Vietnamese Internal Revenue Service and, by the time of Oanh's birth,
was chief of its office in Can Tho.

Everybody knew him. He was rich, and we had a very high standard of living. He lived in a big house that ran between two streets. He built it when he moved to Can Tho in 1937. He had a full-time housekeeper who did everything he wanted, including the washing and ironing. He owned a rickshaw and employed his own rickshaw man. He owned a farm with 30,000 acres and had enough land and houses to be able to give one house to each of his eleven children. He also had three wives. With the first wife he had a son, with the second, a daughter, and with the third, nine more children. I was the fourth child of the third wife. My father had enough money to send the two oldest boys to study in France.

I had a very good life as a young person. I could go anywhere in the city that I wanted. I attended a French elementary school for the first four years. One day my parents asked me to read the local newspaper to them. It was in Vietnamese, and I could not read it! I only knew how to read French. So they decided to send me to a Vietnamese school. I went there through the first half of the eleventh grade. I stopped school in 1962, when I was twenty years old. I had lost time when I changed schools and was embarrassed to be with so many younger students.

My father decided to retire early in 1955. The IRS had wanted him to move to another city, but he refused to go and just retired. He was wild! He gambled and played cards. I used to hear my parents fighting about money, and it made me feel that I had to get a job. So I became a newsreader for a radio station that broadcast to Vietnamese military personnel stationed in the Mekong Delta. After a year of that I got a job working for the U.S. military as an accountant.

Oanh continued to work as an accountant for the U.S. Army after her marriage, until Tra was transferred to Nha Trang in May 1965. There she got a job as an assistant manager for the Bank of America, which ran a branch office in Nha Trang for American soldiers. Asked how she had felt about being an officer's wife, Oanh responded:

All my life in Vietnam there was war. There were soldiers all around me. Military service was mandatory for everyone between eighteen and twenty-seven years of age. Most of the popular songs were about war. So I grew up thinking that I had to do something for my country. I was very proud to be an officer's wife. He left home every morning at 6 A.M. and came back at 8 P.M. and I worked during the day. One day the husband of my next door neighbor was shot down. He did not come back. After that, while I still felt proud, I was also frightened every day until he walked in the door at night.

I asked Oanh why she and Tra had not left Vietnam before the final collapse on April 30, 1975.

One day during the first week of April he came home and told me to leave. His friends' wives and kids had already left. I was sitting on the swing at home. We had just built the house, and as I sat there looking at our lovely coconut and betel nut trees I asked my husband, "Will you go with me?" He said, "No, I do not want to leave my unit." I thought to myself, "If I go, I will miss my house and all of these things that I love," so I said to him, "Wait until the last minute. It took a month for Phnom Penh [capital of Cambodia] to fall." Then a few weeks later, when the last minute came, he was at Tan Son Nhut Airport and could have escaped, but he did not want to leave me behind.

In some ways the end of the war was a big relief for me. At least I did not have to worry any more about his getting shot down. But I was worried because I did not know what they would do to him. Our neighbor was in the Special Police. He used to arrest the Communists, so the Communists knew him. That first night they came to his house and arrested him. He spent three or four years in jail. When they let him out he was very thin and sick. Not long afterwards he died. He was only in his late fifties.

[After my husband left for the re-education camp] I continued to live in the same house and to send the children to school every day. The oldest of our four girls was in the sixth grade then. I tried to earn money by doing all kinds of business. I sold clothing, gold, medicines, coffee, bean cakes, fried bananas, grilled corn—all out on the streets by the curbside, in what we call an "open air market" [*chợ trời*—an informal curbside business]. Some of my businesses were illegal. You were not allowed to sell gold and medicines. I had spent my whole life as a housewife and did not have the experience to do well and to compete in any of those businesses. I just was not making enough money to support the girls. Nobody in my family could help me because they were all in the same boat. I once did go to visit my parents in Can Tho. They gave me some rice, but the soldiers at a Communist checkpoint [on the way home] took it away from me. Finally, I realized that we were not going to make it in Vietnam. I decided to try to escape.

My brother knew a boat captain. Before 1975 he had owned a big fishing boat that could go out to sea and stay for a month. After the Communists came to power they took his boat and hired him to run it and fish for the government. My brother arranged for the escape. We helped him raise the money to pay the captain. There were only 150 people on the boat and 45 were members of our extended family! Everyone left in small sampans and went out to the big boat at night. It was waiting on the Can Tho River. Our plan was to sail to Australia. On the way we stopped at an oilrig off Singapore and asked for directions. They pointed over to the Malaysian shore and said that there was a refugee camp over there. We sailed to it and stayed in the camp for the next nine weeks. There were eight families in our group. We were interviewed in the camp by various countries. We did not know anything about any of them. My brother wanted to get settled as quickly as possible. He said he would go to whatever country picked him first. Australia accepted him, my older sister, two other brothers, and me. But I had another sister who had to go to the United States because she had a son studying there. She begged me to go with her rather than to Australia with the others. She did not want to be alone. So I agreed. We ended up in [an upper Midwestern state] because her nephew had a job there working for [a large computer company].

I came to the United States with no money. We had used all we had to pay for the boat. We only had two pairs of clothing for each of the girls, who were then thirteen, twelve, eight, and five years old. We only stayed in [the place where they were initially resettled] for a year. My first job was as a janitor. I emptied trash for [a large computer company]! I needed to get a second job because I did not want to be living off welfare and food stamps, but the town was so small that I could not find one. My niece told me there were lots of jobs in [the city where I interviewed Oanh and Tra], so I decided to move here.

Describing her life after their resettlement in the new city, Oanh continued:

I do not know what my face looked like during that time. I was too busy to even look in the mirror. The only thing I thought about was making money. I got a job working on an assembly line. I only made $3.25 an hour, and so I went to welfare and asked for help. The woman there was Vietnamese. She was very snooty. She said, "You are making $3.25 an hour, and you are still asking for help? Your rent must be too high. Why do you not move to [a notorious housing project where many newly arrived Vietnamese refugees lived]?" I was so upset. I did not know what to say. I just cried and walked away. Finally, I got a second job working at a convenience store. I got robbed at gunpoint several times. The United States has taught me a lot! After the robberies I got scared, quit, and found a different second job working at a gas station.

Life was very hard until the girls got to the age when they could get part-time jobs and help me support the family. I always worked overtime. The children had to take care of themselves. I would come home from my first job, quickly cook the food, then go off to the second job. I would call home and tell my oldest daughter what to cook. Because of having to take care of her younger sisters, she never got to go to college. The girls did all right, though. They are very nice and sweet. There is one thing that I am sorry about. When I first arrived I did not know how to read a map, so I did not take them to school on their first day. The first day of school is very important. Children need their mama then! I was not able to go to parents' meetings either because I was working two jobs. I still regret it. We are lucky that they turned out so well. They do not have any big problems. I always said to them, "You need to work hard and get good jobs. That is all your father and I want." I encouraged them to study. When children understand a situation they behave well. I reminded them that their father was a pilot. "He is not home now. You have to do well to show him that you love him."

I asked Oanh how she had felt during those years when she as a single mother had worked so hard to support four young children. "I cried all the time. At the convenience store when I was cleaning up I would be sweeping the floor and crying. I slept all right, but I did not eat for enjoyment, just to fill up." Like their husbands in the camps, the prisoners' wives struggled against depression along with poverty, loneliness, and unaccustomed new roles. Even for those already resettled in the United States, their depression often went untreated. This was due in part to prohibitions in the Vietnamese cultural tradition against self-disclosure and to the Vietnamese conception of depression as a personal emotional problem to be managed stoically and alone rather than as an illness. It was also due to the women's unawareness of mental health treatment opportunities available in the United States and to a lack of culturally competent mental health providers.

How, I asked Oanh, did life change after Tra's arrival?

I had worked [in Vietnam] after our marriage, but I was primarily a housewife. Here I was a single mother with children. I had to work very hard to adjust to life. I worked full time in a factory and evenings in a gas station and a convenience store. I was working sixteen to eighteen hours a day! When people at the gas station drove off without paying I would get angry. I screamed at them and gave them the finger. If they came back and swore and gave me the finger, I swore back at them and gave them the finger double! I was not like that in Vietnam. In Vietnam if I heard someone swear, I would turn away and pretend I had not heard it. Before I would not react, but now I reacted. When my husband got here he said that I was not the same woman he had married! While I was moving forward, getting used to a new country and culture, he was being pulled back [into his memories of the old Vietnam]. After he got here he had a long way to go to catch up to me. He had an inferiority complex. Whatever I did he felt like I was being overbearing. I had been making decisions on my own for a long time. That was a big change in the way our roles had been in Vietnam. After he arrived here I went on making decisions without asking him just like I had done for the past fifteen years, but he would get upset. [For example,] when he got here I gave him a set of keys—keys to the house, my car, and a pickup truck I had bought for him. He liked having the truck and was very appreciative. However, a few days later I tried to drive him to the store to show him the way. He did not like it. He said, "The man has to drive." I stopped the car and pointed around at all the other cars. "Look," I said, "here men and women both drive!" After that he was OK with it. You see, in Vietnam the male is the hero, the boss. He takes care of everything.

[Before he arrived] I had prepared myself for various alternatives. Some of our friends, also pilots, came home after their release, stayed together with their wives for a few years, and then got divorced. They just could not make it. I was sure that he and I both loved the children. We tried to discuss our problems with each other when the kids were not at home. We saw our job as setting a good example for the children. For instance, we often tell them that we need money, but that money does not buy happiness. Happiness lies in other things. We are not rich, but we are happy because we know how to create a good and harmonious atmosphere in the family.

Here Tra added,

[Before I left] Vietnam I had anticipated that my wife and I would have a lot of problems when we got together again, but I was not prepared for the problems I had with my children. For example, one day our youngest daughter, a twelfth grader, said she wanted to go over and visit an American friend at her house. My wife did not approve of the way she was dressed and told her to change. She changed, but she was angry and when she drove away she went out of the driveway very fast. I did not like her attitude. I told my wife to call her at her friend's house and tell her not to drive anymore because she was so angry. When she got back we sat all four of the girls down and talked to them.

Oanh explained,

After he got here he did not know much about teenagers or about our kids. He would get angry with them, and I would be caught in the middle. If he had a problem with them or they had a problem with him, they came to me. The girls would complain that he was too old-fashioned.

In the Vietnamese tradition we venerate our ancestors. We always have an altar [for their veneration] in our home. We ask a lot of our children. When we are old they have to care for us. They have to do it with respect, not just with material things, but with emotional things as well. I used to tell the girls, "My life consists only of today. The present is what is important to me. We have to work hard to have a good relationship between us and to keep our family harmonious. When I am dead you can throw my ashes away so that there is no more trace of me. You are free of any responsibility to venerate me. Just respect me and treat me well *now*. Be obedient." In the United States kids can end up living anywhere. That makes it hard for them to come back and visit our graves. It is easier for them [if they do not have the responsibility to venerate us].

Tra and Oanh described with openness and candor the difficulties faced by many former political prisoners and their wives when they were reunited after a separation of five, ten, or fifteen years. Traditional Vietnamese society is patrilineal. Men are responsible for supporting the family and making most of the important decisions. After their husbands left for re-education camps prisoners' wives were forced to assume unaccustomed roles as the main, and often only, provider and the chief decision-maker in the family. When their husbands returned from the camps they expected to resume their previous role as head of the household. Adding to the difficulty of this transition was the husbands' loss of social and employment status after the war. Many needed to have their wives continue to work to help them support the family. It is my impression that the former prisoners' transition back into the family was easier if it occurred in Vietnam, where the surrounding social structure reinforced the resumption of their traditional roles. However, for those like Tra and Oanh who were reunited after the wife had functioned independently for some time in the United States, things were more difficult. In addition to their loss of status, husbands had to cope with a new language that their wives and children spoke much better than they did. They also had to adjust to a cultural tradition in which the roles of men and women, and parents and children, are less clearly delineated than in the old Vietnam. While Tra and Oanh's marriage survived this extraordinary transition, many others did not.

8 / The Pilot's Daughter

*P*huong, the eldest daughter of Tra and Oanh, was ten years old when her father entered the re-education camps and thirteen when she escaped from Vietnam. After her arrival in the United States she had to provide much of the care for her younger sisters because her mother was so busy working to support the family. In her story she reflects on her early memories of Vietnam, her family's flight as boat people, their adjustment to life in the United States, and the effects of her father's long absence on her development both as a woman and as a parent.

Phuong, thirty-one, is the oldest of Tra's and Oanh's four girls. She lives with her Vietnamese husband and their two daughters, ages three and two, in a subdivision close to her parents' home. Her house is a recently constructed, two-story, red brick structure simply and attractively furnished in a contemporary American style. She and her husband both work full-time in businesses that support the local computer industry.

We had met previously during one of my interviews with her parents, and she greeted me in a warm and friendly manner, offering me a cup of delicious chicory-flavored coffee. Phuong is an attractive young woman who speaks English very well, especially for someone who first began to learn the language at the age of thirteen. Since our meeting at her parents' home she and I had corresponded by e-mail, and she understood my wish to supplement the former political prisoners' narratives with the perspectives of other family members.

I began by asking how her father's fifteen-year absence had affected her.

To tell the truth, the effect of my father's absence was more positive than negative. My mother was forced to be a single mother of four children, all girls. She had never before been in an environment where she had to fight for her food. It made her a strong woman. We modeled ourselves after her. We are very independent. I have my mother's strong will.

I am the oldest. I helped her a lot. I would go with her to the gas station [where she worked]. I never saw her being mean to the customers, but she was straightforward. She did not let them step on her.

What are her early memories of Vietnam?

I was thirteen when we left. I have some good memories of the time when my father was still at home. On my birthday he took us out for dinner and cake. We went shopping together. He took my younger sister and me to school. We rode behind him on a Vespa on rainy days. We lived first in Nha Trang, then in Saigon for the two or three years before he left [for the re-education camp]. He did not spend a lot of time with us. I do not recall having a close relationship with him, partly because of our culture, partly because he was in the military. Either our mother or servants took care of us. The man's role was to be the breadwinner. When he was home he was the boss. He did not show his affection. Dad was like that.

Does she have any memories of the last days of the war?

One day my father told us all to get in the car. We had a little Toyota. They were very proud of it and had purchased it just a few months before the fall [of Saigon]. He and my mother were in the front, and we girls were in the back. He said that we were going to the airport. People were running around, and the streets were a mess. I heard people talking about war and the Communists coming. I did not understand it. He took us to Tan Son Nhut [Airport]. He and my mother were having a discussion. They did not know if we could get into the airport or if we should. My mother told us kids to keep praying. We did a good job of that! They were trying to decide whether or not to leave Vietnam. My father told my mother to leave first. She said no. He said he had to stay with his unit. She said, "I am not going without you." Her brothers and sisters were not leaving either, so she decided to stay. We went back home. That night her friend Theresa arrived. She had escaped from central Vietnam and had come to stay with us. My father said that we should all sleep together in one place, the kitchen. He reasoned that it was in the center of the house and surrounded by other rooms. If a bomb came in, it would detonate away from us. Everyone huddled together in the kitchen. I heard the bombs passing over the house—whoosh! Across the street from us there was a large field with electricity poles in it. The next morning [the 30th] someone said that a helicopter had gone down over there, but I did not see it.

On the morning of the 30th my parents said, "Let us go to a friend's house." It was south of downtown and was a much taller building than ours, having four or five stories. We went there, but by the afternoon they said it was all over, so we went home. I saw tanks and soldiers. My mom said, "Do not call them v c [Viet Cong], they will kill you! Call them Ông [mister] and Bà [ma'am]." My father tied a red cloth [the Communist color] around the car's mirror to welcome them. My sister was wearing red, and he used some of her clothing.

Does she remember her father leaving for the re-education camp?

He drove us by the registration station. It was in a school. He said he would have to go for *học tập* [re-education]. I thought, "You have to go to school." He said he would be back in a month. Everyone was very casual about it. No one expected anything. Years later he said he should have remembered what the Communists were like. They had executed his father. My mom's friend Theresa and her two sons were still living with us. Her husband was going to the camp with my dad. They said she would be staying with us for a month, but she ended up staying for a long time. She had French citizenship and eventually went to France before we left Vietnam, but she lived with us for years. It was a good thing because it meant my mother had a friend. Theresa had a nanny who babysat for her children. She was only a few years older than me, but she took care of all of us while my mom and Theresa went out to earn money.

How did Phuong's life change after her father left for the re-education camp?

It was different. Before 1975 we were not rich, but we were comfortable. [After he left] I remember my mom telling me to go out to the market and buy 200 grams of meat to grind up and feed the entire family! There were nine of us, two adults and seven children. We put a lot of fish sauce in it and made it runny to supplement the rice. We also ate a lot of *bo bo* [sorghum] instead of rice. It was not so bad; we just were not used to it. We ate a lot of supplements. I was hungry a lot. My aunt lived fifteen minutes away. She had seven or eight children, and one of them was living and working in the United States. He sent her money. Also, her husband did not have to go to the camp and she was a teacher. She was better off than we were. She had sugar and cooked *chè* [a sweet dessert made of sugar and beans]. She asked us to sell it for her because our house fronted on the street. I remember craving it.

Here Phuong laughed.

My mom does not know this, but after I finished selling the *chè* I used to scrape out what was left over in the pot and eat it. We could not afford to buy it for ourselves.

I do not remember the day my father left [for the camp]. I have no memory of it. One month passed, and he did not return. Then they thought it would be three months, then a year. After that I could hear the hopelessness in Theresa's and my mother's voices. At that time my mother was about the age I am now. I have often thought, "If I were thrown into a situation like that, could I handle it?" It is in the culture. Vietnam is not a wealthy country. People are trained to do anything.

Between 1975 and 1978 I helped my mother. I was the oldest. I went to market with her. For a while we sold roasted corn. We bought raw corn, roasted it, and sold it in front of our house. She had a bicycle. She took me with her. I sat on a big bag of corn on the back of the bike to keep it stable. We used to clean the corn and then roast it and sell it. We did it for a long time, then we switched to something else. She sold cigarettes in front of the house. She kept them in a glass cabinet. At lunch we took a break and closed the iron fence in front of our house, leaving the cabinet inside by the fence. People reached in and stole all the cigarettes! We were innocent. We did not know what people would do. My mother was devastated because she had lost her entire investment. She tried different things. Once she went to Hue [a city in central Vietnam] with Theresa to buy yarn. Whenever she heard that something would sell well she tried it. I would go to the market, sit there, and sell the stuff for her. I remember feeling embarrassed. I did not know how to bargain. By the end of the day we [often] did not sell anything. [During this period] I was still able to attend school. The children were asked to go to meetings of a youth organization to learn more about Ho Chi Minh. My mother said no because she hated them by then, but I had to go. We had parades and I thought it was fun. I did the minimum requirement.

Does she remember leaving Vietnam?

I remember the whole day. It is funny. My mom laughs about it now. She said we would try to escape. It was supposed to be a secret, but I told all my friends at school! I wrote it in their schoolbooks. "Maybe I will not be seeing you next year." I was hinting that I would be leaving. I told my mom. She said, "Why did you do that?" We made one attempt [to escape] in January or February. It did not work. We went down to Can Tho to our grandparents' house, then we came back. Our block leader said, "I thought you had left!" My mother tried to fool him. She said, "We just went for a visit."

The day we left I cooked a pot of rice soup for breakfast. We got up about 4 or 5 A.M. It was still dark outside. We left the pot on the stove, and I remember thinking, "Why are we not washing it?" But we were leaving, so it did not matter. I looked around, trying to remember things. Then we just left, locking our door. We took a bus to the station and caught another bus for Can Tho. We got there by noon. Then we took a very small sampan. I remember how close the water was to my hand. We took the boat to an island where they made bricks. It was the meeting point. My mother told the people there that she had come to see her mother-in-law. It was a small place, and they asked, "What is her name?" She said she did not know. She said to us, "If you see your aunt, ignore her, pretend you do not know her." When it was dark we hid in the engine room of a small boat. I could hear the people coming on board. My uncle, who had set up the trip, could not find his wife, so we had to wait. Finally, she came. They signaled for the big boat to come in. I remember being thrown from the small boat to the big boat. I was scared the people would not catch me. We went down to a small compartment near the engine room. My mother lay there for two days because she was seasick! I remember hearing people saying, "We are stuck because of the low tide." They were worried. The boat was standing still. I went outside and looked around. I saw the moon. It was very pretty, but we were not moving. [After we got going] the trip was smooth. I once saw a dolphin swimming with us.

Finally, we got to an island off the coast of Malaysia. It was a beautiful day, and the water was very blue. I wanted to jump in! They took us in. It was dinnertime, and they fed us ramen noodles. There were not many people on the island. There were eight or nine shelters, just a roof with no walls. They were sectioned off for families: a sleeping and an eating place. We stayed for two months. I enjoyed it. We did not have to do anything. The adults and my older cousins cooked. We ran around and swam and went into the forest. We did not have any money. I remember craving ice—it was so hot! My cousins were either older or younger [than I was]. I was in between and left by myself. I was not lonely, but I would have had more fun if I had had my own group.

We left the island and went to Mersing. We were there for six to ten hours, then flew to Hong Kong. We stayed there one night and then flew to the United States to [the upper Midwestern state where they were first resettled].

We got there in June. I loved it! The first day we saw snow. We took pictures of it and really enjoyed it, the snow and sledding. The people there were nice. A person from the church took us around and showed us the market. A woman taught us English and about the culture. I learned the language well within a year. Of course, I made a lot of mistakes. I remember saying, "I am slipper" instead of "I am sleepy." The kids were nice to me and people helped me. I passed the grade! I went to the library and opened my books, but I had no idea what I was doing.

Refugee children's recollections and experiences of their flight are often very different from those of their parents. Phuong's memories of her escape from Vietnam and resettlement in the United States are filled with fun, wonder, and excitement—a beautiful moon, a dolphin, blue water, and snow. Her mother's memories are of a terrifying journey in which her life and the lives of her four young children hung in the balance and of a painful, exhausting struggle to survive in a new country.

Then my cousin decided to move here [to the city in which she and her parents live]. His mother and family were going with him, so my mother thought, "We will go too and support each other." She used to call me at home after school and tell me what to cook. She is a picky eater, and I am not a good cook. She had me cook easy things like ground beef. I remember cooking a lot of it.

Did Phuong mind having to stay home and cook while her school friends were playing?

I do not remember. I expected it and accepted it. I remember once I had a friend and I wanted to go to her house. I just left with her after school and did not go home. I got in trouble for that! Usually, I went straight home. We had our cousins, and we played with them. I did not go to my friends' houses much. I did not really have to watch my sisters; I was just there. My mother was not much involved in our school stuff. She did not have time. It is fortunate that we all turned out OK and that we did not get into trouble. Last year my sisters and I went out of town together [for a visit] and talked. [We remembered that] my mother had said, "Do not get pregnant, finish school." We did what she said. She made us feel guilty because our dad was not here. We had to do better [than others] because he was not here.

I finished high school and some college. I always worked part-time while I was in school. When I was fifteen I got my first job, at McDonald's. I made my sister come with me because I did not want to work there by myself. She lied and said that she was older [than she really was]. I gave my mom the money I earned. She did not ask me to help her, but I felt that I should. At some point I began keeping a bit of the money for myself. You know, my parents made an excuse for me when they told you that I did not finish school because I was the "second mother." The truth is that I was just not interested. I went to [a local university]. I spent more time working in a grocery store than I did attending school. I met my husband at college. He said, "Why do you not get a better job?" We started working for the same company. He never finished college either. I prefer hands-on learning to book learning.

What does Phuong remember about her father's reintegration into the family after he finally arrived in the United States?

I recall tension between him and my younger sister. At the time my youngest sister and I were at home and my two other sisters were in college. I do not recall much tension between him and me, but he was annoyed with my youngest sister because she was so rebellious. They did not get along. He was more traditional and used to the way children behave in Vietnam. She was an American girl. She said what she thought and acted independently. Do you remember that incident my parents told you about when she backed out of the driveway very fast? My father said, "I am so mad at that girl." In Vietnam you do not act out, even if you are angry. Now my sister says, "Dad did not like me—I was a punk." My mother had been here longer and was used to us.

If my dad had escaped with us, I do not think that we would have turned out this well. He would always have been strict. He would not have let us explore and find ourselves. He would have tried to hold us in and make demands on us. [Since he was not here] we are more open-minded.

Transitioning between two very different countries, immigrant and refugee children like Phuong often experience a strong internal tension between a wish to remain loyal to their parents and their cultural traditions and a desire to fit in with the young people in their new country with whom they attend school. With her mother gone much of the time, working to support the family, and her father in re-education camp, Phuong appears to have experienced less of this conflict and felt that she had more freedom to explore her new world. She was also able to justify her independent strivings by fashioning herself after her mother, a strong, self-sufficient woman whose behavior she tried to emulate.

How does Phuong behave as a parent with her own children? "I will let them have their freedom. My husband will, too. I think I will be open-minded. You can educate, but you cannot control and hold children back."

How does she view her parents now?

We have gotten closer, with our children. They come over to see the grandchildren, and I talk to them more. Sometimes I feel bad for my mother that she had to go through what she did. My dad is less demanding of her now, but he is still very old-fashioned. They are both pretty traditional. You would think that I would be close to my mom, but I am not. She was and still is embarrassed to talk about things with us. She usually holds her feelings back. She does not confide in me. I want my children to be close to me when they are older, to tell me everything.

Oanh's reluctance to share her feelings with Phuong reflects the behavior of most traditional Vietnamese, who are taught to keep their emotions private and to deal with them alone. Phuong's desire for a more open emotional relationship with her own children illustrates how far she has come in the process of adopting the social values of her new country, where openness and self-disclosure are more the norm. Yet she still retains a certain Vietnamese reserve. When she reviewed the draft of the manuscript describing her life, she asked me to leave out some of the more intense feelings she had expressed toward other family members, not wishing to upset or embarrass them.

9 / The Teacher

Quyet is a scholar who earned bachelor's and master's degrees in the United States and taught English at the Vietnamese National Military Academy (VNMA). After re-education camp he returned home and found work as a housepainter. He tried to forget what he had been and focused instead on what he had become, a "new man." Reconciled, at least partially, to his fate, he learned through a friend that the police believed he was working with rebellious Montagnards in the nearby mountains and jungle. His name was on their blacklist, and they were about to arrest him. Fleeing first to his family's home in Saigon, he then sought to disappear in the Mekong Delta region under an assumed identity. Betrayed by the wife of a former student, he embarked on a terrifying voyage as a boat person, finally reaching the United States in 1980. Here he hoped to pursue a Ph.D. in linguistics but was unable to find financial support for further study. A proud and ambitious man, Quyet has struggled to accept his lot and reconcile his personal dreams with the reality of having to work on a computer production line to support his family. His children, heirs to his ambition, pride, and intelligence, have worked hard to achieve the educational and professional goals that his country's defeat and the difficult life of a refugee denied to their father. Still restless and dissatisfied, Quyet continues to try to better himself, upgrading his employment skills while wishing that things might somehow have turned out differently._

Quyet lives with his family in a comfortable, modern house in a suburban town that is home to many of the region's Vietnamese. The living room is attractively decorated in a contemporary style and very neatly kept. We sat and talked at a large, formal dining room table in an adjoining alcove.

Quyet was born in a village in North Vietnam near the Red River.

My paternal grandfather was a member of the village council and owned some land, but he had a hand-to-mouth existence. My father had to become a teacher because there was not enough land to support the entire family. My maternal grandfather was a teacher of Chinese, a learned and educated man who lived in the same village as my paternal grandfather. He was very poor. Not many people wanted to learn Chinese. The only thing you could do with it was to work for the Nguyen dynasty [the last Vietnamese royal house]. The classical exam to become a mandarin was very hard. He chose not to take it because he did not believe in serving the Nguyen dynasty. He was a very proud and dignified man.

Quyet was the eldest of six children. The four oldest were born in the North. The two youngest were born in the South, after the family's immigration there from the North in 1955 following the partition of Vietnam by the Geneva Accords of 1954.[1] Today, all of his siblings live in the United States.

Quyet began his story by describing his father's and uncle's involvement in the August Revolution of 1945:

My father was an elementary school teacher. His brother attended a convent school and initially planned to become a priest, but decided against it and moved to Hanoi, where he got a job working with the French as a finance officer. In 1945 there was a famine in North Vietnam. Out of the 7 million people there, 2 million died. [Around the same time] a Japanese plane that was being pursued by two U.S. fighters ejected its bombs and one fell on our village, killing one of my cousins. [Because of these events] my father and uncle were very angry with the [Vichy] French, the Japanese, and the Allies. They were both excited about the revolution because of their anger at the French and their Vietnamese puppet government, and both supported the

Viet Minh. The Viet Minh promised to unite all the parties, including the Nationalists, who were like the Kuomintang [Chiang Kai-shek's party in China].

During the August Revolution the Viet Minh created a united front that embraced everyone. Then, six or seven months later, they killed off the Nationalists and the leaders of the other parties and became virtually the Communist Party. My uncle and father were very disenchanted by this. My father had stayed in the country with his family to help his mother farm their land. He had to cooperate with the Communists. He was the teacher in the village, the head of the committee of popular education. It was his job to teach the illiterate. He trained them to read and write and do arithmetic. That was all the Communists wanted: to have people educated to the third-grade level so that they could read Communist propaganda.

After four years he had trained enough people and the Communists decided to eliminate him. They did not kill him outright. They sent a double agent to the French. He gave them documents recording what my father had done. They described his initial excitement with the Viet Minh, his support for their cause, and his eagerness to participate in their activities. It was a thirty- or forty-page report! At the end of 1948 the French came to our village and arrested him. They said that he had lied to them in saying that he was neutral. They tortured him for information, beating him brutally, but he had no information to give. He told them, "I was just a teacher." They asked, "How long were you a Communist Party member?" He said, "I never was." They asked, "Did you know the Viet Minh were really the Communists?" He said, "No, I did not have a clue."

The French kept him in prison for seven months. If it had not been for my uncle, they would have killed him. That was what they did after they had gotten all the information they needed from people, they shot them. My uncle worked for the French and knew a Spanish priest who was Franco's [the Spanish dictator's] relative. When my uncle learned of my father's imprisonment and torture he told the priest the truth about him, that my father was not a Communist Party member and that he had only done what he had done to keep his family alive. The priest had influence because of his relationship to

Franco and went to the head of the province, a French colonel. He assured him on his life and honor that my father was not a Communist. The colonel took him at his word and released my father. My father carried the scars of that experience for the rest of his life.

After his release from prison my father moved to the capital of a province that was still controlled by the French and became an elementary school teacher there in a private Vietnamese school that was modeled on the French system. He could not afford to move the entire family, so only my oldest sister and I went to live with him. We stayed there until 1954. Then, three months after the fall of Dien Bien Phu [the decisive battle between the French and the Viet Minh] we moved—first to Hanoi, then to Hai Phong. From there my father put me on a plane for Saigon with a distant cousin who was in the French army. My father and the rest of the family stayed behind. They got me out first because I was the oldest son. Vietnamese parents will sacrifice everything for their first son, even risking their own lives, because he carries on the family and venerates the ancestors. The rest of my family came South by transport ship a few months later.

Once I got to Saigon I started back in with my schooling. I had completed the ninth grade in the North and entered *Hồ Ngọc Cẩn*, a public high school run by Catholic priests. I completed my first *baccalauréat* there, but then I had to leave school because I could not afford to go anymore. I stayed home, took private courses, and studied for my second *baccalauréat*, which I got in 1958. While I was studying for the second *baccalauréat* I also entered the National Normal School and trained to be a schoolteacher. I graduated in 1960. I was good at English, and one of my teachers suggested that I take an exam to see if I could study in the United States. I did well and was selected to go to a college in Georgia. I was not happy with the racial discrimination there. In restaurants and buses and Laundromats there were separate sections for whites and blacks. The president and dean of the college told everyone in the small town where the college was located that another Vietnamese student and I were to be treated as whites. That made the blacks unhappy. I especially remember one incident. I got on a bus and the driver, who knew me, put me in with the whites right behind his seat. A black woman tried to sit down next to me. The driver told her to sit in the back. She got angry and argued with him. Pointing at me she said, "He is colored too. How come he can sit here?" I remember the look of hatred she gave me. But I could not move because then I would have gotten in trouble with the white people.

Finally, I decided that I could not take it any longer and moved to New York. I spent the next two and a half years there at a college upstate. I trained to be a high school teacher, majoring in social studies and receiving my B.A. in 1964. When I returned to Vietnam they told me, "You speak English, so you will be an English teacher." I got an appointment teaching English in a high school. Then in 1967 I was drafted into the army. I reported a day or two late because I had to complete my contract with the school, and as a result I was sent to the boot camp for regular soldiers rather than the one for officers, where I trained for the next three months. Then I was transferred to the officers' candidate school at Thu Duc. I was supposed to be there for nine months, but they only kept me for four and half months because I had been picked to be a teacher at the Vietnamese National Military Academy in Da Lat. They picked intellectuals and people with special skills to teach there. I had studied in the United States and spoke English, so I became an English instructor. I was still only a cadet and was not commissioned for another four and a half months, along with the rest of my class at Thu Duc. The school was modeled after the United States Military Academy at West Point. We looked like an American colony. Some of the junior officers felt that we should not copy the United States. [They said,] "The United States is like the French in disguise." We fought, but not wholeheartedly. It was as if we had betrayed someone. We did not have a good cause. The senior officers thought that they had a cause. We treated them as corrupt, less-educated people. The younger officers were intellectuals. We knew where we stood. We rejected the way things were handled, like the assassination of Diem [Ngo Dinh Diem, South Vietnam's first president] or the appointment of generals as presidents. None of us respected Thieu or Ky [Nguyen Van Thieu and Nguyen Cao Ky, both former generals who became president and vice president of South Vietnam, respectively].

I worked at the VNMA as an instructor during the day and as a duty officer at night. It was our job to defend the academy against a Communist attack. There was a real danger of that happening. Once two rockets landed on our cafeteria. Fortunately, nobody was hurt. It was easy to launch rockets and 82 mm mortar rounds [the Communists used 82 mm mortars; the South Vietnamese and Americans, 81 mm mortars] from the hills surrounding the academy. Then, in June 1971, I was sent to the United States for further training. I went to Columbia Teachers College and got an M.A. in applied linguistics. I was there for twenty-five months. It was fun and I liked being there, but it was located in a dangerous area. Once I saw a professor killed at a street corner by three youths. In July 1973 I went back to the VNMA and stayed there until the war ended in 1975.

I asked Quyet to describe his experiences at the end of the war.

We left Da Lat on April 1st. It was part of the evacuation of the entire army from the central region [of South Vietnam] to the south. It was a tragic retreat. We went in good order, but many of the divisions moving with us had no leadership. There was chaos with soldiers robbing and shooting people. Soldiers without leaders, no matter what their nationality, are like beasts. My general ordered the cadets to shoot some of them. We saw one soldier shoot a man on a Honda motorbike and steal it. We shot him. There we were—the general, 1,000 cadets, and about 500 soldiers—marching in good order and encountering division after division of routed soldiers [fleeing in the same direction] on the route south. It was a mess. We were constantly being shelled by artillery, sometimes from the Communists, sometimes from our own side. To add to the insult, a week before I had sent my wife and children on ahead to the seaside so that they would be safe, but they did not make it. It turned out that they were among the mass of civilians moving along with us, but I did not know that until later.

Finally, we reached Ham Tan and stopped there. The cadets and troops from the VNMA and the School of Political Warfare moved into the town with their weapons and occupied it. Everyone else had to lay down his weapons. I learned there that my wife and kids were among the refugees. She was six months pregnant at the time and traveling with our three children, who were only five, two and a half, and thirteen months old. The children had to walk some of the way. The maid had been carrying them in baskets, but my mother-in-law made her carry her stuff instead. I was really mad at her for that. My wife carried the thirteen-month-old.

After we left Ham Tan we marched on down the road and passed one place where there had been a bombardment. There were bodies scattered everywhere. We soldiers tried not to crush them with our vehicles. As we passed I looked at each body, hoping that it was not my wife or children. She told me later that she had done the same thing as she passed, looking for me. It was a mess. We were disciplined, but other troops would kill you to get your transportation. We called that stretch from Nha Trang to Binh Tuy the "road of terror." It was really scary.

When we got to Binh Tuy my friends and I spread out looking for our families. One of them had a Peugeot, and some of the others borrowed jeeps. We finally found my wife and three children and her mother, sister, and brother. It was like a miracle. They had stopped by the seaside at a beach. There were hundreds of thousands of refugees and soldiers there. Some of the soldiers were raping girls. It was a crazy time. Right after I got back to my unit with my family, the entire school left Binh Tuy on C-130s [four-engine propeller-driven military transport aircraft manufactured in the United States]. The general ordered another guy, a captain, and me to stay behind in command of a support company. We finally got out on a Chinook helicopter. Those things are built to carry about forty troops, but there were ninety people on that one, including my family. I was the last one to get on.

We flew to Long Thanh, near Thu Duc. There I was promoted from first lieutenant to captain by the general. He pinned the insignia on me himself and shook my hand. About a week later we moved to Thu Duc, to the officers' training school. We were told to defend it until the last drop of blood. We had been told the same thing at Da Lat. There were three or four thousand of us, the cadets from the VNMA and the cadets from the infantry officers' school. By the 26th and 27th of April a lot of people had begun leaving Vietnam, including [President] Thieu. We felt we were doing the right thing by staying and defending the country. Then it began to become apparent from the news on the radio that we had lost. On the 27th my wife came to Thu Duc. I told her that I had to defend the school. She said, "You are crazy! Everyone else has left. They are on their way to the United States." She grabbed me and said, "Get the paperwork to leave!" We left Thu Duc on the 27th and went to Saigon, where my mother was living.

April 30th was a day of complete chaos. My mother said to me, "You are an officer, a refugee from the North. You went to the United States twice, and you worked at the VNMA. You have a ticket to hell. You have no chance to survive here." My wife was also afraid for my safety. My mother was vehement that I go. My cousin, brother, and I got on two motor scooters and tried to find a way out. We were heading to the harbor, hoping to get on a naval ship there and escape. As we got close to the Binh Dan Hospital a 130 mm projectile suddenly landed near us. My cousin was scared. He said, "Let us go back. We cannot face this, it is no fun." So we went back to my mother's house.

A couple of days later there was a radio broadcast on the BBC in both Vietnamese and English. It said, "The North has won; the South has lost. The North has embraced a policy of forgiveness. 'Forgive and forget.' All members of the South Vietnamese armed forces must report to the North Vietnamese authorities to be re-educated. Re-education will last for three weeks." The naive people of the South believed what they were told. I had my doubts. The BBC had been told that officers were to bring food and clothing for three weeks. From this they had assumed that re-education would last for three weeks. When I reported they told me the same thing. Bring food and clothing for three weeks. We felt relieved. "They have won, we have lost. There is no need for a purge as in 1946 and 1954 when they killed collaborators. They have changed. They have learned their lesson. What have they got to gain by persecuting us?" We had no experience with the Communist Party so we believed what they told us. To add to the insult, when we reported [for re-education] the political commissar, a major or lieutenant colonel, talked to us like a preacher from the Bible. He said, "You were like lost children. Now you have come back to the arms of your loving mother Vietnam. You are forgiven for your sins and your crimes. All you have to do is go through the re-education program." A lot of us were very excited. "They will forgive and forget. It will be like Grant with Lee, like the United States' Civil War. Now we will work together. We got rid of the French and the Americans, and we are all Vietnamese." That was a trick, and we fell for it. A lot of people, like my father and my uncle, fell for the same trick in 1946.

After the political commissar's speech they took our names and details and sent us home. I lied and said that I was a first lieutenant. That helped me a lot early on, but it caused trouble later. They told me that I could report for re-education either in Saigon or Da Lat. I thought that if I stayed in Saigon there might be a problem. A lot of people knew me there. They knew that my family was Catholic and that we were refugees from the North. Many of my acquaintances turned out to be Communists. If I wanted to lie or hide things [from my past], it would be difficult. So I chose to go to Da Lat. I went back with my entire family. We had a house there with a piece of land, about 150 by 300 feet, and figured that we could plant crops to support ourselves. We did not have any land in Saigon. After my arrival I reported to the hamlet chief. He told me that I could work the land and plant crops and then report later. I had to report to him every day. I also had to report to the district chief. He recognized me because I had taught his daughter English. He had repaired motor scooters and had a shop right next to the VNMA. When I reported to him I bowed my head and he bowed his. He was very polite and called me by my title, *thầy* [teacher]. He asked me if I were surprised [that he was a Communist]. I said, "No, I am not." He said, "I respect you, you are a dedicated teacher, but times change. You need to be re-educated. Believe me, you will not be mistreated here in my district, but my authority does not reach beyond here."

I reported for re-education on May 5th. I was sent to a school where they used to train military police. I stayed there for two months. We did nothing. We were crowded into a barracks that had been used for trainees. We slept in bunk beds, piled on top of one another like sardines. They gave us rice, salt, fish sauce, and sometimes some dried fish. I was hungry all the time. The place was only about 3 kilometers from my home, so my wife was able to bring me extra food every week or two. It was not too bad there. They trained us to sing some Communist songs, and we had a few lousy speeches given by barely literate soldiers. The rice they gave us was filled with gravel. I took a bite and counted fourteen bits of gravel in it. I wondered what was going on. Was it deliberate? I think it was. Maybe they were trying to give us stomach problems so that we would die sooner. [Another former prisoner was told that sand was added "so prisoners will think of their mistakes while they eat."²]

After a couple of months they sent us to Song Mao. It was a base built by the Australians. They had a tactical airfield there made of steel plates and a barracks. We lived in the barracks and got our political education. There was a lot of stuff in my file. You cannot hide everything. My students and neighbors knew I was an instructor and that I had spent six years in the United States both as a civilian and as a soldier. It was really bad to have been connected to the United States. On top of that I was a refugee from the North and a Catholic. If you add up all those things together, you are looking at more than ten years of re-education. Also, I had lied about being a first lieutenant. A "good friend" of mine from the VNMA told them that I had really been a captain and that the general himself had given me my rank insignia. He told the whole story to the Communists. That created a lot of problems for me. I was separated from the others and put in with a group called the "high crimes rabble." They told me that I had been a CIA agent. I denied it. They said, "You were and you still are because you refuse to admit it." Their rationale for believing that I was in the CIA was that I had been sent to the United States as a civilian, taken into the army, and then sent to the United States again.

Having lied to them about being a captain and having them think that I was a CIA agent caused me a lot of problems. The group they put me in included other people who had been closely connected to the Americans, the Australians, and the spies. There were also political warfare officers. We were considered very dangerous and very sinful. We had betrayed the country, sold our hearts, and sold the country to the American imperialists. Our group did not get political education along with everybody else. We had to serve as cooks for the others. We would get our re-education later. The others were taught about Marxism, Communism, and the Communists' policy of "forgive and forget." To be forgiven you had to tell the truth about yourself and your family

munist Party was formed by Uncle Ho [Ho Chi Minh], and about how it had evolved from the Viet Minh. They told us that the policy of the Communist Party was to drive away the French and the U.S. imperialists and to gain independence and freedom for Vietnam. We learned to recite what they taught us by heart. After class we were tested—they called it "the harvest." It included a confession. You had to confess your crimes and those of your father, grandfather, and so on. For example, say your grandfather was a mandarin who worked for the Nguyen dynasty, your father worked for the French, and you worked for the U.S. imperialists. If you admitted those things, you showed that you had "committed yourself to re-education." Some people were stupid and believed this and kept telling them things. They also asked moral questions like "Did you have illicit sex or go whoring around? How many times?" It was like church. You were supposed to tell them whatever you did or read that was indecent, like books glorifying the French or the Americans.

Then there were physical crimes. If you were a private and had killed or wounded a revolutionary soldier, you had shot one guy. If you were a commander, though, you were responsible for everything done by you and your subordinates. If your battalion killed 1,000 men over twenty years, you were responsible for all those deaths. That was a "high crime." Plus, there were 800 of your own men who were killed. That was a "crime against humanity." One of your subordinates in the army might have been a Communist, so you could not lie. You had to tell them everything your battalion did, and you would be held responsible for the casualties on both sides.

After the confession you got an evaluation. A lower-level Communist would say, "Hey, you did a good job [in your confession]." You might then think that you would get to go home early, but you would be wrong. You would just have given them evidence of more crimes to hold against you.

After six months of political training in Song Mao we were allowed to receive visits from our families. Everyone felt very excited, thinking that they were now clear of their crimes. One night a guy raised his hand at a meeting and asked, "Comrade, when do we get to go home?" "What rank were you?" "I was a lieutenant." "What was your position?" "Company commander." "How many revolutionary soldiers did you kill?" "About 350." "Sit down!

You have committed the most heinous crime in the world. You deserve to die, but now, after only six months in camp, you ask if you can go home?" After that meeting people got severely depressed. Several of them committed suicide. When the cadre made that statement people lost hope. "You were nothing but a traitor, a murderer, and a servant of U.S. imperialism. You murdered the good people. What do you deserve? You deserve to die on the spot! Now you can see how benevolent the party is. You deserve to die one hundred times, but the party offers you re-education and then you can go home." I did not fall for it. When they asked me how many American girls I had slept with when I was in the United States, I said, "None. I was a poor student—I only got $8 a day, just enough for room and board. I could not afford to go whoring around." They asked, "How did you keep yourself from doing it?" I said to them, "I masturbated." I also told them that I had studied education, not social studies. I told them that I had learned about the psychology of children, how to motivate them, and educational theories. I did not mention anything about political science and history. If I had, I would have been in trouble. I tried to appear innocent. If I had been like the others and elaborated on everything, they would have kept me my whole life. Even so I was treated as a dangerous enemy.

After passing the theory of re-education and doing our confession we were supposed to do physical labor. We were sent to Luong Son, where we planted cotton. The seed was from the United States. It had been sent to South Vietnam as aid. We planted the seeds in a field next to a small river. It was the first time we had had good water. The water at Song Mao was very dirty—people washed their clothes and went to the toilet in it. This water was clear and running and we bathed in it and drank it. After harvesting the cotton we moved to the other side of the mountain and dug an irrigation canal to bring more water to Luong Son. The canal was in a virgin forest. We lived there. We built our huts out of what we could find, using palm leaves for the roof and branches for a bed. We made our own tools out of scrap metal. The work [of digging the canal] was very hazardous. Three or four feet under the ground it was solid rock. They gave us dynamite to blast the rock, but we had no remote control, just a fuse. When the rocks exploded people would sometimes be killed or injured. We were told that we were working to train our bodies and minds. They talked to us about the origin of the world, and about how men had evolved from chimpanzees. Chimps had become men by organizing, working hard, and learning to use tools. Like our ancestors the chimps we would use tools and become men. It was just another way to justify hard labor, saying that by laboring you trained yourself to be a good man.

After we had been in the camp for about a year and a half someone raised the question of our status. "What do you want to know?" they asked. "Are we POWs [prisoners of war] or what?" "If you were POWs you would demand rights like those American pilots in Hanoi. You are not POWs. You were nothing and you are nothing still. You do not have those rights." After one and a half years of study and work we were told that we had no rights. We were less than animals and not really human.

I asked Quyet to describe how he had felt emotionally during his time in the re-education camps.

Pretty calm. I accepted my fate. I had escaped from the North. My village there had switched back and forth constantly between the French and the Viet Minh. We suffered a lot. Once two shells from a tank hit our house. We were lucky to survive. When French intelligence said that there were Viet Minh in our village the French bombarded us. When the French took the village back the Viet Minh attacked us. Both sides shelled us and small arms fire and mortars showered us. Before I left the North I witnessed Viet Minh purges against anyone who was connected to the French or who owned property. There were three types of rich people. At the top were the *đại điền chủ* [big field bosses]. They were executed immediately by the People's Courts. Then there were the medium rich, the *phú nông* [rich farmers]. They might have saved enough to be able to live on their savings for a year. Sometimes they were killed too. At the bottom were the *trung nông* [medium-rich farmers]. They might have been able to save $50 a year, but usually they had only just enough to eat. They were punished too. If they were accused of rape or exploitation, they might be executed. The People's Court tried and condemned them and then stripped them of their property and wealth. My father's cousin was a *trung nông*. He was put out in front of the church and exposed to the hot sun from morning until evening. At the end of the trial he was unconscious.

I guess I was feeling pretty numb [during the re-education camp]. I had had a lot of experiences with the Communists. Then there were my father's experiences. The Communists used him, and then they tried to use the French to kill him. By the time I got to the camp I knew what the Communists were like. In my confession I told them nothing important in detail that they could use against me. But my six years in the United States, my two American degrees, my seven years in the South Vietnamese Army, and being suspected of being a CIA agent made me think that I was doomed. I accepted my fate and did nothing to damage my honesty, dignity, or integrity. Deep in my heart I was very depressed. On the surface I was pretending to be content. I was mentally numb. I knew that I could be killed at any time. I calmly accepted it. I was waiting for it to happen. I thought, "If they are going to shoot me, they will shoot me, but I will not betray my friends. My friends can hurt me, but I will not hurt them." Like the friend who told my secret that I was a captain. I did not know what my future would be. I had no clue what would happen to us. I was pretty depressed. I was physically tired, so I did not have any trouble sleeping.

Did he consider suicide?

I was Catholic, and they forbid suicide. I am not devout and I do not have much faith, but I had my pride. It seemed cowardly to commit suicide. I would only have done it if I could have used a grenade and killed some of them. Otherwise I never thought of it.

While digging the canal I contracted malaria. It was both a calamity and a blessing. Malaria killed a lot of people. It was the vivax type. People died of a very high fever. Mine lasted for twelve hours. After the fever you were a different man. I was incoherent, but somehow I survived. My body got worse and worse. There were several South Vietnamese doctors in the camp. They had access to medicines and saved my life. They also gave me herbs to relieve the pain and reduce my temperature. I never really got better. I was physically weak and tired easily. My body seemed to give way. I was put on light duty. Before I had cut rocks and carried bamboo, but now I stayed home and wove bamboo baskets for carrying rocks. I had been in the camp for three years. They could not get any information out of me and my body was deteriorated, so they decided to give me back to my wife so that I could die at home.

They sent me to a camp near Ham Tri so that I could get ready to go home. Nearby there was another camp for captains and above, where they grew food for other camps. An incident occurred there in which seven officers escaped from the camp and made it out safely. One of them was a friend of mine. He had told me that he wanted to see me, but I got the message too late. By the time it arrived he was already gone. He tried to sneak home. Some say he made it. Eventually, he was killed in a battle. He never gave up, but just kept fighting. He operated with the Montagnards [a generic name for various ethnic groups living in the mountains along the Vietnamese border—many worked with the Americans and Australians during the war] around Nui Voi [Elephant Mountain].

After I was released I had to travel about 200 kilometers to get home. They gave me a bus ticket and a release paper. It said that I was a P O W. When I got back to Da Lat I was not allowed to do anything. I finally got a job as a painter through the father of my friend's wife. I whitewashed the stucco walls of houses and painted doors and windows. I was not permitted to do any mental work like teaching. I tried to forget what I had been. Now I was a "new man" doing hard labor.

The story should have ended there, but it did not. When I arrived home I was very sick. Everybody gave me health advice and herbs. By some miracle I got strong and healthy again. Each morning I had to report to the hamlet chief. He signed my copybook. Then I rode my bike to the workplace and the work leader signed my book. When I left he signed me out. After I got back to the hamlet I had to sign in again. I got about an hour and a half with my wife and children, then I had to go back to the hamlet chief's office for re-education. Everyone released from the camp had to be re-educated again. It went on from 7 P.M. to 11:30 P.M. every night. We had to learn the lessons and repeat them over and over again. We had to evaluate ourselves and talk about whether we were trying hard enough. Then I went home and went to sleep. There was no time to go anywhere.

Elephant Mountain was about 40 miles from Da Lat. The Montagnards were operating there against the Communists. My neighbor knew Uncle Ho [Ho Chi Minh] [and was well-connected politically]. She found out that I was on a police blacklist. It said that I was a major and a battalion commander of the Montagnards. She told me, "You got promoted! You better leave the city as soon as you can." After she told me that I immediately went to the local police and told them that I wanted to go south to the New Economic Zone [sparsely settled regions to which surplus population was sent] near Ca Mau [a town in the southern Mekong Delta] and work the land there. They asked why. I said, "The soil is richer there. On the land here I cannot raise enough to support my family." They were happy to send me away. The secret police had my name on their blacklist, but the information had not yet filtered down to the local police. I wrote my autobiography [life story, especially those sections considered reactionary by the Communists] in Da Lat, reciting my history, and presented it to the police [for their approval]. [The autobiography had to be presented to the authorities in the New Economic Zone where he was moving.] They put a stamp on it and gave me a release permit. Then I went to Saigon to visit my mother. There I used chemicals to [erase and edit parts of] my story and bought fake papers. I put down in my autobiography that I had only finished ninth grade and that I had become insane. I pretended to be insane so that I could go to another town in the delta without supervision. I went there with my wife and family and two officers who had been students of mine at the VNMA. One of them was married to a woman from that area whose family was closely connected to the Communists, so we were well protected. Then his wife and the wife of the other officer got into a quarrel and in a fit of temper she exposed our true identities. Now I was on the run. I used fake papers. One time I was a teacher and another time I was a nurse. I moved around a lot and made many attempts to escape from Vietnam. The people we paid to help us escape stole our gold and left us behind. We sold our house to pay for the trip, and we lost everything. Finally, I convinced a boat owner that

I knew how to navigate and that I spoke English and some French. I would be able to tell where the ships we met along the way were from. I could contribute. He demanded that I recruit five others who could pay for their trip with gold. I got my brother, my cousin, and a friend, and my cousin recruited a couple of others. I went for free, but the people I recruited had to pay a correspondingly larger share. Finally, we got enough gold. We left Vietnam at 9:30 P.M. on March 19, 1979.

Quyet brought out a rattan cane on which he had carved the history of his flight from Vietnam to the United States.

I called this my "dog-beating cane." Whoever is beaten by it is a dog. I had to carve the story [of my escape] on the cane because I did not have any paper on the boat. On the handle I carved "From Darkness to Light." The people who prepared the boat for the journey did not do a very good job. We only had food and fuel for three days; that was not enough for the entire trip. We spent time in the harbor trying to negotiate for more food and fuel. The negotiations took too long, and somebody told the Communists. The police came with their boat and an armed squad. They intercepted us at 7:45 A.M. on the 20th. One guy fired a shot. Then there was a ferocious fight. We had an AR-15 [a military assault rifle used by the Americans and the South Vietnamese] and a Colt 45 [an American-made pistol] against a whole squad. Our rifle malfunctioned and could only fire one shot at a time. We only had thirty rounds each for the AR-15 and the Colt 45. We shot back until about 9:30 A.M. Finally, we hit one of them and killed him. He was a first lieutenant. After that they did not pursue us anymore and we escaped. We had decided that we would either find freedom or die.

At 3 A.M. on March 22nd our engine stopped. We were out on the high seas, and it was very scary. Finally, we got it started again. The next day at about 10 P.M. we came to an oil rig. We approached it cautiously, putting all the women and children below deck. There were a couple of barges about 100 meters from the rig. I spoke English to a guy on one of the barges. He was Dutch. I told him that I had studied at Columbia and had been captain in the

South Vietnamese Army. He was very friendly. One of our men had been wounded in the gun battle with the police. The Dutch guy gave us medicine, water, oil, food, and cigarettes. On the rig we saw Vietnamese police with A K - 4 7s [military assault rifles used by the Communist troops]. He told us that he could not let us stay because his group worked for the Vietnamese government and we were refugees. He redrew the directions on our map and showed us how to go to Malaysia.

We reached Malaysia on March 24th at 6:50 P.M. The police there told us to wait. The next morning they came and talked to us. They asked for the boat's captain. I told them that I was the captain. "Who is the owner?" I told them who he was and that he had been an army private. Then they asked if we had any money or gold. We said no. They tried to squeeze something out of us. From a Chinese boat they could sometimes get as much as 200 ounces of gold, but we gave them nothing. They asked if we had been robbed. We said no. "Why not?" We told them that we had weapons, including an A R-1 5, and that no one would dare touch us. They told us that they could not take us there. We put out to sea again, and the next day at 12:30 P.M. we reached the refugee camp at Pulau Tenga. We were not allowed to stay there either. On the 27th at 7:00 P.M. we reached Mersing. We stayed there until April 22nd. I worked for a Malaysian police captain using my English language skills. He used me to investigate the other refugees who landed there. I worked as an interpreter/interrogator. The other refugees were jealous because of the good treatment we received [as a result of my work]. On the 22nd the police decided to tow us away. The captain called me over to see him at about 4:30 P.M. He said, "Good news. We are going to tow you to a refugee camp." We thought he meant Pulau Tenga, which was only about a mile away. A small naval vessel, armed with two cannons and two heavy machine guns, arrived to tow another boat and ours. It was windy and rainy. The sea was very rough. They towed us so fast that our boat could not handle it. It was only a fishing boat, with a maximum speed of 17 kilometers an hour and built to work 30 miles offshore. The naval vessel could go very fast. It was scary. The water kept coming in. Finally, our mechanic decided to wreck the engine so that water would get into the hull. Our boat began to sink, and the patrol boat stopped and took us on board. They treated us brutally. The captain was very rude and used obscene language. They tried to salvage the boat, but the next day at about 7:00 A.M. it sank.

They then took us to a remote island, Pulau Permengal. There they transferred us to another boat. So many boats arrived there that they could pick any one they wanted. They did not care how seaworthy it was. If the boat sank, they would not rescue the people. After a week the same naval vessel came back to tow us out onto the high seas. It was April 30th, a fateful day, the day we lost the country and our freedom to the Viet Cong [the anniversary of the fall of Saigon]. I remarked sarcastically, "Maybe we will now lose our freedom to the sea." The captain of the ship summoned me. He said that he would shoot us if we did not obey his orders. He made lots of hand gestures so that the people on our boat would see what he meant. He pointed to the ship's cannons and heavy machine guns. "We are going to use those against you if you cut the rope or try to come back." Then he offered me drinks, whisky, and cigarettes and gave me dinner on his ship. He treated me with respect. Publicly he was tough, but privately he showed emotion. He said, "I feel for you, but it is our national policy that we cannot do anything for you. You fought for the right cause, the anti-Communists." He toasted me, a good-bye toast. Then the ship towed us out to sea. They towed us for eleven or twelve hours. At 7:00 A.M. he stopped the boat. He called to me. "Captain, can you see the mountains over there? There is a refugee camp there." I asked if it were Malaysia. He said no, and then he added, "Remember one thing. Do not ever come back." We said good-bye and left. That afternoon at 1:00 P.M. we reached Pulau Letung, Indonesia.

We stayed at Pulau Letung for about a week, then they moved us to another island called Air Rya. We were the first refugees there. We built our own huts. It was a lot like the re-education camp. We were given food, but not enough. The UNHCR [United Nations High Commissioner for Refugees] had provided sufficient rations, but the Indonesians did not give us the full daily ration, keeping some of it for themselves. It was terrible that humans could rob people like us in those circumstances. Eventually, the UNHCR came to visit and straightened it out. They asked us how we had managed to survive in the camp. We told them that we would eat anything that moved, just like in the re-education camp. We dove down about 8 feet into the ocean to get oysters and shellfish. We tried to fish. We ate crabs, snakes, crickets, and earthworms. The Vietnamese and Chinese believe that eating earthworms can reduce the risk of malaria. In the re-education camps people with malaria would go out and dig up earthworms and swallow them whole. We would eat anything that did not run fast enough to get away, even termites and poisonous snakes. The more poisonous the snake, the better it tasted! We would roast them and eat them. We did not have enough food to eat. The Communists only gave us rice and salt. If we did not eat all those things, we would have died. When we were out planting cotton and digging rocks we were able to catch insects, to fish, to gather vegetables and vines. That is how we survived. There was a well-known Vietnamese pharmacist in the re-education camp who had severe asthma. Some Chinese officers suggested that he eat lizards, the kind that climb on the walls [geckoes]. You would catch it, put it in your mouth, then pinch off the tail, and it would run down your throat.

I finally arrived in the United States in February 1980. I came with my next to youngest brother. If we had left him behind, he would have been drafted into the Communist Army and I could not have tolerated that.

How did Quyet feel when he arrived in the United States?

I had mixed feelings. The United States was like my second home. I had spent six years here and had friends. I was hopeful that I could start building my future. I thought that I could return to school and finish my Ph.D. However, it did not take long for me to see that that was an illusion. There was no money. Who would support it? The reality was welfare. I asked about applying for a grant. They said, "Worry about your stomach first." I was on welfare for a month. I felt disgusted. I found a job working at an Indochinese cultural center as a community resource developer. My job was to meet with civic groups, schools, and universities and tell them about refugee life. I told them how hard it was to escape the war and that if you left Vietnam as a boat person you had a fifty-fifty chance of dying. I had slides and pictures of people who had been raped, robbed, and killed. I was trying to promote sponsorship, especially for homeless children. I worked there for six months. Then the center ran out of money and I was laid off. I worked for the city for a couple of years as part of the CETA [Comprehensive Employment and Training Act] program, but that was phased out by Reagan. Then I worked for the mayor's office for six months helping to find summer jobs for high school students.

After that I was unemployed again. I looked for work with the government, either the city or the state, but I could not find anything that suited my training or skills. I applied for tens of jobs all over the state, but I always came in second. It made me mad. I did not like the politics and the discrimination. Finally, I got sick of everything. My unemployment benefits had run out and I had four children. I did not want welfare. I had to take a job as a production worker [for a computer company]. I did not like the atmosphere. They pushed and exploited people. So I left for another [computer] company. They paid better. I started as a production worker, then became a tester, and finally a technician. That is about as far as I could go. I was with them for twelve years, but I was unhappy with it and upset. My future looked grim. They had a retraining program. I asked to be laid off with a severance package and the retraining program rather than being pushed around. I start the retraining program this January. My goal is to become a computer specialist.

Was it difficult adapting to life in the United States? "I was Americanized before I came here as a refugee, having lived here in the 1960s and 1970s. I had no 'culture shock.' " How about reintegrating into the family?

That may have been a problem for some people. In the late 1940s I left my mother in the countryside [in North Vietnam] and went to the city to live alone with my father. In 1955 I went to South Vietnam alone. I knew that I might never see my parents again. In 1960 I left my parents for the United States and was gone for four years. I was strongly attached to my mother especially, but I got used to it. I knew my parents had gone through so much. My ties to them were strong. When they died I was not there for them. My father died in 1971 when I was in the United States. My mother died in the late 1980s. I was here then too. My feelings are numb. I can get used to almost anything.

In terms of my immediate family, I left home in 1971 [to study at Columbia University]. My oldest child was one year old and my wife was pregnant with our second child. I was gone for twenty-five months. My wife and children could take it, so I could take it. In 1975 I left [for re-education camp] and was gone for three years. I did not know what would happen to me or to my family. I accepted my fate. After 1975 my children were classified as children of the rebels. I had no rights, no Vietnamese citizenship. My children were next to nothing. They could not go to college or work for the government. The Communists tried to force all former Republic of Vietnam troops to live in the New Economic Zones. They wanted all of us to be there, to be ignorant, to be doomed. It was very hard in the camp. I thought about my children all the time. There was no future for them whatsoever.

In 1979 we were separated again. I came [to the United States] all alone. The trip here was hard and scary. I was near death many times. After I arrived I wondered when I would be able to be reunited with my family. Many people could not get their families out. I was very depressed. My happiest moment was when I heard that my wife and family had escaped and been picked up by a German ship. I got a letter from her in Indonesia. They escaped at the end of 1980 and were picked up by the *Cap Anamur* [Island of Light]. It was sheer luck. I knew that ship from being in the refugee camp. They treated refugees well. My wife had taught our daughters the song "Clementine." When the German ship picked them up they sang it for them. My family arrived here on November 13, 1981.

Does Quyet ever think or dream about the re-education camp?

After I was released from the re-education camp and the refugee camp, I never wanted to think about them again. I have never dreamt about them. Maybe I have suppressed all the bad memories. Once in 1963, when I was living in New York, I had a dream that I was surrounded by the North Vietnamese and was a prisoner. I also dreamt about my wife before I met her. When I later saw her I was stunned! We met in Da Lat. A friend of mine introduced her. After we had gone out together a few times I told her that I already knew her from my dream.

Was their marriage arranged? "That was my father's generation. We were quite free. I still had to go through her family. I was from the North and her family was from the central region [*Trung Việt*]. Her mother did not trust Northerners. She was a Buddhist and I was a Catholic. The religions usually did not mix. My mother-in-law objected to the marriage, but my wife was tough and fought for it."

When Quyet looks back over his life, how does he understand and come to grips with the difficult times he has experienced?

I think of it on a global level, not just me. If the United States had not forced Chiang Kai-shek to let Mao Tse-tung go, we would have gotten independence without a lot of bloodshed. Chiang Kai-shek defeated Mao. The United States forced him to join Mao and fight the Japanese. Mao took advantage of this. With the help of Russia he defeated Chiang Kai-shek. I look back and see the bigger picture. In 1945 there was a famine in North Vietnam. Not many people here know about it. The famine gave the Communists the leverage [to take over the North]. When you are drowning you grab anything available to save yourself. I get upset and mad, but I do not hold a grudge against the Viet Cong, not even against those who mistreated me and told me I was nothing. If they had been free and been given an education like you can get here, they would not have said that. "Forgive them for they know not what they do." One day they will understand.

Do you know about the North Vietnamese famine in 1945? The Japanese were about to land in Indochina. The French knew this and gathered up all the farm products, leaving only enough for the people to eat in their homes. Then they dumped everything into Hai Phong Harbor just before the Japanese arrived in Vietnam. The Japanese ordered the Vietnamese to cut down all their crops and plant jute [*cây đay*]. Maybe they wanted to use it for parachutes. Then the Americans came, and there was fighting between the United States and Japan and a naval blockade of the North and the South. In the South they had so much rice they did not know what to do with it. They burned it in the power plants for fuel. By March 1945 in the North all the farmers had run out of food. They starved and died. Out of a population of 7 million people, 2 million died in one month! This helped the Communists gain momentum. I was old enough to read then, and I read in the newspapers about the feelings of the people. Even some Catholic priests joined the Communists because they thought that they had a right and good cause. They thought, "The Viet Minh are not Communists, they are nationalists." My father and uncle believed it. People like me, junior officers in the South Vietnamese Army, were very politically minded. We were drafted and had to fight, but we always had doubts about whether we were fighting for a good cause. The doubts clouded our minds. Higher-ranking officers complied with what the American authorities wanted. We did not believe that we were fighting for a good cause. We fought for pride. The Viet Cong were stupid and they had no sense of right and wrong. They charged at us like wild beasts. We had to fight back. We did not believe what Kennedy, Johnson, and Nixon said. Other Vietnamese refugees are very strong anti-Communists, but I am a bit different. I despise the Communist leadership and feel sorry for their followers. I am especially sorry for all those [in North Vietnam] who have suffered for the last fifty years.

Does he think his experiences have affected his children?

They learned from me to be tough, dignified, and honest. They are proud children, proud of their parents and themselves. Even though I am not successful, they are not bothered by it. They seem to understand. We never yelled at them. We followed the old Chinese proverb "*vô ngôn chỉ giáo*" [Teach by example, not words]. They know we give them unconditional love. Think of my wife's efforts in bringing them here. One woman with four young children escaping from Vietnam! It was quite an achievement. They knew my thoughts were always with them. They are my highest priority. I would sacrifice anything for them. If it had not been for them, I would have tried to achieve my goal [of getting a Ph.D.].

As we finished our conversation and I packed up my things to leave, Quyet added reflectively, "You know, I think I am depressed about not being able to achieve my goals, about not being able to use all my training and get a Ph.D."

Quyet's candid remarks at the end of our interview suggested to me that, despite his successful adjustment to life in the United States and his children's outstanding achievements here, he still wishes that things might have been different. A hardworking scholarly man, Quyet would love to continue the work for which he was trained and to further his intellectual ambitions. However, the realities of life as an older refugee with a family to support, even in a country as wealthy as the United States, have so far denied him this opportunity. After so much suffering and heartbreak he still remains far from the fulfillment of his dreams.

When I went back to visit Quyet to have him review my account of his life story, he told me that he had something he wanted to add. He then handed me a sheet of paper, neatly typed, on which he had written a message to Vietnam's Communist leaders. He explained that he wanted to elevate his story beyond an account of just one person's life and suffering and bring into focus the suffering of the entire Vietnamese people. I have modified the document here and there for the sake of clarity, but have done my best to leave its message unchanged:

I have a few things I would like to say to the Communists. First, you thought you could brainwash us, the members of the armed forces and government of the Republic of Vietnam, but you failed miserably. Yes, let us call a spade a spade. Do not use the word "re-education"—it was brainwashing. Before 1975 a lot of South Vietnamese officers felt some respect for your patriotism and dedication. However, within a few months after you took over the South that feeling was replaced by distrust, disillusionment, and disdain. Do you remember the old Vietnamese saying "*cháy nhà ra mặt chuột*" [After the house burned down the faces of the mice were exposed—meaning, we have seen your true colors]?

Second, by stripping us [the former political prisoners] of our citizenship and our P O W status and by treating us as less than human, you placed Vietnamese people far below the foreigners [you claimed to disdain]—the French, the North Africans, and the Americans. You used to proudly quote your leader's [Ho Chi Minh's] statement that "for every French life we are prepared to sacrifice ten." You did not even realize that the statement suggests that the life of a French soldier is worth ten Vietnamese lives. What a shame! You used to claim that Marxism is the most excellent doctrine and that it represents the highest peak of human intellect. However, by demeaning your own people, by imposing a barbarous doctrine on the innocent, by wiping out the traditional spiritual and moral values of the Vietnamese people, and by ruining the country's economy, you proved the opposite. The South Vietnamese made a joke out of your "*ưu việt* [excellent] doctrine." In speaking of it, they changed *ưu việt* to *u việt* [dark, stupid].[3]

Third, you loudly called for everyone to "forgive and forget." Let me make it clear that we did not, and do not, owe you any apology [for what we did]. Most of us fought bravely simply to defend ourselves. There is nothing wrong with that. When the war was over the past should have been left behind. We could have been your friends and worked together with you to rebuild our beloved Vietnam, but you chose to hold a grudge against us and to treat us worse than animals. It is you who owe us an apology [for that] and especially for desecrating the sacred resting-place of our fallen warriors.[4]

As for the sin of *cõng rắn cắn gà nhà* [bringing a snake to bite the home chickens—referring to South Vietnam inviting the Americans to fight against other Vietnamese], I would assert that *both sides were equally guilty of this, and equally guilty in the eyes of our venerable ancestors* [Quyet's emphasis]. In this matter, neither of us has anything to be proud of—we should both be ashamed! The insanity of a few leaders [on both sides] enabled the weapons manufacturers to test their weapons using our lives, our jungle, and our precious natural resources. What they did was morally wrong and historically unparalleled. Let our children be the judges.

10 / The Teacher's Wife

*L*ike the wives of the other former political prisoners, Quyet's wife,
Trinh, found herself confronting enormous challenges after her husband
was taken away to re-education camp. A teacher and the mother of four
young children, she had to find a way to support her family while continuing to
provide them with parental guidance and discipline. Compelled to work at
several different jobs to earn enough money, she had to leave her children on their
own much of the time and worried about them constantly. In some respects she
was more fortunate than were those women who had been stay-at-home mothers
and knew little of the outside world. Prior to her marriage Trinh had helped her
mother run a business and was familiar with buying, selling, and managing
money. After her husband escaped from Vietnam to the United States he wrote
to her saying that he planned to sponsor them and that they should not try to
escape. Trinh, however, had decided that she could no longer bear life in
Communist Vietnam and that her children had no future there. Rather than
wait several years to be reunited with her husband through the Orderly Departure Program (ODP), she and her children undertook a hazardous escape by
boat.

Quyet's wife, Trinh, is a petite, attractive woman in her mid-fifties.
Like her husband, she is employed as an assembler in the local computer industry. She was born in Da Lat, a resort city in the highlands
where French colonial administrators and businessmen sought a retreat from the heat and humidity of Saigon. Her father worked for the
French as a provincial-level administrator, and her mother, as a jew-

elry trader. "She inspected diamonds. She bought and sold them and helped people pick out the really good ones." Eventually, her father quit his job and, with his wife, opened a vegetable depot, where they sold fresh produce purchased from local farmers to the French. After the French departure from Vietnam in 1954 the vegetable depot was no longer profitable, and so her mother opened a souvenir shop, where she sold local curios produced by the Montagnard people [a generic name for various ethnic minority groups living in the mountains] from the region around Da Lat.

Trinh attended elementary school and high school in Da Lat. "My older brother and sister went to a French school, but my younger sister and I were sent to a Vietnamese high school. Each week we studied both French and English for six hours. I also had to work for my mother in her shop. I spent half a day in school and half a day working. As a result of having to work so much I failed the *baccalauréat* exam many times!" As she said this she laughed and covered her face in embarrassment. How many times did she fail? "I failed the Baccalauréat I twice and the Baccalauréat II twice. I just did not have much time to study." After high school, Trinh spent a year at a teacher training college, graduating in 1967 at the age of twenty-four.

By the time Trinh returned to Da Lat to teach elementary school, Quyet had been appointed as an instructor at the Vietnamese National Military Academy (VNMA) there. A friend of his introduced them. "But my mother did not agree to our getting married because he was a Catholic. I had to keep talking to her to persuade her. It took more than a year." Why was her mother so opposed to her marrying a Catholic? Quyet, who had been helping to translate for his wife, responded.

Many Vietnamese did not like the Catholics. They insisted that there was only one God, while the Buddhists had many gods. They would not permit Vietnamese Catholics to have ancestor altars in their homes. The Vietnamese did not like that. They believed that it was important to show your gratitude to your parents and to your deceased ancestors. This provoked a lot of strong feelings against the Catholics. That is why so many of them were persecuted. Also, to marry me she had to convert to Catholicism.

After their marriage, in 1969, Trinh continued to teach. A year later their first child, a girl, was born. By the time the war ended on April 30, 1975, they had three girls—ages five, three, and one—and Trinh was pregnant with a fourth child. Quyet had to leave his young family in May 1975 to begin his re-education camp ordeal. Reflecting on his departure Trinh said,

It was a very difficult time. I had one child about to be born and another who was only one year old, and there was no one to help me. I did not know when he would be coming home. I did not think it would be soon. I had to plan my future without him. I was lonely. For the first two months after he left I had to go through a political education course to learn about the new regime. All the teachers had to go. It was an all-day program, and I had to leave the children home by themselves. I locked the door and the gate, and the five-year-old had to take care of the other two kids. The atmosphere in those political meetings was stifling. You were supposed to denounce your husband, your father, the old government, and the Americans. I just listened. I did not write down or say anything. A few of the teachers condemned the former regime, but most did not. Like me, they just sat and listened.

Here Quyet added, "I do not know how she got away with it! The ones who did say something were probably just 'kissing ass.' "
Trinh continued,

After my son was born in September I had three months off, but then I returned to work at the school. I worked there for five hours in the morning, then in the evening I had to work for a couple more hours teaching illiterate adults to read and write. Whenever I went to work I had to leave the children alone, and I worried about them a lot. Each day before I left I prepared a bottle for the baby, heated it, and wrapped it in a towel. I set an alarm and told the three-year-old, "When the alarm rings you have to feed your brother." She used to test the milk on her hand to be sure it was not too hot. I told her not to worry about his diapers, that I would change them when I got home, but she said, "I can do it," and changed them anyway. It was pretty nerve-wracking because the diaper had safety pins!

Was her salary from the school enough to support the family? "No, but I had some gold saved up. We had hidden it and had not declared it. I sold it to buy food. Also, in the afternoon when I was not teaching I bought vegetables from local farmers to sell at the market to make a little extra money."

Did people treat Trinh differently after her husband was sent away to re-education camp?

My neighbors, like the old lady who helped my husband to escape from the police, did not like the Communists. They did not treat me any differently. And most of the teachers at the school were in the same situation I was in. Their husbands had taught at the VNMA and were also in re-education camps. When one of us got a letter from her husband in the camps, she would pass it around and share it with all the others, even though it was a personal letter. We all read the letters and cried together. Even the schoolchildren saw through the policies of the new regime and made jokes about them. Each time I read them the story about how Uncle Ho [Ho Chi Minh], returning from exile in China, had kissed the soil of Vietnam, the kids would call out, "Liar!" They also had a word game they used to play. Every classroom had to have a picture of Uncle Ho. The Vietnamese words for putting a picture in a frame are *lồng khung*. They would point at Ho's picture and make a pun by reversing the letters to *liệng cống*. That meant "Throw it in the gutter!" Outside of the school and my neighborhood, however, it was different. The principal made us visit the parents of all of our students each week. I had fifty-three students in my class! When I went out to visit them people on the street would point at me and say, "She is an officer's wife. I hate her! Kill her!"

Was Trinh able to have any contact with her husband while he was in the re-education camps? "Yes, I was able to visit a few times. I had four children, and one of them was a baby, so it was hard to go as often as I would have liked." Did he seem different? "He looked older and skinnier. He was not any different emotionally. I loved him even more when he was in the camp because he seemed to be suffering a lot. Like him, I had to write down my autobiography, starting with my great-great-grandfather. I had to write down that my husband had spent time in the United States. Because of his time there I was not sure if he would ever be able to come home."

I asked Trinh to describe her emotional state during the time Quyet was in the camps. "I had no future in Vietnam. My future looked cloudy and dark. My children would not have a chance to go to school. I was very depressed, but I was not completely hopeless." How did she cope with having such a bleak future?

He was gone. I had no hope of him coming back. I assumed I would have to raise the children by myself. So I focused my energies on their educational future. I figured that I would send them to school until the government said that they could not go any more or I ran out of money. If I did not make enough money from teaching, I decided that I would find a different job selling things so that I could make more money.

Was there anything in her early life that helped prepare her to cope with the situation in which she found herself?

I had helped to run my mother's gift shop for five or six years before I got married. I knew about buying and selling and how to manage a business and money.

My husband came to the United States two years before we did. When he escaped from Da Lat I sent the children to my mother-in-law's place in Saigon and went with him to the delta [Mekong Delta]. After he was betrayed there I moved around with him for a while. Then when he finally escaped from Vietnam I moved back to my mother-in-law's house. She was nice to me, but my sister-in-law was very mean. There are always problems with sisters-in-law in Vietnam! I tutored neighborhood children to make extra money. When my husband finally got to the United States he wrote back to me, "Do not try to escape. I will sponsor you." He had heard horrible stories about women being raped and men being killed by pirates. My friends told me the same thing, "Do not try to escape, you will die at sea. There is a 90 percent chance that you will die!" But my life was so bad and I was so desperate that I decided to try to escape anyway. I had no house and no money. I had tried to escape three times before, and each time the leader of the group had cheated us. They took our gold and then left us behind. I had sold the house to finance one of our escapes. For the fourth attempt I had to borrow some gold from my sister. When we finally got to the United States I said to my children, "Even after I am dead and your auntie is dead you still have to send back money to your cousins in Vietnam. It was her money that allowed us to escape."

Each time I tried to escape I told the children's teacher what was going on. She was sympathetic to us because she wanted to escape too. I told her that if we did not make it, would she please let the girls come back to school? She could just say that the girls had been away for a couple of days visiting their auntie. When we finally did escape I sent her a present to thank her for her help. Since there were five of us we could not all go to the boat together. The Communists would have known that there was something up. So I always sent the two older girls on ahead to the boat owner's place to wait for the rest of us. I wrote my husband's name and address on the inside hem of each girl's shirt and told them, "If we are separated and you escape alone, write a letter to your father at this address and he will sponsor you."

We were very lucky that last time because we only had to stay at sea for three days and two nights before they picked us up. When I saw the rescue ship I read its French name, *Port de Lumière*. I said to the captain of our boat, "Stop, that is a French ship, they will pick us up!" The ship was actually German [-registered]. Its name was *Cap Anamur* [Island of Light]. They were out looking for boat people because they had heard what happened to them and they were eager to help us. When I got on board the ship I was carrying all four girls. I was so tiny that they were amazed I could do it and they took a picture of us! All we had were the clothes on our backs. They gave us T-shirts with the ship's German name on the front and its French name on the back. We were put in cabin 15. I was so happy to get on board that ship! I was finally able to start thinking of the future again. I wanted the children to at least graduate from college in the United States. I had always wanted them to study abroad. We had sent them to a French kindergarten before the end of the war to prepare them. I thought that they would be too narrow-minded if they spent their entire lives in Vietnam.

When we finally got to the United States I said to my husband, "Your and my lives are no good anymore, we are too old. We have to work for our children's future."

I turned to Quyet and asked if he had felt the same way.

Initially, I had hoped to work on my Ph.D. I had no idea when my family would be able to come to the United States. I had hoped to sponsor them for the ODP program and that might have taken five to ten years. I was quite worried when I heard that she planned to escape by sea. But when I heard that they had made it I was very happy. When I knew that they were on their way here I had to rethink my plans for the future.

Does Trinh think that all of the turmoil surrounding her and her husband's departure from Vietnam affected the children?

No, I do not think it had much of an effect. They matured very early. The two older ones had to take responsibility for the two younger ones. Each time I woke them up for our escape attempts it was always very early in the morning, about 3 A.M. They understood without my saying anything that they had to follow their mom and not complain. They knew that they were going to see their father. If I had not escaped from Vietnam, it would have been terrible for them. They would have grown up listening to and believing what the Communists said. As little children they were proud to be part of the elite students' group, to be "nieces and nephews of Uncle Ho" and to wear red neckerchiefs. I was worried that if we stayed in Vietnam, they would be influenced by the Communists' teaching.

At this point in our conversation Trinh stopped talking, and I noticed that she was crying. I asked her why she was sad.

A couple of months ago I got very upset. I was visiting my niece and nephew and noticed all the things they had, computers and nice clothes. When we got here we had nothing. I only made $3.25 an hour. My husband had been laid off. We did not have enough money to buy toys for them. I told my son how upset I had been about that. He said, "If you had been rich, then we would not be what we are now—hardworking, good students, all college graduates with good jobs. If you had been rich we would be spoiled. So you do not need to feel bad." But as a parent you do feel bad when you cannot give your kids everything you would like to give them. We were so poor then, we had nothing. So we focused on their schooling and on having them go to college.

I asked Trinh if all the ups and downs in her life had changed her as a person. "Going through all those ups and downs did change my personality. It made me a more difficult person." What do you mean by difficult? "I am more sensitive and easily hurt." Quyet added,

Let us say that we had not lost the war and were still living in Vietnam. She would have had a much easier life. I would be a professor at the VNMA and maybe also at Da Lat University. People would have shown her respect, and the future for us and for our children would have been very bright. Sometimes she looks back on that and feels sad. She would have been better off financially and socially. Here we meet Vietnamese who have less education than we do, but they have made a lot of money and feel that they are better than we are. That upsets her. She is very happy that the children have done so well, but sometimes she thinks back on how life might have been and it makes her feel sad.

I asked Trinh how she had adjusted to the cultural differences between Vietnam and the United States.

The first few years it was difficult. We were caught between two cultures. My relatives and friends told me, "Watch out for the girls." My oldest daughter wanted to go away to school. Everyone told me, "Do not let her go off and live by herself. At colleges here the boys and girls sleep together!" So I did not let her go. She went to a local college instead and lived at home. Now she is mad at me. I was afraid for the girls when we first got here, but later on I relaxed. We let the other kids go away to school. It is hard for my oldest daughter that she had to stay home while the younger ones got to live at their colleges. She still has some emotional scarring from that and some resentment toward me.

11 / The Politician

*T*he people whose lives are depicted in the next five chapters are members of a single family—a father, a mother, their son, their grandson, and their daughter-in-law. The father, Hung, grew up during the French colonial period, came of age during the first Vietnam War (between the French and the Viet Minh), and became a politician during the second (between the South Vietnamese and Americans and the North Vietnamese). He was incarcerated after the war and, because of his high position in the government, was sent to a re-education camp in North Vietnam. Sustained in his ordeal by the love of his family, his experiences in the camps made him a simpler man and taught him what is really important in life.*

Hung was born in 1924 in a rural village in the Mekong River Delta, the most fertile agricultural region in Vietnam. "The village was surrounded by rice fields and fruit trees. It was near the Mekong River, so fish were plentiful. There were two seasons, rainy and dry. Although the people had to work hard they were friendly and there was enough food for everyone. My father was a rice farmer, and our family was poor. We had to rent the land we farmed." The eldest of four children, Hung was the only one to receive a formal education. "My two younger sisters and younger brother stayed home to take care of the house and the farm. In Vietnam in those days very few parents could afford to send their children to school and only the daughters of the rich were educated. Ninety percent of the population was illiterate."

Hung attended local schools that reflected Vietnam's colonial history. His first year was in the Chinese school, where he learned to read *chữ nôm,* the Chinese characters modified and adapted to represent the Vietnamese language. This pictographic alphabet was gradually replaced by roman script (*quốc ngữ*), introduced to Vietnam by Portuguese and French missionaries in the seventeenth century.[1] Alexandre de Rhodes, a French Jesuit, created a dictionary of the Vietnamese language in roman script, listing words in Portuguese, Latin, and Vietnamese. After spending a year in the Chinese school Hung entered the local elementary school, established by the French after their conquest of Vietnam in the nineteenth century. "I went to school through the fifth grade. That was as far as you could go there. To continue in school I would have had to attend a school in another village. But that school cost money, and my family was too poor to send me. So I went to work helping my family grow rice."

Hung, like many older Vietnamese, idealizes his youth in the years prior to 1945, describing it as happy and relaxed.

I had a lot of free time and taught myself to play a large, two-stringed instrument that looks something like a banjo. It was popular then for young people to form amateur music groups, and I joined a small band with some friends to play traditional Vietnamese country music. Some evenings we played soccer, running around the village field in our bare feet. Sometimes we went to the local casino to gamble or just sat around talking and smoking marijuana. It was legal then [to smoke marijuana].

How did the French colonial government treat the Vietnamese? "They treated us well. They educated people. They did not want the people to be slaves." Hung's retrospective view of the French may have become more nostalgic over the years and certainly differs from that of many other Vietnamese of his generation. Although most Vietnamese respected French cultural traditions and often sought to emulate them, they resented the French colonization of their country, and some worked actively to overthrow the French. Hung did acknowledge one of the more disagreeable aspects of French rule, taxation: "There were two different rates, one for the rich and a lower one for the poor. If you paid taxes, you were a citizen. If not, you were not a citizen. It was important to be a citizen in those days because it made it easier to travel. All you had to do was to show your identification papers."

The French also imposed a military draft for which all young Vietnamese men had to register. Those chosen randomly through a lottery system served three years in French military forces.

I was eligible for the draft in 1945, but because of the turmoil in Vietnam around the end of World War II I did not have to become a soldier. The Vietnamese government was very unstable then. The Japanese, the French, the Viet Minh, the Hoa Hao, and the Cao Dia were all fighting one another.[2] After 1945 there was only war and fighting. I hated death. I hated the war. In my region there was a lot of fighting. There were bombs and the noise of war all the time. There was a lot of fighting and a lot of dying. Dying was so easy. I had friends who were killed and injured. You heard a gunshot, and you knew that someone had been killed. There was no justice then. I was afraid of the war and the killing and I hated it.

Despite the war raging around him, Hung was ambitious and sought ways to improve himself.

I saw the future of most of my friends and acquaintances as bleak. There was only poverty, hardship, and difficult times. I did not want to spend my life as a farmer like the rest of my family and friends. I wanted to live in the city and have a career so that I could do more interesting things. I was artistic and admired writers and singers. I liked to draw and used to sketch pictures of people in the village. I also liked fashion and finally decided to become a tailor. I studied with a tailor in a nearby town. Then I went to Saigon and worked for a tailor there so I could learn about the latest fashions.

In 1949, when he was twenty-five years old, Hung married. His future wife was a local girl from a nearby village. Asked what had attracted him to his wife, Hung responded,

I did not really know her. It was time to get married, and I did what my parents told me to do. A matchmaker arranged the marriage. That was the tradition. The matchmaker would learn that one family had a son and another family had a daughter. He would go to the family with the son, tell them about the girl, and see if they were interested in considering a marriage. If they were, the son and his family would go to the girl's home to meet and talk with her. They would observe how she greeted them, how she poured tea, and how she looked. Then they had about ten days to decide if they wanted the boy and girl to be married.

What would happen if the children did not want to marry? Hung laughed at this question. "Children would never disagree with their parents in those days. We have a saying in Vietnam, '*áo mặc không qua khỏi đầu*' [your shirt never goes above your head]. It means that children have to obey their parents."

After his marriage, Hung returned to his native village and set up a tailor shop. Asked about his and his wife's dreams for their life together, Hung responded, "We hoped to earn enough money to be comfortable, to be able to take care of our families, and to give our children an education." Hung and his wife eventually had eight children. The first, a son, was born in 1950. A second son, Bach (see "The Politician's Son"), was born in 1953 and was followed by two girls and four more sons.

In 1953 the twenty-nine-year-old Hung decided to change his career from tailoring to a more profitable one in which he could exercise his artistic abilities. With the support of his parents he attended a private school for photographers in Saigon, the largest city in Vietnam and soon to be the capital of the Republic of South Vietnam. His wife and son remained behind in the village, where he went to visit them on weekends. He enjoyed the school and, after a few months of training, was able to return to his village and establish his own photography studio. "I took and developed the photographs myself. The automated developing equipment of today was not available then. Most of my business was taking pictures of villagers for weddings and other formal occasions. The photo shop is still in business in the village. My oldest son runs it."

Hung's business flourished and his young family grew steadily larger, but in 1962 he was drawn into the tumultuous and dangerous world of local politics. "There were corrupt officials in my district who made extra money by falsely accusing people of being Viet Cong [v c]. They made the people pay a bribe to avoid arrest. They accused some of my neighbors of being Viet Cong. It made me angry. I knew them and they were not Viet Cong. I decided to take the officials to court." In the litigation-mad world of contemporary America such behavior might seem tame and almost second nature, but in the corrupt, wartorn South Vietnam of the early 1960s it was unusual, highly courageous, and very dangerous.

I was afraid that they would murder me for accusing them. Life was cheap in those days, and there were a lot of guns. I ran away to Saigon and hid. The local newspapers started writing about the case, and it soon came to the attention of the provincial government. The government decided to intervene rather than let the case go to court. They removed the district chief and the police who supported him from their positions.

As a result of his courage in challenging the corrupt district bureaucracy Hung became something of a local hero and was encouraged by his friends and neighbors to enter politics himself. He also received support from the government in Saigon.

I was attracted to politics by the opportunity it offered to help people. It is in my personality to love and help others. To do so I needed a position in the local government. I also wanted to help the national government fight the Communists. The Viet Cong were already very active in my area. They came to hate me because I worked to make the government trustworthy and good. [The Viet Cong had told the people that the government was corrupt and stole from them. My efforts to restore the integrity of the government caused] the people to lose confidence in the Viet Cong. This eroded their base of [popular] support.

Hung was elected to political office in 1965 as head of the village council, roughly equivalent to an American town council. "It was our job to protect the citizens, to ensure that the village chief did his job, and to make local laws." Hung was elected to two terms, each lasting two years, but did not complete his second term, as he was elected in 1969 to be a representative to the provincial assembly (equivalent to the house of representatives in an American state). Hung was a member of the Democratic Party, the party of Nguyen Van Thieu, president of the Republic of South Vietnam. "I was attracted to the party because they were against the Communists, and I wanted to fight the Communists. I saw it as a battle between good and evil, with Ho Chi Minh as the chief evildoer. The Communists were not good citizens, they were evil men."

Hung was elected to two four-year terms in the provincial assembly, but only served one year of his second term because of Saigon's fall to the Communists on April 30, 1975. He had no national political aspirations, but he did meet the nation's leaders, including President Thieu and Vice President Nguyen Cao Ky, at a meeting in Saigon. I asked him how he had felt about Thieu and Ky. He responded, "I remember them as being very opposed to the Communists. They treated me kindly." It is of interest that Hung spoke so blandly and uncritically of both the French and the Thieu-Ky regimes. His subsequent remarks about the Americans were also nonjudgmental. All of his hatred was reserved for the Communists, who he denounced as "evil." It is not clear to me whether he actually saw the political world of Vietnam in such simplistic, black-and-white terms or still felt that he must speak loyally of the old government. He may also have been reluctant out of politeness to say negative things about people who had been allies of the United States.

Asked when he began to sense that South Vietnam might lose the war, Hung responded,

In 1972 and 1973. During that time the Communists were getting very strong, and I began to fear that the war was lost. I felt this especially when the Paris Accords were signed on January 27, 1973.[3] I knew the Communists would not respect the treaty. I felt very sad. I was worried for the nation. I foresaw then that without American support, we would lose the war.

Why was South Vietnam defeated?

The Communists got the people's support. They lied to the people, and the people believed them. The Southern government did not want to bomb the areas where the Viet Cong lived among the people because they did not want to kill innocent civilians. If they bombed them, the Viet Cong would tell the people to go on strike against the government. They would say, "The government is not protecting you, they are killing you."

Here too Hung reserved his criticism for the Communists and their deceitful tactics. He might equally well have attacked the Americans for refusing to provide the support they had promised to the South Vietnamese government as part of its acceptance of the Paris Accords.[4]

Did Hung consider fleeing Vietnam at the end of the war like so many of his countrymen?

I wanted to go. I was afraid the Communists would capture me and put me in jail. But I did not have the opportunity to flee. [During the last days of the war] I felt very sad and depressed. [As he said this, Hung appeared to me to be quite serious and unhappy.] On April 30th [the day Saigon fell] I stayed home. I was afraid to go outside the house or anywhere else. I had had an important position in the provincial government and had been a leader of the Democratic Party. I knew it was only a matter of time before they came to put me in jail or kill me. Ten days after the fall of Saigon I was put in a re-education camp.

On May 10, 1975, Hung was told to report to the village security office. Several vc officials met him there. "It was very confusing. They had no titles, and I did not know them. [vc and North Vietnamese Army officers usually wore no rank insignia.] He was interrogated politely over a two-hour period by two of the vc. "They asked me to confess 'voluntarily' about my job and my position in the Democratic Party. They asked me to talk about my background, my politics, and the duties I had performed. After the interview I was told to go to a re-education camp, bringing along enough supplies for a one-week stay. Of course they lied. It was not for a week. It was for nine years, most of them in North Vietnam."

The vc permitted Hung to return home to get clothing and supplies. "I brought along enough clothes, food, and money for a week. I did not know they were lying." When he returned to the village office a large truck was waiting to take him and a number of others to the re-education camp. "We were taken to an open field by a rice mill near a small river. We waited there for several hours, until a ship came to take us to the camp. It was located on abandoned land a few miles away."

Hung described life in the camp as "very difficult. We spent the days digging an irrigation ditch to be used in growing bananas and pineapples. Each day we got two small bowls of rice with salt. There was no meat or vegetables. The guards threatened us, trying to make us afraid. It was verbal abuse. They said, 'You belonged to the Democratic Party and took advantage of the people by taking bribes.'" Asked how he had felt during this period, Hung responded, "Very sad and confused. I was not used to physical labor. We did not get enough food. We were out in the hot sun digging the irrigation ditch and planting bananas and pineapples. I frequently caught cold. We worked eight hours a day, six days a week. On Sunday we did not have to work, but we did have to attend re-education meetings."

After three months Hung and his fellow inmates were transferred to a second camp about a mile away. There conditions were much the same as in the first camp.

I felt very confused and stressed. I began to think that I would never get to go home. My wife was allowed to visit. She came once to the first camp and three times to the second. She was only permitted to stay for half an hour. She brought small amounts of food—fish sauce, sugar, and sausage. Before she could give it to me the guards had to check it to be sure that there was nothing I was not allowed to have.

In 1977, approximately two years after he had left home for re-education camp, Hung and a few other prisoners were taken from the camp to an unknown destination.

We were considered to be the most dangerous prisoners. They thought that I might be a problem because of my prior position in the old government. We went by bus to Saigon, where we boarded a ship, the *Sông Hương* [the same ship on which the Pilot was transported to the North]. There were about 1,000 other prisoners on the ship. They were all men, either government administrators or military officers. I knew a few of them, but not many. The ship was very dirty, especially the lavatories, which were quite unsanitary. We were kept in the hold. It was very crowded. We were given two packages of noodles and half a can of condensed milk each day. We did not know where we were going. I asked, but they would not tell us. Everything was kept secret. We all felt very sad and depressed.

When the ship got to its destination we were handcuffed together in pairs and led ashore. I saw a sign reading "Hai Phong" and knew that we were in North Vietnam. There were a lot of buses waiting for us. As we walked toward the buses people threw stones at us and shouted insults. I thought that it must be a setup by the Communists, not an expression of what the people really felt.

At the buses they divided us up and sent us to different camps. Mine was about 2 miles from Hanoi. I could see the city in the distance.

Hung was to remain in the camp for the next seven years.

Conditions in the new camp were much better than in the other camps I had been in. It was very structured and organized. Every few months the Red Cross and other organizations would come to visit. They interviewed people in the camp to see how the conditions were. Normally, the camp was dirty, unclean, and very crowded, but before the visitors arrived the people in charge hid some of the prisoners in the fields, leaving only about half the prisoners in the camp. They cleaned things up and tried to give the impression that it was for "re-education," not a place where people were threatened and tortured. They had pigs hanging in our huts, let us play soccer, and dressed us up nicely. However, we were forbidden to speak foreign languages, even though some of us knew French and English, and we were not allowed to talk to the visitors directly.

Everyday life in the camp consisted of "working eight hours a day, six days a week. The prisoners were divided into groups. Some raised vegetables, others were carpenters, others cut down trees, still others grew rice. On the seventh day we had lectures in which they demeaned the former government and encouraged us to follow the new government." Was Hung ever tortured or beaten? "No, it never happened to me. The Communists were smart. They did not kill you outright in the camps by shooting you. Instead they slowly tortured and terrified you. A few prisoners who did not follow the camp's regulations were punished. They were handcuffed, put in a dark room, isolated from the other prisoners, and given less to eat." I asked whether people had died in the camps. "Many! Starvation and hard physical work caused people to get sick. It was very easy to die. It had nothing to do with your mental state or personality. It was just that there was not enough to eat and there were no medicines."

Sometimes Hung and his fellow prisoners would talk together "about the old days, history, and politics. We discussed what might benefit us and disadvantage the Communists. But you had to be very careful who you talked to and had to know each other well because there were a few spies [the 'antennas' described in previous chapters]."

During the seven years he was in the camp Hung received a total of nine visits from his family, who traveled from the south to Hanoi by train, a distance of approximately 1,000 miles.

If it had not been for those family visits, I would have starved. They brought supplies. The guards always checked through the supplies before they gave them to us. The first couple of visits we were only permitted to spend about an hour together. The guards sat next to us, listening to our conversations. After those first couple of visits my family was allowed to stay for one to two days. During our visits my wife and I talked about the family and about our love for them and for each other. We could not say anything else because the guards were always listening.

When I asked Hung about his mental state during the time of his imprisonment in the North, he replied, "We were all very sad. We kept hoping that the Communist government would fall and that other countries would come and rescue us. We especially hoped that the Americans would come because they had helped us fight the Communists before."

I asked Hung if, as the years passed, he had begun to lose hope. "No, I never forgot how bad the Communists were and I never gave up hope. I could never forget how much I hated the Communists." Did he ever bemoan his fate and wonder why all of these horrible things were happening to him? "I did not think so much about my own fate as of the fate of my country. From the time when the French first conquered Vietnam in the nineteenth century until now, we have never been at peace."

After seven years in this camp Hung and his fellow inmates (approximately 1,000 men) were transferred by truck to another camp a few hours south of Hanoi. "They did not tell us where we were going or why they were taking us away. The new camp was dirty and unsanitary. It was more like a jail than the other camp had been. It was very crowded, and we were dealt with in large groups rather than individually. We continued to do gardening work, but our diet was worse— only rice, salt, and bindweed."

Eight months after his transfer, and shortly before Tet (the Vietnamese lunar New Year celebration) in 1984, Hung was released from the re-education camp and sent home.

They told us that we would be leaving three or four days before we were released. All the prisoners were taken to an open field. There they read out some of our names and isolated us from the others. Then they told us, "You get to go home and be reunited with your families. We forgive you." For the next three or four days we were given extra food to show people on the outside that the camps were not really so bad. When we left the camp they gave us a piece of paper with our name, date of release, and destination, along with a train ticket home.

Did his experience in the re-education camps change his life?

Certainly. It affected me greatly. In the camps I continued to hate the Communists. The longer they kept me in jail, the more I hated them. They could not re-educate me because I knew them too well. I knew their true colors. It is too bad that other nations do not know the Communists as well as we do. As President Thieu used to say, "Do not believe what they say—watch what they do." After I returned home from the camps I could see that conditions in Vietnam had greatly deteriorated. I felt sad and hurt for the people who had to live under the Communist government. There is no future for them.

I asked Hung what enabled him to survive in the camps. Without a moment's hesitation he replied, "The love [*tình yêu*] of my family. I thought of them often in the camp, of my wife and children and my elderly mother." To comfort himself he read books and papers supplied by his family.

They were books and papers published by the Communists, but I would do anything to pass the time. And I wanted to know what was going on. To really know the Communists you have to learn their weaknesses. I can talk about the Communists and the camps forever. The Communists are manipulative and evil. They falsely accused innocent people. They buried them alive. They tied their hands behind their backs and threw them in the river.

Hung returned home to the same house he had lived in before his incarceration. He still had his family, a garden with trees and vegetables, and the photo shop, which his family had continued to operate during his absence. "After returning home I decided to let my oldest son run the shop because I was too old." Returning home did not mean Hung was free.

Over the next three years I had to stay in my house after dark. Once a week I had to present myself to the village security office. If I wanted to leave the village, I had to get permission. Sometimes I would be asked to do unpaid community work like cleaning the streets and digging irrigation ditches. [Physically] I was much weaker than before because there had not been enough to eat in the camps. [Emotionally] I was very disturbed. I kept envisioning the camp and always felt afraid and worried. I had trouble sleeping and was depressed. To some extent I still feel that way whenever I think of the camp.

Does Hung ever feel as if he is still in the camp? "Not here in the United States, but I did when I was in Vietnam. Sometimes I dream about the camp. I hear the bell ringing. They had a bell they used to ring every morning at 5 A.M. to call us to work. Then I wake up and realize that I am here and not in the camp and I feel very relieved."

In January 1992, when Hung was sixty-eight, he and his family immigrated to the United States under the auspices of the H.O. Program (a program that permitted the immigration of former political prisoners to the United States). Only his two older sons and their families remained behind. His oldest son stayed on to run the family photo shop, and continues to do so to this day. His second oldest son, a former officer in the South Vietnamese Army, also remained in Vietnam, coming to the United States separately with his family in 1996.

Asked how he feels being in the United States, Hung replied, "I feel more at peace. I have escaped from hell to freedom." Is life different here than he thought it would be? "When I first came I had imagined things would be different than they really are. In Vietnam I had heard that the United States was a paradise. When I got here, I had to adjust to reality."

12 / The Politician's Wife

Hung's wife, Tho, is a woman of the old Vietnam. Born into an affluent family in the Mekong Delta, she received a brief formal education and then stayed home to help her parents and siblings care for their house and farm. Her marriage to Hung was arranged, and she assumed the traditional wife's role of subservience to her husband and his wishes, focusing her energies on the family. When he was sent away to re-education camp she had to adapt to the unaccustomed position of being head of the household. Initially overwhelmed by her new responsibilities, she found the strength to carry on for the sake of her husband and her children.

Hung's wife, Tho, is a sixty-eight-year-old woman from the same province in the Mekong River Delta, but from a different village. Her family were also farmers, but they were much more affluent, owning the land they farmed.

My paternal grandfather was a wealthy landowner. He owned a plantation and rented out his land to farmers. They paid him back for the land with rice. They also had to help him at family functions like weddings and funerals. Out of respect for him they set aside their own responsibilities and volunteered to cook and clean at festivals. His land was very good. It lay close to the Mekong River, and the river kept bringing down fresh soil. The area was well known for its tangerines. He raised them for sale in Cho Lon.[1] When my grandfather died he divided up the land among his children. Since my father was the only boy he got a larger share than his sisters did. Like his father my father raised tangerines for sale in Saigon. This and the land we owned gave us a higher standard of living than the other people in our neighborhood [*xóm*]. We were also respected because of my grandfather's position as a large landowner.

There were five children in Tho's family. She was the youngest and had two older brothers and sisters. The oldest, a brother, was sixteen years older than she, while the youngest, a sister, was four years her senior.

In my day girls were not educated, and I only went as far as the third grade. My oldest brother went to school for seven or eight years, and my younger brother went for about five. Parents were afraid to let their daughters learn to read and write because then they might write love letters to boys! My parents were very strict with me. They would not let me go to concerts, fearing that I would meet boys and fall in love. My mother would have let me, but not my father.

How did she spend her time as a young girl? "My older brothers were married and their wives came to live with us. I helped them with cooking twice a day, and when I finished I went out and helped the family take care of the tangerines." Did she do anything for fun? "My parents did not let me go anywhere, so I just helped out around the house and garden. Sometimes I went grocery shopping or fished in a small pond on our land." Growing up Tho was closest to her sisters, and after they got married she felt closest to her mother. "My sisters both lived in the same neighborhood as we did. I spent a lot of time with them. In Vietnamese families we tend to love the youngest child the most, so they paid a lot of attention to me."

I asked Tho about her first meeting with her husband.

In Vietnam a young man's family first goes to the girl's home [the process is called *đi coi mắt*—literally, "to go to see the eyes"] to see what she looks like and to observe how she greets them and pours tea. I remember being very nervous. I was wearing a dark blue *áo dài*. I went out and greeted his parents and the matchmaker, but I forgot to greet him. Then when I poured the tea my hand was shaking so much that I spilled it.

What was her first impression of her future husband? "I peeked out through a hole in the wall. I thought he looked very attractive and fashionable because he lived in Saigon and dressed like the people there. At that time people in the country dressed very differently from those in Saigon. A person from the city was pretty conspicuous." How was her marriage arranged?

My father had not decided if he wanted us to marry, but then he went to a party and overheard that [my husband's] family was very good. He persuaded my mother to let me marry him. As for my husband, he accepted what his parents wanted. He was especially eager to do what they said because his younger brother had married a woman from Saigon without their permission. At that time people in the country thought that Saigon girls were too advanced, intelligent, and fashionable and not focused enough on the family. As a result his mother refused to attend her son's wedding.

How did she feel about getting married? "I really did not have any say in the matter. Once my parents made the decision I had to do what they said."

I asked whether the disparity in income and social standing between her and her husband's families had been a problem for them.

Not really, even though his family was poor and he had lost his father at an early age. My father had spent time in France and had an open mind. He had gone there as a soldier in World War I and fought in France and Africa. [He went because] my grandfather believed that the wealthy landowners should set an example. My father did not care if my fiancé was poor, only that he had a career. In those days most people were farmers and anyone with a skill or trade was respected.

After their marriage Hung set up a tailor shop in his home village and Tho left her home to live with him and his family. "Being a daughter-in-law in a husband's family is fairly difficult. Every day I had to get up early, about 4 A.M., to sweep the front yard, get water, and help with the cooking. His family treated me well, but I had to do a daughter-in-law's duty."

As their family grew Hung began to consider ways of making more money.

As a tailor his income was limited. He could only make a certain number of pairs of trousers each day! As a photographer he could make a lot more money. At that time photographers were highly respected and earned a lot. Fifty years ago in Vietnam photography was still something very new. Cameras were expensive, and if you had one, children in the village would surround you to see what it was.

Despite the promise of more money, however, "I begged him not to do it. But men had a lot of power in the family [in those days]. If they made a decision, that was it. All I could do was cry and try to persuade him not to do it." Hung left his tailor shop, village, and family for the next six months to study photography in Saigon. Tho explained: "It was not a big problem for me. I took over the management of the shop, and the three employees and three students who worked there kept the business going."

After completing his training Hung returned from Saigon and established his own photo studio, which over the years became a very successful business. The family continued to grow, and life settled into a routine. A major turning point came when Hung decided to take on the corrupt district officials who had accused people in the village of being Viet Cong (v c). Tho explained:

[The people they accused] were our neighbors. They came to him and complained about how they were being mistreated. Hearing their stories made him angry, and he decided to help them. Initially, I tried to stop him from doing it. I said, "Do not get involved. Our family does not have any power or authority. Let [the corrupt officials] win." But he said, "Do not worry. The righteous people always win."

Hung's success in having the corrupt officials removed led to an invitation to run for office as head of the village council. Again Tho tried to dissuade him. "I never wanted him to get involved in politics, but if he wanted to do something he just did it." Although her husband's involvement in politics, first at the village and later at the provincial level, did not immediately affect her life, it was the reason for his lengthy postwar incarceration in the re-education camps. This experience had a profound effect, not only on him, but also on his entire family.

Asked how her life had changed after her husband was taken away to the re-education camp, Tho responded,

After he left I had to take care of our seven children and the photo shop by myself. The shop did not do well. My husband had been the primary person involved in it, and after he left none of us really knew how to run it. Also, people were afraid to patronize the shop because he was in a re-education camp. Even our relatives and his best friend stayed away. It was like we had some dangerous illness, an infectious disease, and people were afraid they might catch it. They did not want to get involved and get in trouble with the government.

The social ostracism described by Tho was probably most severe in the years immediately following the end of the war, when anti-American feeling was at its height. It was more likely to occur in contacts with those who were either Communists or their sympathizers or those who had lost relatives to American or South Vietnamese military action. However, even those who were more neutral appear, at times, to have turned their backs on "collaborators" for fear of contaminating themselves by contact with the new government's enemies.

"Each month all the wives of men who had been sent to re-education camps were asked to come to a meeting. The purpose was to re-educate those of us at home. They told us not to open businesses and take advantage of people. Instead they wanted us to stay home and farm." The wives of other prisoners were some of Tho's most important social supports.

Those of us who were in the same situation became very close. We loved each other more than before. We shared information about things like the government's visitation policy for the camps. People who did not have husbands in the camps stayed away from us. My son was in the military. After he was sent away his best friend's wife began to ignore my son's wife—not even saying hello on the street—because it might be bad for her husband's reputation.

I asked Tho if their standard of living had changed after her husband's departure for re-education camp. She replied emphatically,

Yes! Life changed a lot. Every night I waited until the children were in bed and could not hear me, and then I cried because we did not have enough money for me to visit him. The day after my husband left people from the government came and made a list of everything we had. They took some things like our TV and my son's military clothing, saying that it was "the people's property." Fortunately, they left a lot of things, even the photo equipment. In that sense I was lucky. My best friend lost everything she owned. With my husband, our primary provider, gone I had to sell our possessions to support the family. I sold pots and pans in front of the house. Even so there was not much to eat. Meat and fish were rare. We mixed sweet potatoes with rice just to fill our stomachs.

Eventually, Tho began to receive monthly visitation slips from her husband permitting her to visit him in the re-education camp. She took these to the district security office, where she was issued a travel permission slip. Both the visitation slip and the travel permission slip were necessary for her to visit the camp. "We had trouble getting together enough money to pay for transportation to the camps, but I felt very sorry for him and went as often as I could. After he was sent to the North we were at first allowed to visit only every two years, then once a year. Initially, we were permitted to bring along only 6 pounds of supplies. Later this was increased to 50 pounds."

Asked about her emotional state during this time, Tho responded,

I hated the Communists very much, but I mostly worried about my husband, especially after he was sent North. For a long time after he was sent there they lied to us, saying that he had been sent to the Chi Hoa prison in Saigon. I was depressed and melancholy and cried all the time. Every time I got permission to go see him I had to worry about where to find the money to get the things he wanted. I lost my appetite and had trouble sleeping. Still I had to do the best I could to take care of the family. I went to see my mother-in-law, and she suggested that I start selling fried bananas in front of the house to make extra money for the things my husband needed. I tried it, and it worked! I also started selling things from the photo shop to help pay for the trips North.

My husband was gone for nine years, seven of them in the North. In those nine years I got to visit him seven times. During our visits we did not have much privacy. I had to lie to him and say that we had enough to eat and that the children were going to school. I did not want him to worry about what was going on at home, especially about the children's schooling, because he valued education so much. In reality the children were not allowed to go to school because of their father's position in the old government. For example, my daughter had done very well in high school. After her graduation she wanted to go on to college. There was a priority list to determine who got admitted. If your family were Communists, you went to the top of the list. If they worked for the old government, you went to the bottom. Since her father and brother were both in re-education camps, she did not get accepted. One of my sons was expelled from school because of his father's former position, and the two youngest were not permitted to attend.

They were told, "You cannot go to school because your father was a former assistant to the United States government."

Such institutionalized discrimination was a common experience for the children of former political prisoners and for the children of others closely connected to the old regime and the Americans, such as the Amerasians.

Prisoners' letters to and from their families were read and censored. Tho showed me the collection of letters, carefully and lovingly bound in leather, that she had received from her husband and son during the period of their incarcerations. "During the time they were in prison they wrote many letters home, but the letters were censored, so they had to be careful what they wrote. Even though my husband was starving in the camp he had to write that they were being treated well. To let us know what was really going on he began to write his letters in a kind of code." To this day her husband and son will not reread the letters they wrote so many years ago. "It brings back the memories of the camp too powerfully. My son still has nightmares about the place."

In 1984, nine years after her husband was first imprisoned, Tho learned by accident that he was about to be released. One of her sons had gone to the North to visit his father. During the visit he learned from Hung that he was going to be leaving in a couple of days, and he immediately sent a telegram home to inform his mother. This account demonstrates the unpredictability of prisoners being released from the re-education camps. In most cases neither they nor their families had any idea when they were coming home and were usually given only a few days notice prior to their discharge.

When I asked Tho whether her husband seemed different after returning from his long and brutal incarceration, she responded,

He seemed simpler. Before the camp he had been a picky eater. Now he ate everything and tried not to waste food. His thinking was simpler too. Before he was always very firm in his views. Afterward he was more flexible.

199

He used to say to the children, "If you have been to a re-education camp, you learn to value what you have." Before he had been a big spender, but now he liked to save money. He will only buy coffee if he can get a second can free! He used to be a very fashionable and trendy dresser. Now he says, "I buy my clothes at Goodwill. They are just as good!"

Conditions for the family had begun to improve during the two years prior to Hung's release. "Our daughter had a small business in Saigon selling paper and pens, and I sold pots and pans in front of the house." After Hung's return his oldest son reopened the photo shop. "He did not have official permission to do so, but some of our old customers began to ask us to come take photos at weddings and festivals and develop them. We did not make much money, so the government did not notice. Finally, we got official permission to reopen the business."

I asked Tho if she ever thinks about the time during which her husband was incarcerated. "I still have nightmares about it. Sometimes I dream I am on the train heading back up North to visit him. Then I wake up and realize that I am lying here safely in bed." How does she like living in the United States? "I am used to things now, and I like it here very much. I still have a son and daughter living in Vietnam. I went back there recently for a month or two and did not like it. It was too hot."

13 / The Politician's Son

Bach, the second son of Hung and Tho, was a university student during the latter years of the war but was drafted and forced to give up his studies and his dream of becoming an engineer. He fought as an infantry officer, leading his men on operations against the Viet Cong (v c). After the war he and his father were both sent to the same re-education camp. Bach was released after five years and returned home, subsequently establishing a flourishing photography business in Ho Chi Minh City. Despite his professional success and affluence, however, he decided to immigrate to the United States, giving up everything for the sake of freedom and his children's future.

Bach, the second child of Hung and Tho, was born in 1953. I met him in his tiny wood-frame rented house a few miles away from the home of his parents. Above the mantelpiece hung a large black-and-white photographic portrait of him as a young man in his South Vietnamese military dress uniform. I asked him about the picture. "It was my graduation picture from Dong De [an army training program in South Vietnam]. I was twenty years old when it was taken." Does he remember how he felt at the time? "I thought I was going to die. Dying was really easy then. I wanted the picture as a remembrance for my family."

Bach was born and grew up in the same village as his father. He attended the village school through the ninth grade and completed the tenth through the twelfth grades at a public high school modeled after a French lycée.

After completing the twelfth grade I took a test, *Tú Tài 2*,[1] to qualify for the university. It was very difficult. Those who passed entered the university. Those who did not went into the military. There was one public university in Saigon, which had faculties specializing in different fields—medicine, law, engineering, and science—and also two private universities. I wanted to study engineering, but my grade on the qualifying exam was not high enough, so I had to do science.

Bach began his university studies in the fall of 1971, two years before the final withdrawal of American troops and less than four years before the fall of Saigon and the collapse of the Republic of South Vietnam. "I liked the university a lot because I majored in math, my favorite subject." Unfortunately, Bach's time at the university was brief. In April 1972 all the universities in Saigon were closed. Setting off for class one day he found a large sign on the university gate reading *"Tổ Quốc lâm nguy, Bạn làm gì để cứu tổ quốc?"* (The nation is in peril; what can you do to help?). He also learned that the government had lowered the age of military service to seventeen. It was clear that he would have to go into the army.

I asked Bach how he had felt about having to give up his university studies.

I felt very sad because I could not fulfill my dream of getting a university degree. I was surprised to see that sign at the university. I had been reading the papers and watching TV and knew that things were bad, but my classmates and I kept studying and hoping that we would not have to go into the army. Now I knew I had to go; there was no escape. If I did not go, I would be arrested. There was a schedule for entry into the military posted at the university. It was based on the month and year of your birth. I had a month before I had to go, so I went home and stayed with my family. I felt very sad. I had three girlfriends and had not been very close to any of them, but now I spent a lot of time with them because I knew I would be sad and lonely in the army and I wanted to have somebody to write to.

Bach presented himself in Saigon for military service and was transported to Quang Trung, a training camp about 6 miles from the city. There he spent the first three months learning the rudiments of soldiering, such as marching and marksmanship. The next two months were spent on a political assignment, getting to know the people in the area, a type of civil affairs program. Having graduated from high school and passed the university qualifying exam, he was then sent to officer candidate school in Nha Trang. There he trained to command an infantry platoon. He learned how to lead troops, to set booby traps, and to build fortifications.

I did not like it very much. I was really sad to be in the army. It was my dream to be an engineer, and now I knew that my dream was not going to come true and I would not be able to complete my education. I was also afraid that I would be killed. I felt like I had no future. Surprisingly, given how much I disliked the course and how sad I felt, I did quite well and had very high scores. There was one benefit to that. If you had high scores, you got to choose the [army] division in which you served, so I chose the one in my home province.

The base to which Bach was assigned was only about 20 miles from his hometown, and once in a while he was permitted to go home and spend the day with his family. Initially, he served as the supply officer of his infantry battalion, then after a year he was given command of a company of *Nghĩa Quân* (Popular Forces—the Vietnamese equivalent of the National Guard). He and the 200 men under his command were stationed in a village only a mile from his home.

"I hated going into the army. I was forced to go, and the training was difficult, but after I got out into the field I liked it. I liked the soldiers. They loved one another and treated each other well. I also began to understand how evil the Communists were and could see a purpose to my military service." Bach gave an example of the Communists' behavior: "We were fighting in a village. After the fight the Communists would hide in the church or in the people's homes. They knew we would not fight in those places because we did not want to hurt the people." Bach said that he was shot at

three or four times, but never hit. After a battle I would go home and sleep. The next morning I would get up, have a cup of coffee, think about it, and feel very scared. But then I would remember my duty and not be afraid. I still dream of the fighting. I see myself leading my troops out on patrol. It happens when I am very tired. Once back in Vietnam shortly after I was released from re-education camp I was sleeping next to my wife. It was very early in the morning and a caged bird we had in the room began to whistle. I thought it was the sound of a rocket coming in, jumped out of bed, and yelled to my wife, "The Viet Cong are coming; let us hide!"

The war ended for Bach on April 30, 1975, the day Saigon fell to the North Vietnamese Army and the v c.

I was in charge of two bridges along the highway leading to Saigon. The night before my commanding officer had told me to keep the radio on. He called every fifteen minutes for a while, then we heard nothing. At about noon on the 30th we heard a message over the radio [from the last South Vietnamese president, General Duong Van Minh] stating that all soldiers were to surren-der. I had no orders [from my commander] and did not know what to do. A lot of South Vietnamese soldiers were passing by over the bridges. I was afraid that if I left, the Viet Cong would blow up the bridges and I would be sent to jail. However, if I stayed, I might be captured. By about 4 the next morning most of the other soldiers had left, but a few of us were still there. An older woman who lived near the bridge, whom I had befriended during my time there, came over to me and said, "What are you doing here? Nobody knows who is in charge. Why not come to my house and I will protect you?" She had a son who was a soldier, and she liked me because I used to talk with her when she crossed the bridge. She was afraid that the Viet Cong or my own men would shoot me. I was very confused about what to do. I just could not decide. What she said about my being shot made sense, and so I finally decided to go with her. At about 5 or 6 in the morning some friends of mine came to her house and told me to head south with them, but she told me to stay with her, saying that they did not know where they were going. I waited at her house, looking out toward the bridge through a hole in the metal gate. Around 10 o'clock I noticed that the Viet Cong had put up their flag at my post on the bridge. I waited about thirty minutes and then decided to go over and talk to them. I walked up to the Viet Cong commander and said, "I am in command here. There is somebody senior to me, but he left last night." The Viet Cong told me where to put my rifle, the radio, and a typewriter we had at the post. Then he asked me some questions: "Who was your commanding officer? Who worked for you? Who was in charge of the four platoons in your company?" I stayed there talking with him for about an hour. He did not really know what to do with me, so he wrote out a note with his signature on it saying that I had been interviewed and could go home.

How did it feel talking with the enemy? "I was not afraid. He was polite. I felt sad that the country was lost."

After his interview with the v c commander Bach walked the mile or so to his parent's home.

When I got there the Viet Cong had just arrived in a big G M C truck and were taking my parents' things, their T V, furniture, everything. Even now when my mother hears a big truck she gets frightened. I did not see my father, so I walked up to the second floor of the house. There I found my mother sitting on the bed crying. I saw five or six Viet Cong with guns trying to carry our stuff down the stairs. They had presented my mother with a piece of paper saying that they had come to take our things because my father had stolen them and they belonged to the people. Seeing my mother crying I felt angry. I still had a knife, a pistol, and some grenades, and I was ready to use them. I said, sarcastically, imitating the Viet Cong, "This stuff was stolen from other people. Let them take it." I was trying to provoke the Viet Cong, trying to make them angry so I could shoot them. My mother's older sister was sitting next to her on the bed, comforting her. Seeing how angry I was she took me outside and tried to quiet me down. She said, "Calm yourself. Give it up. Accept that you have lost and do not do anything."

After that my father and I stayed at home, waiting to be called. I threw my weapons away in the river.

Did Bach and his father talk about what might await them? "We knew that the future was bleak; neither of us had a future. After about a month a loudspeaker announced that all officers of the former government had to go sign up for re-education camp. I turned myself in a couple of days before my dad. When I got to the village office there was a big truck waiting for me." How did he feel as he got on the truck? "I sat there hoping that the sooner I went to re-education camp, the sooner I would get out. I thought I would only be gone for about a month. I was still hoping that I could go back to the university and complete my education." Who was on the truck with him?

My commanding officer, the one who left the night before I surrendered, was there. He had been hiding somewhere. When he heard the announcement he came out and got on the same truck. He is ethnic Chinese, and he showed up carrying a condensed milk can filled with pickled white radishes. The Chinese love to eat them. That was all he had! He said, "By the time we have eaten half this can we will be home again." We had been told to bring enough money and supplies for fifteen days. I had brought a mosquito net, two sets of clothes, and some salted pork, but no other food. I was not frightened. I kept thinking, "The sooner I go, the sooner I get home."

The Viet Cong drove us out to a big empty field. There were no people, animals, or houses to be seen. They told us to build a barracks and said, "The sooner you finish the job, the sooner you can go home." That made us work harder, ten hours a day. We were anxious to get it built so that we could go home. When we finished the job we even had a celebration and put up a sign that read *"lễ khai giảng khóa 1/75—học tập cải tạo sĩ quan chế độ cũ"* [opening of the first class of 1975, re-education camp for officers of the old regime]. I thought to myself, "Well if this is the first class, then there are bound to be others. [We will not be here long.]" I was wrong. There was only one class, but it lasted for years.

In the camp there were no tables or chairs, so we just sat on the ground. The camp was near the river, and the soil was wet. We stripped the bark from trees so we could sit on it and keep dry. A couple of days after my arrival my father was brought to the camp. His job was to pass out the rice they supplied to us. One day he said to me, "Well the rice is all gone, so I guess we will be going home tomorrow." But we did not. The Viet Cong were very manipulative and lied a lot. For example, when we left for the re-education camp they said, "Bring enough supplies for fifteen days," not "Camp will last fifteen days."

In the camp our ration consisted of salt, pepper, rice, cucumbers, and a little meat. During those first two years I was very hungry all the time, so hungry that I could not sleep. I drank water to quiet my hunger, but then I was up half the night going to the bathroom. I craved meat. At night I thought and dreamt about it. Once a friend of mine was punished by being placed in a metal shipping container [out in the hot sun]. He kept pounding on the box and calling to the guard saying, "Give me two pounds of meat and I will die." He was losing his mind. The next day he died.

They punished us for silly things like writing to our wives and saying that it was lonely in the camp and that we did not like it. A friend of mine used to write music. He had written a piece for his wife that read, "Maybe I will not be coming home to you." Later that day they told us to bring all of our things outside and spread them out for inspection. They found his music. For writing it they put him in isolation and he died.

My father and I were together in the camp for five months, then he was transferred to another temporary camp because of his high position in the government. During the time we were together we slept next to each other. When he was transferred I thought that I would never see him again. Being transferred to the North was a bad thing. [Prisoners considered to be more dangerous to the new regime were sent there.] The day he left I walked with him for a long way toward the new camp. The guard asked me, "Are you going too?" I said no and turned around, watching my father walk away. The camp in which he stayed waiting to be transferred was about 3 miles away. My father was too old to do physical labor, so he stayed in the camp. I was one of the youngest, only twenty-one, so I got all the hard jobs. Whenever the rest of us went out to work there was always the risk of stepping on a mine. Every time my father heard a mine exploding he worried, thinking it might be me. One day I saw a man from his camp. He told me, "Yesterday your father wanted to carry water out to the workers so he could see if you are all right, but they would not let him." I told him to tell my father that I was fine.

How were Bach's spirits in the camp?

All the prisoners were very obedient. Before the camp they might have been tough guys, but in the camp they did not dare talk back. One day about ten prisoners were taken out and shot. There was no reason for it as far as I could tell. At about 5 P.M. they called their names, had them stand in front of the barracks, and said it was time for them to go to work. Then they were led away and shot. If they called you out to work in the afternoon, it meant that they were going to shoot you. I saw it happen many times. In one of the camps there was a guard who shot people when they were going to the bathroom. No reason, he just shot them.

I was surprised to hear about this random, senseless shooting, as I had not heard such things described by the other former political prisoners. On a later visit to Bach I asked him if I had understood him correctly about the guard's actions. He confirmed what he had told me before and then added,

He was crazy. The other guards did not behave like that. But when the camp director found out about what he had done, he did not punish him, he just sent him to another camp.

Once we were in a camp not far from the Cambodian border. It was during the Vietnam-Cambodia War. The Viet Cong placed Claymores [anti-personnel mines] around the camp. We thought that they were to protect us, but they aimed the Claymores at us! They said that if the Cambodians attacked, they would kill us first because we were their enemies too. The prisoners who were religious prayed that the Cambodians would not come.

All told I was in four different camps over a five-year period.

Why was he incarcerated for so long if he was only a junior officer? "[I assume that] it was because of my father's high rank and because I had fought against the Viet Cong. Most of my friends were only in the camps for three years." Three days before he was released from his fourth and final camp Bach's name was read out over a loudspeaker. He was separated from the other prisoners and told that he was going home.

At first I could not believe it. I had lost hope that I would ever go home. For the next three days they fed us a lot and then they gave us money for the trip. I was so happy to be going home. The ferry took me across the river to get a bus, and I did not look back once because I was afraid that they might make me return. When I told the bus driver I had been in a re-education camp he said I could ride for free.

Bach was released in 1980, at the age of twenty-seven. At home he went to work in the family photo business. During the first year after his release, he had to stay in the village, signing in each week at the village security office. In 1981 this restriction was lifted, and he moved to Saigon to live with his wife's family. He and his wife had met in 1974 when she came to his village to visit relatives. She was three months pregnant when he left for the re-education camp. "I first saw my son when he was one year old. I carried his photo around with me in the camp. [He showed me the tattered, worn photo of his son, then a toddler.] It is my most valuable possession. After he was born my wife went to live with her parents in Saigon."

In Saigon Bach worked for two years in a government photography shop.

I was very good at photography, and they asked me to supervise the shop, but because of my background [as a former political prisoner], I refused. I thought that the workers I would be supervising would take advantage of me because I had been a prisoner. In 1983 I opened my own small shop in [a district of Saigon]. My wife took the orders, and I developed the photos. Over the next four years the business grew a lot. We had customers from all over because we had color developers and most places outside the city did not. For the three months after Tet [the Vietnamese lunar New Year, a time of celebration and picture taking] there was so much work I hardly slept at all. I was so busy working that when the mosquitoes bit me, I did not even notice. I was motivated to work hard because I had been in the camp for five years and had not been able to support my family. In the camp I got nothing for my work, but in the shop I did.

The photography business continued to grow and eventually did so well that in 1989 he was forced to go into partnership with the government.

They did not know how to run a business. They said that it was my choice about the partnership, but if I had not agreed to join with them, they would have closed me down. When they saw all the money I was making they broke the contract and bought me out. With the money I made in the sale of the business I opened two shops in Saigon and three in the provinces. We still own two of them and our old house in Saigon.

I asked Bach why he had decided to leave Vietnam when his business was doing so well.

I had applied for the H.O. Program [a program that enabled former political prisoners to immigrate to the United States] before the business got so successful. We learned that we had been accepted about the time my son graduated from college. He was at the age when he would be drafted into the military. Because of my history [as a former political prisoner] he would have been sent to a work battalion and could have been sent to the jungle and gotten sick.[2] So we decided to come here for his sake. Even though we had made a lot of money, there was no security or safety in Vietnam. At any time a policeman could come to take us away and we would have to go. It was even more precarious because we had money. We wanted my son to get more education. Now he is living out my dream of becoming an engineer.

Doan Van Toai underscores Bach's comment about the lack of due process in postwar Vietnam.[3]

Vietnam today is a country without any law other than the arbitrary directives of those in power. There is no civil code. Individuals are imprisoned without charges and without trial. Once in jail, prisoners are taught that their behavior, attitude and "good will" are the key factors in determining when they may be released. . . . In fact, they never know when they may be released—or when their sentences may be extended.

Former political prisoners were especially vulnerable to this capricious abuse of power. After their imprisonment in the camps their Vietnamese citizenship was taken away and was not restored until they had completed various re-education requirements in their communities. It was the perception of those I spoke to that their citizenship could be taken away again by the government at any time as a consequence of real or perceived misbehavior.

I asked Bach to tell me about his new life in the United States. "We have more freedom, it is safer, and my son can get an education. It is harder to make money. I work as a shipping clerk at a tile company, and my wife stays home to be with the kids. I applied for work in a photo shop, but I did not get the job despite my experience. I think the problem is my English." Does he still think about the re-education camp? "For the first year after my release I had nightmares that the Viet Cong were coming to get us and shooting at us and I would hide under the bed. I still have dreams of leading my men on patrol." Did the experience in the camp change him in any fundamental way?

The Communists have done a lot of bad things, especially the camps. They did not re-educate people. They simply made us hate them more. They did not change people, but they certainly changed their families. There is a high rate of divorce among former political prisoners. Their families were left for years without a father figure. Some of their daughters became prostitutes, and some of their sons became thieves.

A number of former political prisoners and their wives commented to me about the destructive effects of the re-education camps on families. As has been noted earlier, wives were often forced to become the family's primary provider after their husbands were sent away to the camps. Absent the entire day selling in the market, mothers returned exhausted, with only enough energy to prepare the evening meal and crawl into bed. As a result children spent considerable time unsupervised—"being raised by the streets," as one former prisoner told me. Although the same might be said of the children of impoverished families in many parts of the world, including the United States, the prisoners' children bore the additional burden of social ostracism and discrimination for being the children of "collaborators." Schools, the other places besides the home where they might have been supervised and disciplined, were sometimes closed to them because of their fathers' status. In addition it was reported to me that during Vietnam's impoverished postwar years teachers were often compelled to take second jobs to supplement their meager salaries. As a result they did not have the energy to supervise and discipline their students as they might have in the past. Whether such conditions drove the prisoners' children into theft and prostitution, as Bach maintained, is unclear. However, they would certainly have put them at increased risk for the development of emotional and behavioral problems. Hopefully, future research will address the long-term developmental effects on previously normal middle-class children, such as those of the former prisoners, of an almost overnight descent into long-term poverty, prejudice, and discrimination.

14 / The Politician's Grandson

*B*ach's son Anh, the grandson of Hung and Tho, is studying engineering at a local public university, living out his father's dream. Although he has adapted successfully to American life, he is sometimes troubled by the racism he encounters here. He is also caught up in a decades-long conflict between his father's family and his mother. This conflict, originating twenty-seven years ago, before the end of the Vietnam War, continues to the present day.

By the time I was able to arrange interviews with Bach's wife and son a number of changes had occurred in the family. They had moved out of their rented house and purchased a home near Bach's parents in a neighborhood where many Vietnamese families live. Arriving there for the first of our interviews I noticed a sign in front of the house offering film-developing services. Bach had discovered a Konica photo-processing machine at a garage sale and purchased it, and he now operates a home photo shop on weekends when he is not working at the tile company. He advertises in the local Vietnamese newspapers and hopes to expand his business soon to "American" photographers. Bach seemed to me to be immensely proud of his accomplishment and happy at last to be able to pursue his own profession.

I arrived at the house to interview Bach's twenty-four-year-old son Anh, whose picture Bach had carried with him during his five years in the re-education camp. Bach's youngest daughter, who appeared to be about twelve years old, opened the door. She and her younger brother were home alone watching a video of a Vietnamese movie. After determining who I was and why I was there, she invited me in, offered me a drink, and telephoned Anh to ask him to come home for the interview. He arrived a few minutes later with his girlfriend, an attractive young Vietnamese woman about the same age as he is.

Anh is a slender twenty-four-year-old man who is studying electrical engineering at a local university. He sat on the edge of the sofa while we talked, speaking in strongly accented but fluent English. His openness and candor struck me as a contrast to the more reserved and traditional manner of the older Vietnamese I had previously interviewed. "I arrived in the United States with my family in May 1996, when I was almost twenty-one years old. We came on the H.O. Program [a program that enabled former political prisoners to immigrate to the United States]. At that time you had to have been in jail for at least three years to qualify. My dad was in for almost five years. I have heard recently that they have lowered the time requirement to two years, although I am not certain about that." I asked Anh if he had any memories of the time during which his father was in the re-education camp.

My mother was two months pregnant with me when he entered the camp. By the time he got out I was only five years old, so I do not remember much. I do remember reuniting with him. My dad's family lived in the countryside. My mom took me to their house to meet him. He, my grandmother, and my dad's older brother were already there when we arrived. He and his brother look a lot alike, and they tried to see if I could tell who was who. My father was really poor back then. He had just gotten out of the re-education camp, and he had nothing. There was a guy in the village who had been a sergeant in his infantry unit. He was much older than my father was. He had a house in the village and needed someone to care for it, so he let my dad, mom, and me live there rent-free. We shared the house with a poor teacher. We only stayed there for about six months and then moved to Saigon.

The family's move to Saigon was prompted by a longstanding conflict between Anh's family and his father's family dating back to before

1975. Anh poignantly described the conflict and its effects on his mother's and his own emotional lives. Later, however, after reviewing a transcript of what he had said, Anh and his parents requested that I not share its details. As Anh put it, "My mother and I do not mind, but my dad is worried that it might make things worse between us." The reluctance of Anh's family, like some of the other former political prisoners and their families, to completely "bare their souls" may trouble some readers. However, as Anh and his mother revealed in their private conversations with me, it is not that complex emotions and inner conflicts are absent from the Vietnamese psyche. Rather the Vietnamese are far less willing than we are to share their inner lives.

I asked Anh whether the conflict between his family and his father's family still exists. He replied,

Yes, but they have papered it over. On the surface things are OK, but they do not see my father in the same way they used to. To them he is a rebel [who defied their authority]. It is really weird because I am the oldest grandchild and in our culture the oldest boy in the family is everything. When my grandparents are dead I will be the one who keeps their picture [on the family altar] and venerates them. I am the one who has that privilege. So now they pretty much [act as if everything is OK], but I can tell how they really feel.

My dad borrowed some money from a rich distant relative so that he could get established in Saigon. We stayed with my mom's family there for the first four years. Then we moved to another district, bought our own house, and lived there until we moved to the United States. After we got to Saigon my dad tried to find a job, but he did not have any luck because all he knows is photography. Then a friend of my mom's family, a powerful VC [Viet Cong] who had been a double agent during the war, introduced my dad to the local government photography company. Back then there was one big photography company per district. The government owned and operated it because the government owned all the businesses. My dad worked for the photography company in [a district of Saigon—Anh did not want to share its name because he was concerned that such identifying details might cause trouble for relatives still living in Vietnam]. He worked there from 1981 or 1982 until 1984 or 1985. He took pictures, developed them, and did everything. He also had an [illegal] private photography business on the side. He had so much private business that he needed to hire somebody to help. Back then in Vietnam they only did black-and-white photos. Then color pictures became popular, so he switched to that. He learned how to do the processing on his own. In 1985 things changed so that you could work for yourself rather than just for the government. He did not have the money to buy the new color equipment and set up his own business, but he had a friend with money who became his partner. They worked together for a couple of years, then they had a disagreement and broke up. My dad bought him out. By then he had worked for two years and had earned back all the money that they had invested.

My dad then rented part of a kiosk right in front of the main market. The kiosk used to be a newspaper stand, and my dad had one side of it. My mom fixed it up so that it looked really nice, with a glass cabinet [to display the photographs]. He built up the business and had a lot of customers. Then in 1986 the government set up the first photo Minilab in Saigon. [The Minilabs were automated color photo-processing businesses.] We were worried about the competition from the Minilabs, thinking that it would hurt our business. But the people in the Minilab could not work the machine. It was new technology, and all the instructions were in English. After the first couple of months their pictures were still turning out really bad, so my dad started to feel pretty good. He said, "They can open as many Minilabs as they want to!"

My dad had so much business that he was working twenty hours a day, but he still could not get it all done in time. So he decided that he had to do something [to speed things up] because otherwise the customers would get tired of the long wait and take their business elsewhere. In 1988 Vietnam was into the đổi mới [renovation] period, and so he went to talk to the director of his district's government photography company. My dad proposed a business deal to the director. The idea was that they would buy and operate a Minilab together. The director was new and not making any money, so he was interested in starting the business. It was the first Minilab owned jointly by the government and an entrepreneur. We sold everything we had to put into the business, even our bicycles. For the rest we got a loan. It would have been impossible to get the loan without the help of the director of the photography company. He got the loan for my dad. The business went really well. After a year they had earned back all of their investment, although we still had loan payments to make. Then the director tried to kick my dad out of the business, thinking that by then he had learned enough and could run it by himself. He tried to cover up what he was doing by saying that his superiors had told him that they did not want my dad there anymore. He said that he had argued with them and fought for my dad, but that they had insisted. We did not find out until later that he was making it all up.

My dad told us that he was glad they were kicking him out because it was a business deal with the government and hard to get out of on your own. The government bought him out, so he had enough money to start his own business. He bought an old photo-processing machine from a lady who did not know how to operate it. He started his new business in [a different district of Saigon—here again Anh did not want the exact location revealed out of concern that it might identify them to the Communist authorities]. From that point on my dad was on his own. The business grew, and he opened a second business in our house with his sister and a friend as partners.

I asked Anh how the re-education camp experience had affected his father.

I cannot really say from my own experience because I did not know him before the camp. My mom said that he changed. He focused more on the family. He realized that he was just a pawn in the political struggle. He focused on making his family wealthy and did not take part in politics anymore [unlike his own father, the Politician]. He just did not care. I know my dad had bad experiences in the camp. He is still scared of that time. They did not sentence you. They kept you there for as long as they wanted. When they released him he did not believe it. He had to ask his friends, "Is it really true?" Sometimes he still has nightmares about the camp. I remember one time when we were still in Vietnam. We had a parrot in the room where they slept. It made a noise during the night, screeching, and my dad started screaming because he thought it was incoming artillery. I was sleeping upstairs and I heard him scream. In the morning he, my mom, and I talked about it. When he heard the noise he had jumped out of bed so that he could hide. [This is Anh's version of the story told earlier by his father.]

How did his father's absence in the re-education camp affect Anh's mother? "She had to work really hard. She smuggled food. Back then they called all private buying and selling 'smuggling' because the government owned everything. She went out to the countryside, bought fruit, and took it back to Saigon for resale." How did it affect your life that your father was away in the re-education camp? "The only thing I remember is that I wanted to spend more time with my mother, but she was not home much because she had to work. My maternal aunt and uncle took care of me."

Did Anh have any problems growing up in Vietnam because of his father's history as a former political prisoner?

I did not notice any discrimination until I graduated from high school. In Vietnam you take an examination to see who gets to go to the university. The top 1,500 examinees are admitted, and the other 30,000 fail. They do not have open admissions like they do here. When you fill out the application for the exam they ask what your parents did during the time when the old government was in power. If your family had something to do with the VC, you got extra points on the exam. Say your dad was a VC soldier and he was killed. You would get two or three extra points. You needed about twelve points to pass the exam. Those extra points were a lot of help. Other than that the discrimination was not so bad. By the time I was in high school we had đổi mới, so the discrimination was less obvious. It was worse for people who grew up before I did. My uncle, who is older than I am, was expelled from school in the tenth grade because his dad was in re-education camp [and had worked for the old government]. That made my dad really angry. It just was not fair.

How far did Anh get with his schooling in Vietnam?

I went to university there. I attended the Hanoi Foreign Language University. Its headquarters is in Hanoi, but there is a campus in Saigon. In Vietnam the university lasts for four years. I finished three years, and then my parents decided to come here. My mom's brother pushed us to come. He said, "You should take advantage of the opportunity." My dad was reluctant because he was making a lot of money and we had a very good life style, but my uncle kept pushing him. He took my dad to the place where you apply for the H.O. Program. Once the paperwork was completed they invited us to come to the United States, but we were not sure we wanted to go and so we postponed it. Eventually, we decided to come. We knew our life would be better here.

How did he feel about the decision? "I had mixed feelings. The people I had known who had been abroad looked good and had done well, but I had to give up a lot [including my university studies]. At the time we left we were doing really well and were pretty rich."

I asked Anh how he had managed to learn English so quickly and well.

My dad had a friend in the re-education camp who was an English teacher. He had been an interpreter for one of the generals, so he must have been pretty good. After he and my dad were released they lost contact with one another, but then they met again one day walking along the street. [My dad asked him to tutor me, and I studied with him for several years. As a result,] I did not have any problems with English after my arrival, so my adjustment was not really that hard. [In addition,] Saigon was a pretty sophisticated place, so it was not such a big transition [coming here to another city].

I asked Anh whether he had experienced any discrimination in the United States. He asked what I meant by discrimination, and I said, "Because you are Asian and from Vietnam." He responded immediately: "All the time. People on the street give you dirty looks and talk behind your back. They try to insult you. It is worse if you do not speak English because then they think you are stupid." Has he experienced discrimination at the university here? "It is better in school because the people there are better educated. They know that discrimination is wrong, so they try to hide it, but deep down I believe there is discrimination." What makes him think that? "When I have an interview I just sense that they are not as open as they would be if I were white." Are his friends all Vietnamese or other Asian kids? "My best friend is Vietnamese, but at school I have friends of all types." Would he date a white girl? "Sure, I would be happy to. You cannot hate everyone."

Bach, Anh's father, had entered the room toward the end of our conversation, and I congratulated him about his new photo business. I asked the two of them to tell me more about how he had acquired the photo-processing machine. Anh said,

My dad saw the photo machine in some guy's backyard, uncovered [and exposed to the elements]. He loves the photography business. So I called the man for him and we bought it. Dad bid very low at first and they did not respond. He talked to all of us at home that night, and we suggested that he make a fair offer. He did and he got it. He bought it in November while we were still in the rental house. The photo machine needed a lot of work, but we got it going. It is in the basement. He was not sure it would work when he bought it, but he loved it because it was a reminder of something familiar. Buying it was a bit like gambling [because he did not know if he could get it to work again]. He called an old friend in Vietnam who is an engineer. He helped my dad a lot. Now it works perfectly, just like a new one at Wal-Mart or Costco.

15 / The Politician's Daughter-in-Law

A fter the war ended Hoa, the wife of Bach and the mother of Anh, endured poverty, the social isolation of being a former officer's wife, and also a bitter conflict with her husband's family. Even after moving to the United States the family conflict continued, making her adjustment here all the more difficult. Although the effects of the conflict are somewhat muted by her relative independence from her in-laws here as compared to Vietnam, it continues to intrude into her family's daily life.

Hoa, Bach's wife, had been reluctant to speak with me. The interpreter told me that there were some things she did not want to talk about. Hoa was apparently afraid that if she did talk with me, she might tell me more about her life than she wanted to tell me. Having just heard Anh's tale about what had been going on between Hoa and Bach's family, I understood her reluctance.

As I concluded my final interview with Ahn, Hoa returned home from work. She had recently taken a job at the airport assembling the utensil and condiment packs that are distributed to passengers with meals. I greeted her and inquired about her new job. She told me that she enjoyed it and was glad to be working. I then turned to Bach and Anh and reiterated how much I would appreciate it if Hoa would agree to talk with me. I explained that while a lot has been written about the former political prisoners' experiences, very little is known about the experiences of their wives and family members. They spoke with her, and after some discussion she agreed to be interviewed.

I returned a few weeks later to meet with her. Bach's former company commander in Vietnam was visiting them for the weekend, trying to decide whether to move from California to a house across the street. Bach introduced him to me. "During the war we worked together all the time. If I were patrolling down one side of a river, he was patrolling down the other side." We talked for a while about their shared experiences in the re-education camps. They had just listened to a tape that details the experiences of the prisoners in an especially notorious camp, Trại Kiên Giang. "That is where they sent the people who got 'special treatment,' meaning that they were never going to get out," Bach told me. "It sent chills up my spine listening to that tape. The author recounts at one point how the Communists told him that he could leave [the camp]. Then as he was going out the gate they said to him, 'Not yet, come back,' and forced him to return. Remember how I told you that I could not look back at the camp when I left? I was afraid the same thing would happen to me!" Both Bach and his friend agreed that food, or rather the lack of it, had been their main preoccupation in re-education camp. "On the tape the former prisoners talked about how there were only three things we did not eat—maggots, flies, and mosquitoes. Everything else we ate."

After our short talk Bach and his friend excused themselves, and I was left alone with Anh and Hoa. They sat together on the sofa, with Anh functioning as my interpreter. I felt somewhat uncomfortable at first because I knew of Hoa's reluctance to discuss her early life with Bach and the difficult relationship they have with his family. I began by asking what it was like for her during the time her husband was in the camp. "It was the same for everyone [we were all in the same situation]. I had to work hard and do things that I had never done before. I had been training to be a teacher, but after my husband left I had to sell peanuts on the street. That is the kind of work that only the poorest people do." How did the experience of his being away affect her emotionally? "I felt shocked and sad." Did people treat her differently than they had treated her before Bach went to the camp? "Yes. As an example, my husband's closest friend began to associate with the Communists after 1975. One day he saw me selling things on the street. He would not even look at me and ignored me as if I were a complete stranger. He did not want to get involved [with someone whose husband was in the camps]." Who did she turn to for emotional support? "My family in Saigon." Here Anh turned to me and said, "Do you remember what I told you about my dad's family?" He then gave me a look that seemed to imply that given the state of relations between Hoa and Bach's family prior to Bach's incarceration, Hoa was not going to be getting any support from them.

I asked Hoa what she had worried about in those days. "Waiting. The Communists had promised that he would be back in one week. They said that the earlier you went for re-education, the sooner you would get home. My husband was one of the first to go. They did not sentence people [so you had no idea how long they would be away]. I kept thinking, 'Maybe he will come home tomorrow.' Then the next day I would think, 'Well, maybe tomorrow.'" I asked Hoa if she understood why so many people, like her husband, went into the camps voluntarily? Anh replied for her:

I can answer that. The South Vietnamese did not like the Communists, but the war had been brutal. When it ended and the Communists were in power the people hoped that the Communists would treat people differently than they had during the war. Most people thought [naively], "If I go for re-education right away, I will get out sooner and can do something with my life." The people who did not believe the Communists, who thought that the Communists would kill them, ran away. Some became outlaws, hiding out in the city without identification cards.

I responded that several political prisoners had told me that they did not resist because the Communists had tricked them. They lied to them about how long the re-education camp would last, got people's hopes up about a new era of reconciliation and cooperation,[1] and then when everyone was locked up they revealed their true intentions. Anh agreed and added,

The trick was even more sophisticated in Saigon. When the Communists called people in for re-education camp they told their families not to send food, but to give them money for their meals. They told them that they would need enough money to pay for seven days' worth of meals. During that seven-day period, restaurants in Saigon catered in the food for the re-education camp men. When word got out about their good treatment people in Saigon thought that the Communists must have been telling the truth. "Maybe they do want to get along with us," they thought. Men who had not reported in for re-education said to one another, "It does not look like it is going to be so bad." So they turned themselves in voluntarily. Only after everyone presented himself and they were all locked away did the Communists say what was really going to happen.

Hoa added, "They told my husband to bring along only enough food for one week. We all fell for the trick."

Truong Nhu Tang, a founder of the National Liberation Front (NLF)[2] who fled from Vietnam in 1979, provides an insider's view of the Communists' approach to winning people's trust. "The Communists are expert in the arts of seduction and will go to any length to woo you over to their side, as long as they don't control the Government. But once they are in power they suddenly become harsh, ungrateful, cynical and brutal."[3] After the war ended hundreds of thousands of South Vietnamese like Bach and his family appear to have fallen for these "arts of seduction" and turned themselves in for re-education camps without a struggle.

Despite the ongoing conflict with her husband's family Hoa lived in the countryside near them for over a year after Bach's departure for re-education camp. A villager let her live rent-free in a small bungalow, and she sold peanuts on the street to earn money for food. Hoa said that she had remained in the countryside for several reasons. First, as an officer's wife she feared that the Communists would harass her own family in Saigon if she were with them. Second, she was two months pregnant with Anh and wanted to stay close to her husband's family so that they would accept her child. Third, she and Bach were not officially married. As a result, permission slips to visit him in the re-education camp were sent to his family, not to her. She had to be nearby to ensure that she received them.

After Anh's birth Hoa decided to move back to Saigon to be with her own family.

Things were better there. Saigon seemed the same [as it had before the war]. The Communists did not pay much attention to the women, only to the men. After I returned to Saigon I bought food in the country and sold it in Saigon. It was hard to make money back then. I had to earn enough to get milk for Anh, to help my family, and to visit my husband. I did not see my friends much. I just worked and stayed home with my family.

I asked Hoa how the end of the war had affected her life. "Everyone was affected by the end of the war. Some fled the country, others moved to other parts of Vietnam." How did she feel after the war ended? "I felt sad. Each night before I went to sleep I sat up thinking sad thoughts about how things might have been [if we had not lost the war]." How was her appetite during that time? "I did not have any trouble with my appetite; there was just not enough to eat. Everybody was in the same boat—it was something you had to endure. I was young and was not involved in the political issues of the time. I did not care who governed the country as long as life was OK."

How did Hoa's husband seem when she visited him in the re-education camp?

He had changed. He was skinnier and he smelled bad from the mud. Everyone in the camps was like that. I once gave him a bar of soap. He used it for three years and still had some left at the end! He had to use the outside container of a sandbag [a very rough burlap or synthetic material] as his towel. You were not allowed to talk much or to touch during the visits. They were afraid that you might give the prisoners something they were not permitted to have. The guards watched and listened while you talked and checked thoroughly through everything you brought to make sure that there were no weapons.

Did you take Anh along with you when you went to visit your husband?

When he was very small I took him. The road to the camp was difficult to walk on because of flooding. I also had to walk a long way. I was only able to visit my husband once during the first year. Then they increased it to every four months, and finally, to every two months. After a while they also let us write letters to one another, but they censored the letters before delivering them. Sometimes I could not afford to visit the camp. When I did go I took along food for my husband, things like ground peanuts with salt, fermented shrimp paste [*mắm ruốc*], noodles, and unrefined sugar."

Did her husband's personality seem to change while he was in the camp? "He was still the same person, but he was sad. At first our visits were very sad, but after a while you got used to it. I felt that everyone else was in the same situation that I was in and that I was not alone." After his release from the camp how did he seem? "Emotionally, he was the same. Physically, he was very skinny. He looked like a v c, not like my husband any more!" I mentioned that the two of them had only been together for two years before her husband left for the re-education camp and were then apart for five years. How had the long separation affected their relationship? Hoa answered simply, "It enhanced it. Initially, I was scared because after he returned home the local authorities came by and checked on him all the time. I was afraid somebody would try to take revenge on him [for being in the old government's army]."

How was their life together after Bach came home from the camp?

"It was hard to make a living. His family paid him just enough money for himself [not enough for the three of us]. My husband was and is very involved with his family. He listens to them, but in the end he does what he wants. In a sense he is a kind of rebel in the family." Would things have been different between Hoa and Bach's family if they had remained in Vietnam? "Before my husband came home from the camp I stayed away from his family. I did not want to be yelled at. But when he came home he worked for his mother [in the photo shop], and so I became dependent on her. Here [in the United States] things are better because we can be independent [of his family]."

Since Hoa had brought up the sensitive issue of her husband's family I asked if she would mind telling me how she and her husband had met.

My grandmother lives in the same area as his family. [I was down visiting her] at the end of the year. Early one morning I was trying to catch the bus back to Saigon to visit my mother. My husband saw me waiting in the street, but we did not talk. Later on I was back in the village at his dad's photo shop making copies of materials I needed to apply for a teaching job. We met there. Initially, we were just friends. We eventually became boyfriend and girlfriend, but we were not married. Then there was an accident. I was visiting my husband out at the army base where he was stationed. It was not far from the village where he lived. A drunken soldier there tried to pick a fight with him. The soldier pulled out a gun. It discharged accidentally and shot me in the leg. My husband felt responsible and insisted that I stay with him at the army base for a couple of months while I recovered. Asian people believe that if a couple stays together that long, they are tied to one another. From that point on in everyone's eyes we were married.

I asked Hoa if she could tell me a bit about her own family.

They are all still in Saigon. We call them whenever we can afford it. I still miss them and Vietnam. I grew up in a happy family. There were nine children, and I was the second oldest. My parents were very kind and gracious. They owned a pharmacy in the countryside. My mother ran it. My uncle owned a bus company and was a millionaire. My father helped him to manage the company. He was sort of like a dispatcher of the buses, checking to see that they were O K before they went out. I attended school through the eleventh grade. In Vietnam you can teach elementary school after you have completed your ninth grade certificate.

Despite the pain of leaving her own family and friends behind in Vietnam, the movement of Hoa's family to the United States improved her life in a way that might not be obvious to most Westerners. In Vietnam practical and traditional requirements would have compelled Hoa to live with, or at least under the control of, her mother-in-law. Given the tension in their relationship one can imagine that her existence there would have been painful. Here in the United States, where independent nuclear family living is far more easily accomplished and much more acceptable socially than in Vietnam, Hoa can live apart from her in-laws and develop a life of her own.

It was interesting to me to observe how Anh appears to have chosen to affiliate with and protect his mother and her family rather than his father's family. In traditional Vietnamese society the father's family's eldest son is the person responsible for the continuation of the father's family line and for the veneration of their ancestors. While Anh appears prepared to accept this responsibility, his emotional allegiance is to his mother, who has suffered with him at the hands of his father's family. Living now in a society that encourages its members to follow their own desires, Anh is caught in a conflict typical for a generation transitioning between two vastly different cultural traditions. His duty as a Vietnamese oldest son pulls him toward the family of his father, but his heart draws him closer to his mother. Adapting to the ways of his new homeland, he feels comfortable expressing his inner conflict, even to a stranger. However, in the end he yields to the authority of his more traditional father and asks that the details of the conflict be concealed.

16 / Conclusion

I began this long journey with very different expectations about what I would find at its end than has actually been the case. Knowing what I did about the former political prisoners' lives—wars, re-education camps, poverty, ostracism, discrimination, and immigration at an advanced age to the United States—I expected to find men and women who were shattered and bitter about their fate. Instead I found mostly tough, resilient, and often philosophical people interested in getting on with their lives and not overly preoccupied with the past. Sharing my surprise at their equanimity and sanity with friends and colleagues, I was reminded that the ordeals endured by the former prisoners and their wives were so grueling and unforgiving that only the strongest would have survived. Those who were less resilient would have died in the camps or after their release or would never have undertaken the enormous challenge of becoming refugees. It was also suggested to me that former political prisoners who are doing poorly here may not have been referred for interviews or may have chosen not to participate. A Vietnamese acquaintance of mine, who escaped from Vietnam as a boat person, offered a somewhat different explanation for my findings. "The Vietnamese," he said, "keep a lot inside their heads." Several of the people I interviewed mentioned that they were more "difficult" people now than they had been prior to their re-education camp experiences. They were more sensitive, sad, irritable, and angry. The superficial calm and acceptance that I observed in my interviews with them may have masked an inner torment that they did not feel comfortable sharing with me.

I have no way to determine the completeness or emotional and factual truthfulness of what I was told other than by comparing the content of the former political prisoners' narratives and by relying on my instinctive and trained responses to other human beings. After many hours of listening to the former prisoners and their family members talk about their lives, it is my belief that they were truthful and, within the limits of their cultural tradition, fairly open about their experiences. Several, in fact, were open to the point that they felt they had told me too much and asked that I modify and soften their remarks. While some may have omitted certain details or events that cast them in an unfavorable light, their stories have an internal consistency that persuades me of their veracity.

I come away from my encounters with the former political prisoners and their families filled with a sense of immense admiration and even awe for their achievements. What they have successfully endured is beyond my capacity to fully comprehend. As I learned of their protracted suffering and recurrent ordeals I could not help but wonder how I would have borne up under similar circumstances. In facing the more mundane trials of my own life I have been fortunate to be surrounded by loving family and friends and supported by the material wealth of the United States. Many of these women and men, on the other hand, bore their far greater and more prolonged suffering not only alone, but without any idea of when, or if, it would end. Putting one foot ahead of the other, often without any reason to hope, they appear to have emerged largely intact from a process that would have shattered or deformed many of us. Aside from their privileged social status and comparatively high educational levels in the old Vietnam, most did not appear to come from especially remarkable backgrounds that would have prepared them to face such trials. Their temperaments and philosophies varied considerably. Some were inherently optimistic and positive, while others seemed more cynical and negative. And that, I suppose, is the ultimate secret of resiliency. One never knows if it is present until it is tested.

What lessons can be learned from the lives of the former political prisoners and their families? To begin with, I believe that certain personal characteristics were associated with better psychological and functional outcomes. One of these was the capacity to develop, or fall back on, some philosophy or belief system that helped them to endure the endless days, weeks, months, and years of a degrading confinement and subjection to hard labor, starvation rations, and brainwashing. Whether it was a book by Dale Carnegie, French writers who advocated Stoicism, or a mind cleansing and breathing technique based on yoga, they found a shelter for their minds and spirits that shielded them from the brutality to which they were exposed.

Another important adaptive characteristic was the ability to focus on the here and now and on one's day-to-day survival rather than yielding to the seduction of the past and dwelling on all that one had lost. Especially in the time after their release from the re-education camps, the former prisoners had to find a way to forget what they had been and to focus on what they now were and could become. This was very difficult while they were still living in Vietnam, where opportunities for employment were few and most felt that they had no future. Many anticipated a far brighter future in the United States, only to find that racial discrimination, advanced age, their lack of American professional credentials, and their limited financial resources made the achievement of their career goals very difficult. Those able to find or develop a fulfilling role for themselves here, however humble, seemed to me to be much happier than those who felt that they were degraded and humiliated by working in jobs far below their capacity.

Finally, there is the vital importance of family support. Those who believed that their families, and especially their children, understood and respected their suffering, valued them for it, and did not condemn them for their apparent "failure" in life appeared to me better adjusted than those who felt unappreciated and blamed. Over and over again I heard the former political prisoners and their wives find validation and justification for their sacrifices in the brighter future they had secured for their children by immigrating to the United States.

If there is a political lesson to be learned from the former prisoners' lives, it is that the United States, when intervening abroad, should listen carefully to what those it supports really want for themselves and for their country. Several of the former prisoners I met reflected sadly on their lack of a "righteous cause" during the Vietnam War and on how this had affected their ability to fight their more highly motivated adversary. One of the former prisoners put it this way:

It seemed to me like we were fighting for the Americans, not for our own country. Many of the junior officers felt that the Americans were only "the French in disguise." We did not want to join the Communists because we had seen what they were like and what they had done to the people, but we also did not want to help the Americans. We have a proverb in Vietnam that sums up our situation then: "To avoid stepping on the watermelon's rind you slip on the coconut's skin." We had no good choice. When we fought it was because we had to. The Communists charged at us like wild animals. We had to defend ourselves and mow them down. I fought because I did not want people to say that I was a coward, but I did not believe in what I was doing.

The Communists, initially under the guise of the Viet Minh and later as themselves, took advantage of Vietnam's historic struggle to free itself of foreign domination, whether from China, France, Japan, or the United States. As Doan Van Toai recounts it,

In the beginning, when talking to the other resistance fighters . . . Ho [Chi Minh] never referred to communism. . . . Not communism, but the struggle against French colonialism, was Ho's great theme. . . . People spoke of "patriotism" and "independence," but never communism or class warfare. It was not because the peasants were in love with communist ideals that they hated big landowners, but because such individuals were the creatures and protégés of the French."[1]

Americans were told that they were fighting a war to prevent a democratic country from being taken over by the Communists and to stop the spread of Communism in Asia. However, in the eyes of many Vietnamese the United States was simply the last in a long line of colonial powers trying to use Vietnam for its own purposes: "[The Americans] had come, as they put it, 'to protect South Vietnam's people from Communist aggression.' In fact, it seemed clear to me and my friends that they were here because Vietnam had a role to play in America's own worldwide confrontation with communism. As far as we could see, care for the Vietnamese people had precious little to do with it."[2]

The zealous anti-Communism that blinded many Americans to the issues that were important to the Vietnamese also made it difficult for Americans to accept any criticism of their own behavior. As one of the former prisoners told me, "You had to endorse everything the Americans did and said or you were 'anti-American.' They could not tolerate any criticism of what they were doing. You were either 100 percent for them or you were against them." Looking back at the Vietnam War from a perspective of twenty-five to thirty years, one can begin to appreciate how painful the American presence must have been for many Vietnamese.

The French at least had brought with them an ancient culture, which many Vietnamese found they could appreciate in some ways. . . . Now something else was happening, something more pervasive; less comprehensible and consequently more ominous. The Americans' material power was overwhelming, crushing, devoid of culture—except for a democratic ideal, which was grotesquely caricatured by Saigon's rulers."[3]

The former political prisoners and their family members that I met in the course of writing this book were uniformly grateful for the opportunity to live in the United States. Here their neighbors and the police no longer torment them for being on the losing side and for having "sold out" their country to foreigners. Their children have the opportunity to attend college and graduate school and to build successful lives. Yet in speaking with them I often wondered how they must feel to have been rescued by the very people whose unpredictable involvement in Vietnam—at times overbearing, overwhelming, and insulting, and at other times almost nonexistent—might be viewed as a major reason for their own loss of country and social standing. None of the former prisoners or their wives voiced strong resentment toward the United States for its failure after 1973 to intervene militarily or to provide adequate support for South Vietnam. Perhaps they were reluctant to criticize the Americans out of politeness and a desire not to offend people in their new homeland. Perhaps, after so many broken dreams, disappointments, and years of suffering, they had simply become resigned to their fate and recognized that the way to a meaningful future lies in moving forward, not back into the immutable past. One of the former prisoners who reviewed the manuscript for this book offered another explanation. He blamed the Communists, not the United States, for Vietnam's and his own desperate years after the war.

In my opinion the cruelty of the Communists is due to [the] nature of Communism. Not only the Vietnamese, [but also] the Russian Communists were [very] wicked. That we were badly treated was not the [fault] of the United States [for] reconciling [so] slowly with the Vietnamese Communists after the war. [The] Communists thought [that] the USSR was the best [country] in the world. They thought [that] they could [make advances] without Western technology. They were the most stupid and uneducated leaders in the world.

I asked several of the former political prisoners if there are ways in which the U.S. government could have helped them after their arrival here. They responded by saying that, more than anything else, they would have appreciated assistance in purchasing a home. For a Vietnamese, they said, owning one's own home has a great traditional and symbolic value. It is the center of the extended family and the site where one's ancestors are venerated. These two organizing principles of Vietnamese life are the spiritual and material links between past, present, and future generations. As impoverished newcomers to the United States, the former prisoners found it impossible to purchase homes. They had to spend years in government-subsidized housing or in the homes of friends and relatives before they could accumulate enough money for a down payment and establish a credit rating to secure a loan. Being without a permanent home added to the former prisoners' postmigratory experience of disorientation and displacement and made them feel rootless in their new country. They requested that the U.S. government provide other newcomers like themselves with home loans as soon as possible after their arrival.

From my perspective there are also a number of other areas in which Americans might be able to make a difference in the lives of the former political prisoners and their families. They are resilient and courageous human beings, but their virtues should not blind people to their needs. These men and women want what Americans all want for themselves—opportunities to improve their lives. To take advantage of and to create opportunities, they need good English language skills, expedited retraining or re-certification in their professions, and further education to acquire a marketable occupation. If they are compelled to work at entry-level jobs just to support their families and escape welfare, it is unlikely that they will have the time and energy to develop their English language skills and to retool in the fields in which they have been trained. Scholarships, grants, and low-interest educational loans would have helped men like the Doctor, the Teacher, and the

Politician's Son to re-enter their professions rather than to take whatever jobs they could find just to survive.

Several of the former prisoners and their wives were having difficulty bridging the enormous cultural divide between Vietnam and the United States. In Vietnam men enjoy considerably more status and power than do women, and adults exert much more control over their generally more obedient children than is the case in the United States. Traditional Vietnamese husbands, especially those who had been separated from their families during the transition between Vietnam and the United States, found the challenges to their roles as husbands and fathers perplexing, humiliating, and infuriating. Often their wives were now the primary breadwinners in the family and their children were more independent and defiant of their parental authority. They felt dishonored within the sanctuary of their own homes. This was a serious blow to their self-esteem, already damaged by their loss of social and economic standing at the end of the war, by their demeaning conditions in the re-education camps, and by social ostracism and job discrimination after their release. Education for them in the cultural differences between Vietnam and the United States and support groups to help them adjust and find their way here might speed their recovery and adjustment.

Although it was the men who were imprisoned and tortured, their wives also suffered greatly and experienced many traumatic events. A number of the former prisoners and their wives had clear symptoms of depression and/or Post-Traumatic Stress Disorder (PTSD). Although all were able to function adequately, I believe that they would benefit from culturally competent mental health treatment. Unfortunately, such services are often the first to be cut when public budgets are trimmed. People wanting to provide such treatment for the former prisoners and their wives require a number of skills. First, they need to have a knowledge of Vietnamese cultural traditions that may impede standard Western therapeutic approaches. Potential barriers to the former prisoners and their wives entering or continuing in psychiatric treatment include a reluctance to disclose their feelings to strangers, even professionals, and a belief that they must cope with their emotions alone. The Vietnamese do not have a tradition of "talk therapy" and often approach it with skepticism. Second, therapists interested in working with them must have the emotional capacity to listen to a great deal of very painful material without becoming withdrawn, aggressive, saccharine, or condescending. Third, therapists need to develop a deep respect for all these people have overcome and accomplished. They are, in the truest sense, survivors who have endured the seemingly unendurable.

The former political prisoners and their wives have, in many respects, lost both their past and their future. While their children will carry on their name and memory, and perhaps achieve what fate denied their parents, official public acknowledgement of their suffering and sacrifices is nowhere to be found. Their memorials in South Vietnam, and even their military cemeteries, have been desecrated and destroyed by the Communists. Aside from disparaging remarks about them by the Vietnamese Communists as the *nguy* (puppets) who sold out their country to the French and the Americans, it is as if they had vanished from Vietnam and never been a part of its history. It has often occurred to me that there should be a memorial here in the United States erected with public funds to honor the former prisoners' and their wives' sacrifices during and after the Vietnam War and to respect the memory of the country they served. Like the Vietnam Memorial in Washington, D.C., it would be a place to which they could take their children and their children's children to show them what they were and to give their lost cause a symbolic representation. They are Americans now and the United States owes them some recognition for the part they have played in its history.

In this book I have presented only one perspective on the Communists' behavior in postwar Vietnam, that of the former political prisoners and their families. Having listened to them talk for so many hours about the brutality of the re-education camps and their degradation and impoverishment at the hands of the Communists, it feels to me almost disloyal · and obscene to consider any other perspective. However, a full accounting of their lives requires some attempt to reflect on the actions of the other side—the Communist government of Vietnam.

The end of the Vietnam War did not bring a bloodbath, as many had expected. The Communists did not systematically murder all those who had been their enemies. Civil wars are bitter affairs, and one could be forgiven for thinking that what did happen was not the worst possible outcome. Cambodia, Vietnam's neighbor to the west, provides an example of how terrible things could have been in the horrible genocide that followed the Khmer Rouge victory in 1975. A better outcome would have been one such as the Vietnamese Communists appeared to be proposing after their victory.[4] The defeated South Vietnamese were led to believe that the new Communist government wanted to "forgive and forget," that it planned to reconcile with its enemies and then utilize their skills and abilities to build a new Vietnam. As a Communist supporter of this approach has written,

Considering the length of the war and its destructiveness, the policy we were about to implement was magnanimous and humane. Many of us felt that it was also wise. Treatment of this sort would be likely to reorient people, who had been shocked by their defeat and were now experiencing considerable anxiety about their own futures. A humane approach to such psychologically vulnerable individuals would have a good chance of winning their allegiance.[5]

However, as the stories of the former political prisoners and their families illustrate, what the Communists actually did was far from humane and appears to lie somewhere between the two extremes of genocide and reconciliation.

After their triumph in 1975, the Vietnamese Communists appear to have suffered from the "victory disease." Their doctrine, strategy, and beliefs had brought them an almost unbelievable success over both internal and external enemies, including what was then arguably the most powerful nation on earth, the United States. The uncompromising approach that had won the war was then turned toward winning the peace, with disastrous results for Vietnam's economy, international standing, and people, including a number of the victors.[6] It took at least ten years for the Communist Party to recognize and rectify some of its early errors by initiating a new economic policy (đổi mới, or renovation) and to begin talks with the United States aimed at ending the trade embargo. The re-education camps were, in part, a reflection of the Communist Party's extreme and isolated approach to problem solving in the immediate postwar period.

I asked the former prisoners if they thought the United States could have done anything to help them while they were still in the re-education camps. Several suggested that sending food to the camps would have been the most valuable contribution. Food, or rather the lack of it, was the dominant theme of their re-education camp years. I wondered whether the Communists would have allowed such food assistance to be delivered to them. "Maybe not all of it, but some," was the response. "If the United States had sent ten parcels of food, perhaps only two would have been delivered to us, but that would have been far more than what we had."

It is my belief that the U.S. trade embargo had a devastating effect on the civilian population of Vietnam and, by extension, on the lives of the former political prisoners and their families. Witnessing the effects of the embargo personally during my visits to Vietnam in 1990 and 1993, it seemed to me that the people Americans had punished most were the weak and the vulnerable, like the former political prisoners and the Amerasians, not the leaders and policy makers. If the United States had been able to reconcile more quickly with Vietnam after the war, it might have been able to influence and ameliorate the treatment of its former allies and friends and might have helped to prevent a great deal of suffering and loss of life. The United States' failure to achieve a more rapid reconciliation with Vietnam was certainly not one sided.

The Vietnamese Communists placed many obstacles in its path. However, I am persuaded that by failing to achieve full diplomatic relations with Vietnam until very recently, the United States must bear some of the responsibility for what happened to the former political prisoners and their families after the war.

What do I carry away with me after listening to the life histories of the Vietnamese former political prisoners and their family members? First, that the victims of war, no matter whose side they are on, are complex, sensitive, and vulnerable human beings. Wherever the United States and other countries send their soldiers around the world, they must keep in mind the worth and dignity of those they encounter and never treat them as anything but their equals. Second, that the suffering of the victims of war does not end when the peace treaties are signed and the troops go home. A country in which a war has been fought does not move smoothly and quickly into a tranquil peace. At best there is a painful, protracted period of healing and recovery that may not fully end until the generation that has fought and endured the war has passed from the scene. Third, that the United States should be very careful where and how it intervenes around the world. Americans must be sure that the people they assist share the same vision for their country's future that the U.S. government does. One former political prisoner who reviewed the manuscript for this book told me, "I hope people in the U.S. government pay attention to this point [about listening to what other people want for their countries]. The U.S. goes around the world acting like the big boss. It gives money to third world countries like Vietnam. Then it says, 'OK, now you have to do things our way.'" Fourth, that if the United States does go to war, it cannot simply abandon its friends and allies afterwards, leaving them behind to the mercies of its enemies. By the act of intervening in their lives the United States has assumed a responsibility for what happens to them. Fifth, that Americans must recognize war for what it is, not for what they often see depicted in films and on their television screens. It is not like a movie or a video game that ends when the power is turned off. It is not clean, surgical, or antiseptic. It is a grinding, brutal interplay of complex forces that often develops a sustaining energy and momentum of its own, driving people and governments in directions that they neither anticipated nor desired. Americans must remember that the destructive processes they unleash in a few weeks or months of emotion may live on for decades and haunt their dreams forever.

NOTES

1. C. V. Vien, *The Final Collapse* (Washington, D.C.: Center of Military History, U.S. Army; U.S. Government Printing Office, 1983), p. 48.

2. R. S. McKelvey, *The Dust of Life: America's Children Abandoned in Vietnam* (Seattle: University of Washington Press, 1999).

3. Lacquerware is a traditional Vietnamese art form brought to Vietnam from China in the fifteenth century. A solid color lacquer is applied to porous woods, polished to a high gloss like porcelain, and then decorated or painted with other different colored lacquers (P. Huard and M. Durand, *Viet Nam: Civilization and Culture,* rev. 2d ed. [Hanoi: École Française d'Extrème Orient: 1994], pp. 204–7).

4. N. L. Jamieson, *Understanding Vietnam* (Berkeley and Los Angeles: University of California Press, 1993), p. 363.

5. Ibid., p. 364.

6. The ODP was a bilateral agreement reached in July 1979 between the U.S. and Vietnamese governments to permit the legal and safe immigration of Vietnamese to the United States.

7. See, for example, T. T. Vu, *Lost Years: My 1,632 Days in Vietnamese Reeducation Camps* (University of California, Berkeley: Institute of East Asian Studies, 1988); T. V. Doan and D. Chanoff, *The Vietnamese Gulag* (New York: Simon and Schuster, 1986).

8. See, for example, M. C. Smith-Fawzi, E. Murphy, T. Pham, L. Lin, C. Poole, and R. F. Mollica, "The Validity of Screening for Post-Traumatic

Stress Disorder and Major Depression among Vietnamese Former Political Prisoners," *Acta Psychiatrica Scandinavica* (1997: 96): 87–93; R. F. Mollica, K. McInnes, T. Pham, M. C. Smith-Fawzi, E. Murphy, and L. Lin, "The Dose-Effect Relationships between Torture and Psychiatric Symptoms in Vietnamese Ex-Political Detainees and a Comparison Group," *Journal of Nervous and Mental Disorders* (1998: 186): 543–53.

9. E. Hemingway, *A Farewell to Arms* (New York: Scribner Paperback Fiction, 1945), p. 291.

10. J. McCain, *Faith of My Fathers* (New York: HarperCollins, 1999).

I. INTRODUCTION

1. V. T. Truong, *A Viet Cong Memoir* (New York: Vintage Books, 1986), p. 271.

2. Ibid., p. 272.

3. Ibid., p. 274.

4. N. L. Jamieson, *Understanding Vietnam* (Berkeley and Los Angeles: University of California Press, 1993), p. 364.

5. M. C. Smith-Fawzi, E. Murphy, T. Pham, L. Lin, C. Poole, and R. F. Mollica, "The Validity of Screening for Post-Traumatic Stress Disorder and Major Depression among Vietnamese Former Political Prisoners," *Acta Psychiatrica Scandinavica* (1997: 96): 87–93. An unpublished study by Pham et al., cited in the Smith-Fawzi article, surveyed the camp experiences of a group of former political prisoners evaluated at the Indochinese Psychiatric Center in Boston. It found that "51% reported having been beaten, 39% reported having been placed in a sack, box or container, 86% had witnessed others being tortured, and 10% had experienced mock execution."

6. Smith-Fawzi et al. This study reported that 86 percent of the sample of former political prisoners still had PTSD an average of nine years after their release from the camps.

7. Only a few accounts in the scientific literature document the intensity of the former political prisoners' suffering and the effects of that suffering on their

mental health. These studies describe a very high prevalence of psychiatric disorders among them (35 percent to 90 percent), even when compared to other Vietnamese refugees (18 percent to 79 percent). W. L. Hinton, J. C. Chen, N. Du, C. G. Tran, F. Lu, J. Miranda, and S. Faust, "DSM-III-R Disorders in Vietnamese Refugees: Prevalence and Correlates," *Journal of Nervous and Mental Disorders* (1993: 181): 113–122; R. F. Mollica, K. McInnes, T. Pham, M. C. Smith-Fawzi, E. Murphy, and L. Lin, "The Dose-Effect Relationships between Torture and Psychiatric Symptoms in Vietnamese Ex-Political Detainees and a Comparison Group," *Journal of Nervous and Mental Disorders* (1998: 186): 543–53.

8. "H.O." has been variously interpreted as short for "Humanitarian Operation" or, by the Communists, as an abbreviation of the Vietnamese words for "re-education camp"—*học tập cải tạo*.

9. U.S. Department of State, *Fact Sheet: East Asian Refugee Admissions Program* (Washington, D.C.: Bureau of Population, Refugees, and Migration, January 18, 2000).

10. K. V. Nguyen, *Vietnam: A Long History* (Hanoi: The Gioi Publications, 1993); Federal Research Division, Library of Congress, *Vietnam: A Country Study* (Washington, D.C.: U.S. Government Printing Office, 1989).

11. Nguyen, p. 240.

12. Federal Research Division, p. 143.

13. Ibid., p. 110.

2. THE DOCTOR

1. The *baccalauréat* exam, adopted from the French, was a "comprehensive, nationwide final examination. . . . It was like the college boards and a high school transcript rolled into one — but because of its immense prestige, it was more than that. . . . For colonial high school students, it was a coveted golden key to privilege and status" (D.V. Toai and D. Chadoff, *The Vietnamese Gulag* [New York: Simon and Schuster, 1986], pp. 60–61).

2. PTSD typically follows a traumatic event or events in which one was confronted by death or the threat of death or serious injury to oneself or

others and experienced feelings of fear and helplessness (American Psychiatric Association, *Diagnostic and Statistical Manual of Mental Disorders, Fourth Edition* [Washington, D.C.: American Psychiatric Association, 1994], pp. 424–29). After the event one reexperiences it in upsetting recollections or dreams, avoids stimuli associated with it, has a sense of emotional numbing, and experiences heightened arousal, with problems such as difficulty sleeping, being easily startled, and having trouble concentrating. In addition to the experiencing of symptoms, the diagnosis of PTSD requires that the symptoms significantly impair one's ability to function in daily activities such as work or family life. PTSD is common among refugee populations, prisoners of war, and torture victims. Symptoms often improve with the return to a safe environment and the passage of time, but they can also be quite persistent. Most of the Vietnamese former political prisoners I interviewed reported that their PTSD symptoms were most intense in Vietnam during the years after they were released from the camps and diminished or disappeared once they reached the United States. None reported that their symptoms presently interfere with their daily functioning, although several studies have suggested that PTSD often persists for many years in former political prisoners. (M. C. Smith-Fawzi, E. Murphy, T. Pham, L. Lin, C. Poole, and R. F. Mollica, "The Validity of Screening for Post-Traumatic Stress Disorder and Major Depression among Vietnamese Former Political Prisoners," *Acta Psychiatrica Scandinavica* [1997: 96]: 87–93; R. F. Mollica, K. McInnes, T. Pham, M. C. Smith-Fawzi, E. Murphy, and L. Lin, "The Dose-Effect Relationships Between Torture and Psychiatric Symptoms in Vietnamese Ex-Political Detainees and a Comparison Group, *Journal of Nervous and Mental Disorders* [1998: 186]: 543–53.) For those interested in the problems confronting victims of violence and therapeutic approaches to working with them, Guus Van der Veer provides an excellent review in his book, *Counselling and Therapy with Refugees and Victims of Trauma* (West Sussex, England: John Wiley & Sons, 1998).

3. T. T. Vu, *Lost Years: My 1,632 Days in Vietnamese Re-education Camps* (Berkeley: University of California, Institute of East Asian Studies, 1988), p. 91.

4. C. V. Vien, *The Final Collapse* (Washington, D.C.: Center of Military History, U.S. Army; U.S. Government Printing Office, 1983), p. 3.

5. The two Trung sisters (*Hai Bà Trung*), Trung Trac and Trung Nhi, are early heroes of Vietnam's struggle for independence. They led an unsuccessful revolt against Chinese domination in Vietnam and in 43 A.D. drowned themselves to escape capture by the Chinese (P. Huard and M. Durand, *Viet Nam: Civilization and Culture*, rev. 2d ed. [Hanoi: École Française d'Extrème Orient, 1994], p. 28). Tran Hung Dao was a general serving under the Vietnamese king Tran Nhan Ton. Faced by an invading Mongol army, the king wanted to surrender, but Tran Hung Dao persuaded him not to. He reportedly said to the king, "Sir, if you wish to surrender, please first cut my head off. As long as my head is still on my shoulders, the kingdom will continue to exist" (ibid., p. 37).

3. THE ENGINEER

1. What Americans refer to as the Vietnam War was actually the Second Indochina War or, as the Vietnamese Communists call it, the Second War of Resistance. The First Indochina War, or the First War of Resistance, was the war between the Viet Minh and the French.

2. C. V. Vien, *The Final Collapse* (Washington, D.C.: Center of Military History, U.S. Army; U.S. Government Printing Office, 1983), pp. 46–55.

3. T. V. Doan, "A Lament for Vietnam," *New York Times Magazine,* March 29, 1981.

4. THE TAILOR

1. During the war South Vietnam was divided into four large military zones called "Corps." The northernmost zone was denoted as "I Corps," and the region to its south was denoted as "II Corps."

5. THE SPY

1. The stretch of road mentioned by Sang was described by Bernhard B. Fall in his book *Street Without Joy* (Mechanicsburg, Pa.: Stackpole Books, 1961). Fall was later killed in an ambush there.

6. THE PILOT

1. His enlarged thyroid may have been due to an iodine deficiency, a common problem in Vietnam. Its rapid resolution in France probably reflects an improved diet with more iodine.

2. Pleiku is a city in the Vietnamese Central Highlands. In 1975 it was the headquarters of South Vietnam's Military Region II. Its evacuation, which began on March 16, 1975, turned into a rout. The military convoy that was redeploying from Pleiku to the coastal city of Tuy Hoa became entangled in a mass of refugees fleeing Pleiku. Over the next few days Communist troops attacked and seriously disrupted the convoy. Psychologically and militarily, this was a major turning point in the war and helped to accelerate the precipitous withdrawal of South Vietnamese forces from the northern and central provinces southward toward Saigon.

3. I believe that this comment relates to the 1972 North Vietnamese offensive in South Vietnam. The NVA brought tanks for the offensive down along the Ho Chi Minh Trail.

4. C. V. Vien, *The Final Collapse* (Washington, D.C.: Center of Military History, U.S. Army; U.S. Government Printing Office, 1983), p. 3.

5. N. T. Truong, *A Viet Cong Memoir* (New York: Vintage Books, 1986), p. 158.

9. THE TEACHER

1. During this period approximately 900,000 North Vietnamese, many of them Catholics, moved to South Vietnam. About 100,000 South Vietnamese moved to North Vietnam.

2. T. V. Doan and D. Chanoff, *The Vietnamese Gulag* (New York: Simon and Schuster, 1986), p. 18.

3. Quyet explained to me that in the South Vietnamese dialect, *u* and *uu* are almost undistinguishable. The northern dialect differentiates them more clearly.

4. Here Quyet refers to the Communists' destruction of the South Viet-

namese Army Cemetery, Nghĩa Trang Quân Đội—the Vietnamese equivalent of Arlington National Cemetery.

II. THE POLITICIAN

1. Federal Research Division, Library of Congress, *Vietnam: A Country Study* (Washington, D.C.: U.S. Government Printing Office, 1989).

2. The Hoa Hao—formally the Phat Giao Hoa Hao ("perfect" Buddhism)—is a Buddhist sect founded in 1939 by the monk Huynh Phu So. The Cao Dai is a syncretic religious sect founded in 1926 by Ngo Van Chieu, an official in the French civil service. Its patron saints include Victor Hugo and Chiang Kai-shek, and it has a very colorful and elaborate "Holy See" in Tay Ninh, west of Saigon. Its leadership includes a pope and cardinals, a number of whom are women. Both the Hoa Hao and the Cao Dai operated as highly organized communities with a nationalistic orientation and with large, well-trained armies.

3. For an interesting description of the South Vietnamese government's reaction to the Paris Accords, see C. V. Vien, *The Final Collapse* (Washington, D.C.: Center of Military History, U.S. Army; U.S. Government Printing Office, 1983), pp. 19–26.

4. Ibid., p. 264.

12. THE POLITICIAN'S WIFE

1. Cho Lon means literally "big market." Once a separate city, Cho Lon and Saigon gradually grew together, and Cho Lon became the main commercial district of Saigon. Before 1975 it was home to a half million ethnic Chinese. Many of them left Vietnam when the Communist government cracked down on private enterprise and entrepreneurs.

13. THE POLITICIAN'S SON

1. *Tú tài* was the Vietnamese term for the French *baccalauréat*. Bach is referring here to passing the Baccalauréat II exam, the qualifying test for university entrance.

2. Other Vietnamese refugees, especially Amerasians, have told me similar stories about the children of "collaborators" being sent to work battalions rather than to military units, perhaps because of perceived unreliability or disloyalty to the new government.

3. T. V. Doan, "A Lament for Vietnam," *New York Times Magazine,* March 29, 1981.

15. THE POLITICIAN'S DAUGHTER-IN-LAW

1. N. T. Truong, *A Viet Cong Memoir* (New York: Vintage Books, 1986), p. 271.

2. The NLF was formed in South Vietnam by a group of individuals frustrated by President Ngo Dinh Diem's perceived lack of support for the reunification of Vietnam and his increasing dependence on the United States. The NLF joined and, in the South, became virtually synonymous with the Communist Party, the Việt Nam Cộng Sản, or Việt Cộng (VC). In popular parlance, the NLF came to refer to the political arm of the Communists in South Vietnam, and the VC, to their military arm.

3. T. V. Doan, "A Lament for Vietnam," *New York Times Magazine,* March 29, 1981, p. 8.

CONCLUSION

1. T. V. Doan and D. Chanoff, *The Vietnamese Gulag* (New York: Simon and Schuster, 1986), p. 31.

2. Ibid., p. 72.

3. Ibid., p. 73.

4. N. T. Truong, *A Viet Cong Memoir* (New York: Vintage Books, 1986), pp. 271–72.

5. Ibid., p. 272.

6. Doan and Chanoff; Truong.

GLOSSARY

Some of the abbreviations, locations, persons, and terms used in this book may be unfamiliar to readers, especially those who are not acquainted with Vietnam and its modern history. These elements are defined when they first appear; this glossary serves as an additional reference.

Antennas—Name given by the former political prisoners to those prisoners who functioned as spies for the re-education camp authorities.

Army of the Republic of Vietnam (ARVN)—The army of the Republic of South Vietnam; allies of the United States during the Vietnam War.

Associated State of Vietnam—To counter Viet Minh successes, the French granted Vietnam associated statehood within the French Union in 1948. The Emperor Bao Dai was named as the country's titular leader. Associated statehood status was meant to convey the appearance of independence to Vietnam while in reality maintaining it under French control.

August Revolution—A nationwide series of uprisings in August 1945 led by the Viet Minh against the French, the Japanese, and those affiliated with them. The revolution was triggered by widespread starvation in the North, the fall of Japan, and the anticipated arrival of the allies. The culmination of the revolution was Ho Chi Minh's declaration of Vietnamese independence on September 2, 1945.

Bao Dai—Last emperor of the Nguyen dynasty and of Vietnam, Bao

Dai was head of state under the French-controlled Associated State of Vietnam from 1949 until 1955. His prime minister, Ngo Dinh Diem, overthrew him and became president of the Republic of South Vietnam.

Battle of Dien Bien Phu—Dien Bien Phu is a northern Vietnamese town near the Laotian border. The French seized it in November 1953 as part of their strategy to combat a Viet Minh offensive in Laos. The Viet Minh laid siege to the French garrison at Dien Bien Phu on March 13, 1954, and on May 7, 1954, after a series of hard-fought battles, the French surrendered. France's defeat at Dien Bien Phu led to the Geneva Accords, the French withdrawal from North Vietnam, and the partition of Vietnam at the 17th parallel.

Black Pajama Cadres—Nickname given to the South Vietnamese Rural Cadres program. The name came from the black, long-sleeved shirts and trousers typically worn by Vietnamese farmers. The goal of the cadres was to infiltrate rural areas, disguising themselves as part of the local population, so that they could give early warning of Viet Cong movements and help identify Viet Cong collaborators.

Central Intelligence Organization (CIO)—The South Vietnamese equivalent of the U.S. CIA.

Demilitarized zone (DMZ)—As a result of the Geneva Accords, Vietnam was temporarily divided at the 17th parallel into two military regrouping zones. French troops were withdrawn from the northern zone and concentrated in the south, and Viet Minh troops were withdrawn from the southern zone and concentrated in the north. On either side of the military demarcation line between the two zones a DMZ no wider than 5 kilometers was established. Combatants were prohibited from stationing troops within this zone. It was the intent of the Geneva Accords that the demarcation line would no longer be necessary after the holding of Vietnamese national elections in July 1956. However, these elections were never held, and the demarcation line and DMZ became the permanent border between North and South Vietnam. The DMZ continued to designate the no-man's-land between the two countries until the fall of Saigon, on April 30, 1975.

Democratic Republic of Vietnam (DRV)—Name given to North Vietnam by the Viet Minh after independence was declared in 1946 following the August Revolution.

Đổi Mới—Literally "renewal or renovation," *đổi mới* was a policy of economic and political reform introduced in 1987 by Nguyen Van Linh, general secretary of the Vietnamese Communist Party.

Đồng—Vietnamese monetary unit. In 1990 its official exchange rate was approximately 10,000–11,000 *đồng* to U.S. $1.

Duong Van Minh—Known as "Big Minh" because of his size, Duong Van Minh was an army general and the last president of the Republic of South Vietnam. He gave the orders for the final surrender of the South Vietnamese armed forces and formally surrendered to the North Vietnamese Army (NVA) and the Viet Cong (VC).

Hanoi—Capital city of Vietnam, located along the Red River in northeastern Vietnam.

Hue—City in central Vietnam; the former Vietnamese imperial capital. In early 1968 Hue was the scene of a major battle between Communist forces and American and South Vietnamese troops during the Tet Offensive.

Ho Chi Minh—Founder of the Indochinese Communist Party and the Viet Minh, Ho Chi Minh was president of North Vietnam from 1945 until his death in 1969. Historically, he has been described as Vietnam's Mao Tse-tung and as "the founder and leader of the Vietnamese revolution" (N. T. Truong, *A Viet Cong Memoir* (New York: Vintage Books, 1986], p. 312). His name is a pseudonym meaning "he who enlightens"; he was born in central Vietnam in 1890 as Nguyen Tat Thanh.

Ho Chi Minh City—Formerly known as Saigon, the city was renamed for North Vietnam's founder after the final defeat of South Vietnamese forces in 1975.

Ho Chi Minh Trail—Complex series of paths, trails, and roads leading from North Vietnam through Cambodia and Laos into South Vietnam. The Ho Chi Minh Trail was the major supply route for Communist forces fighting against American and South Vietnamese forces during the Vietnam War.

H.O. Program—Special program under the Orderly Departure Program (ODP). The H.O. Program enabled former political prisoners who had been incarcerated three or more years in re-education camps and who had served in the South Vietnamese armed forces or government to immigrate with their immediate families to the United States.

Montagnards—Generic name given to various ethnic minority peoples living in the mountainous regions of Vietnam. These groups are distinguished from one another linguistically and by their diverse cultural and historical traditions. The Americans and Australians recruited Montagnards to fight with them against Communist forces in the South. The Vietnamese Montagnards best known to Westerners are probably the Hmong, many of whom were resettled after the war in the United States.

National Liberation Front (NLF)—Extralegal political movement founded in 1960 by southern intellectuals and nationalists who wanted to overthrow the Diem regime and liberate South Vietnam from U.S. domination. It eventually evolved into the Communist Party organization in South Vietnam.

New Economic Zones—Sparsely populated, often remote areas of southern Vietnam designated as resettlement sites for the surplus population of larger cities, especially Ho Chi Minh City. These areas were ostensibly intended to relieve overcrowding and increase economic productivity, but they often appeared to function as places to send persons considered undesirable, such as Amerasians or former political prisoners.

Ngo Dinh Diem—A nationalist and first president of the Republic of Vietnam, Ngo Dinh Diem was assassinated by his own generals in 1963 in a CIA-backed coup.

Nguyen Cao Ky—A former air force vice marshal, Nguyen Cao Ky served as South Vietnam's prime minister from 1965 to 1967 and as its vice president from 1971 to 1975. At the end of the war he escaped from Vietnam and opened a liquor store in California.

Nguyen Van Linh—A northerner who spent most of his political life in the south and was a leader of the Viet Cong in Saigon, Nguyen Van Linh became secretary-general of the Communist Party in 1986. Under his leadership many socioeconomic reforms were introduced, including the policy of *đổi mới* (renovation). In 1991 he was replaced as secretary-general by Do Muoi.

Nguyen Van Thieu—An army officer trained in France and the United States, Nguyen Van Thieu became president of South Vietnam in 1971. He escaped from Vietnam in 1975 and went to live in England.

North Vietnamese Army (NVA)—Formally the People's Army of Vietnam (*Quân Đội Nhân Dân Việt Nam*), the NVA fought against the American and South Vietnamese armed forces in South Vietnam.

Orderly Departure Program (ODP)—Bilateral agreement reached in July 1979 between the U.S. and Vietnamese governments. Its purpose was to address the dangerous and illegal departures from Vietnam of refugees such as the boat people and those escaping overland through Cambodia. The ODP permitted the legal and safe immigration of Vietnamese such as the family members of people already resettled in the United States, former U.S. government employees, Vietnamese Amerasians, and former political prisoners and their families.

Pétrus Ký—Pétrus Trương Vĩnh Ký (or Jean-Baptiste Pétrus) was a noted Vietnamese scholar of the nineteenth century. A Roman Catholic priest and widely read author, he helped to educate Vietnamese about the cultural differences between themselves and the Europeans. Graduates of the famous high school in Saigon named after him were among South Vietnam's educational elite and continue to have active alumni organizations abroad in many Western countries.

Phoenix Program—Program organized and directed by the CIA and aimed at identifying and arresting or killing Communist cadres operating among South Vietnam's rural population. It united the efforts of various South Vietnamese intelligence organizations charged with detecting and eliminating Viet Cong agents and provided their operatives with counterinsurgency training. The program proved to be quite successful at disrupting the Viet Cong's rural organization and infrastructure.

Pleiku—Town in the central highlands of southern Vietnam. Pleiku was a marketplace for the local Montagnard people. During the war it became a South Vietnamese headquarters for operations directed at Communist supply routes from the Ho Chi Minh Trail into South Vietnam.

Republic of South Vietnam—Name given to South Vietnam in 1955 after it became an independent state under President Ngo Dinh Diem.

Southeast Asia Treaty Organization (SEATO)—A mutual self-defense alliance composed of Australia, France, Great Britain, New Zealand, Pakistan, Thailand, and the United States. John Foster Dulles, U.S. Secretary of State under President Eisenhower, proposed and developed SEATO to counter the threat of Communist expansion into Southeast Asia. A subsequent protocol to the treaty added Cambodia, Laos, and Vietnam to the nations protected by SEATO.

United Nations High Commissioner for Refugees (UNHCR)—Established in 1951, the UNHCR is the United Nations organization that deals with rufugees. The UNHCR was very active during the Vietnam War, dealing initially with internally displaced Vietnamese refugees and then leading and coordinating international efforts to cope with the massive flight of refugees from Indochina that began with the fall of Saigon, on April 30, 1975.

John W. Vessey—A former chairman of the U.S. Joint Chiefs of Staff, General Vessey was appointed in July 1987 by President Reagan as special emissary to Vietnam. His task was to negotiate with the Vietnamese government about the fate of Americans still listed as missing in action (MIA) in Vietnam and to address other humanitarian issues, such as the Amerasians and re-education camp prisoners. He continued to function in this role under the administrations of Presidents Bush and Clinton.

Viet Cong—The term "Viet Cong" (VC) was a contraction of *Việt Nam Cộng Sản* or Vietnamese Communists. This was the term used by the Americans and the South Vietnamese to designate their guerilla adversaries in the South. The Viet Cong referred to themselves as the National Liberation Front (NLF).

Viet Minh—Formally the *Việt Nam Độc Lập Đồng Minh Hội* (League for Vietnamese Independence), the Viet Minh was founded by Ho Chi Minh in 1941. It was a union of nationalist groups opposed to the foreign domination of Vietnam. Led by Ho Chi Minh, the Viet Minh fought against both the French and the Japanese.

Vietnamese National Military Academy (VNMA; *Trường Võ Bị Quốc Gia Việt Nam*)—Located in the mountain resort of Da Lat, the VNMA was South Vietnam's military academy. Modeled after the United States Military Academy at West Point, the VNMA was the primary site for the training of career military officers for the South Vietnamese armed forces. Unlike West Point, the VNMA trained officers, not only for the army, but also for the air force and the navy.

The French founded the VNMA in 1948 in Hue as the Vietnamese Regular Officers School. President Nguyen Van Thieu was one of its first graduates. In 1950 the school was moved to Da Lat. Until 1954 all of its commanders and instructors were French. After the departure of the French, the Vietnamese, with American support and assistance, took over its command and instructional duties. In 1959 a South Vietnamese presidential decree established the VNMA as a university.

INDEX

Amerasians, Vietnamese, xi, 199,
239
"antennas." *See* informers
Army of the Republic of Vietnam
(ARVN), 36, 250
Associated State of Vietnam, 10, 250
August Revolution (1945), 9, 143,
144, 250

baccalaureate exam, 244
Bao Dai (last Vietnamese emperor),
10, 19, 250–51; and Japanese
puppet government, 9;
overthrown, 11
Bien Hoa (air base), 107
Binh Tuy, retreat from, 148
Black Pajama cadres. *See* rural cadres
boat people, x, 12–13, 51, 126,
136–37, 162–63, 174–75

Cambodia: Khmer Rouge in, 238;
Vietnamese war with, 13, 208–9
Cao Dai, 180, 248

Cap Anamur (German-registered
ship), 164, 174–75
Central Intelligence Agency (CIA),
151, 152
Central Intelligence Organization
(CIO), 71, 75, 79, 251; training
for, 76
Chiang Kai-shek, 144, 165, 248
children of former political
prisoners: adjustment to life in
U.S., 140, 228, 235–36; arrival in
U.S., 137–38, 214; conditions of
life in U.S., 132, 137–39, 214,
219–20; conditions of life in
Vietnam after fathers' departure,
46, 54, 127–28, 135, 136,
171–72; discrimination against,
in United States, 219–20;
discrimination against, in
Vietnam, 53, 65, 66, 95, 198–99,
210–11, 218, 249; effects of
fathers' absence on, 54, 133,
139–40, 175–76, 212, 218;

fathers' departure into re-education camp, 134, 135; feelings about coming to U.S., 219; reactions to end of war, 133–34; recollections of escape from Vietnam, 136–38; relationship with fathers, 129–30, 133, 139–40, 166; reunion with fathers, 139, 214

China: cultural influences of, 179; Vietnamese border war with, 13

Cho Lon, 12, 248

chữ nôm (Vietnamese pictographic script), 179

Communists, Vietnamese: behavior toward former political prisoners, 237–39; former prisoners' views of, 4, 55, 100, 156, 166, 167–68, 183–84, 188, 189, 190, 203–4, 232, 234

confessions, forced, 42, 47, 69, 80, 81, 152–54, 156, 185

coping strategies: of former political prisoners, 5, 8, 21, 25, 30, 44–45, 53, 56–57, 58, 63–64, 67–68, 69–70, 75, 118–19, 155–56, 163–64, 189–90, 229, 230–32; of prisoners' wives, 5, 173, 229, 230–32

Da Lat, 19, 146, 169, 170; retreat from, 147

Da Nang (Tourane), 8

deception: Communist tactics of, 87–88, 224; used to lure former political prisoners into re-education camps, 40–41, 80–82, 112–13, 185, 206–7, 223, 224

demilitarized zone (DMZ), 21, 251–52

Democratic Republic of Vietnam (DRV), 252; establishment of, 9–10; postwar social and economic policies, 11–12

depression: in former political prisoners, 53, 156, 167, 185, 188, 236–37; in former prisoners' wives, 173, 176, 236–37

De Rhodes, Alexander, 179

Dien Bien Phu, battle of, 10, 60, 106, 145, 251

discrimination, former political prisoners' experience of, xiii, 7, 145–46, 163

divorce rates, 28–29, 95, 212

Doan van Toai, 41

đổi mới (renovation), 216, 218, 252; effects on re-education camp, 6, 93

đồng (monetary unit), value of, 50, 93, 252

Dong Cong (Roman Catholic religious order), 88

due process, lack of in Vietnam, 211

Duong van Minh, 23, 38, 78, 112, 204, 252

education: in postwar Vietnam, 54; in prewar Vietnam, 178–79

escape: from re-education camps, 84–85, 85–86, 93; from Vietnam, 120, 158–60

famine (1945), 143, 165–66

First War of Resistance. *See* French–Viet Minh War (1945–1954)

former political prisoners: adaptation to life in United States, xiii–xiv, 7, 27, 54, 67–69, 98, 99, 128–31, 162, 163–64, 167, 191; backgrounds of, 4, 13–14, 20–21, 32–34, 59–60, 72–76, 103–8, 143–46, 178–83, 201–2; departure from Vietnam, xiii, 7, 27, 51–53, 120, 158–60; divorce rates among, 28–29, 129, 212; effects of loss of status on, 7, 27–30, 167; employment in U.S., 27–30, 66, 67, 99, 162–63, 211, 213, 220; feelings about leaving Vietnam, 53, 54, 98, 159; lives in Vietnam after camps, xii, xiii, xx, 4–5, 6–7, 26–27, 47–50, 65–66, 95–96, 120, 157–59, 190, 209–10, 214; postwar employment in Vietnam, xiii, 26, 27, 49–50, 58, 65, 120, 157, 178–79, 209–10, 215–17; reactions to Communists'

deceptive tactics, 40–41, 69, 113, 149–50, 167, 185, 186, 187, 203–4; reactions to U.S. role in Vietnam, 109–11, 146, 166, 232–34; reactions to war's end, 37–38, 62, 78–79, 112, 184–85, 205–6; reasons for coming to U.S., 66, 210–11; reasons for leaving Vietnam, 51–52, 98, 158, 210–11; understanding of their fate, 8, 30, 165–66, 188; Vietnamese reactions to, 95, 119, 186, 209; wanting to stay in Vietnam, 96; women among the, 92. *See also* depression; Post-Traumatic Stress Disorder

France: colonial policies toward Vietnam, 9, 179–80; conquest of Vietnam, 8–9; and famine of 1945, 165–66; military training in, 107; re-establishment of colonial control, 10–11; role in release of former prisoners, 5, 25–26; role in Vietnamese educational system, 18, 20, 33, 124, 145, 179; torture of prisoners by, 144–45; Vietnamese resistance against, 9, 18, 143–44

French–Viet Minh War (1945–1954) (First War of Resistance), 10, 104, 246; effects of, 19–20, 155–56, 180

Geneva Accords (1954), 32; and cease-fire between France and Viet Minh, 10; and national referendum, 10, 11; and partition of Vietnam, 10, 60, 73, 106, 143, 251–52

Go Cong, 79

Hai Van Pass, 77
Ham Tan, retreat from, 147–48
Hanoi, 252; French recapture of, 10, 252
Hán văn (Chinese script), 17
Hoa Hao, 180, 248
Ho Chi Minh, 110, 136, 158, 168, 172, 183, 232, 252; and foundation of Communist Party, 9; jokes about, 92, 172
Ho Chi Minh City (formerly Saigon), 253
Ho Chi Minh trail, 111, 253
H.O. Program, 7, 51, 52, 66, 96, 120, 191, 210, 214, 244, 253; prisoners not qualifying for, 94, 95, 100
Hue, 252; fall of, 76; French recapture of, 10
Hugo, Victor, 248

Independence Day, Vietnamese, 9; and release of prisoners, 6, 94
informers, 158; in re-education camps, 25, 44, 63, 70, 83, 118, 151, 156, 188, 250; prisoners' reactions toward, 44

Khmer Rouge, 13, 238
Kissinger, Henry, 109

lacquerware, xi, 242
landowners: control of rice production, 9; lifestyle of wealthy, 17–19, 192–93, 194; Viet Minh treatment of, 32, 106, 155–56
Long Khanh, fall of, 22, 77–78, 148–49
Luong Son re-education camp, 154–55

Malaysia, treatment of boat people by, 160–61
Mao Tse-tung, 165
marital relationships after re-education camps, 48–49, 120–21, 128–31, 226–27
marriage, Vietnamese traditions of, 18–19, 35–36, 61, 69, 73, 97–98, 105, 108–9, 165, 170–71, 181, 193–95, 227, 228
medical treatment: in postwar Vietnam, 26, 52, 54; in re-education camps, 45, 89–90, 115, 118, 156–57, 162, 187;
military service of former political

prisoners: entry into, 20–21,
34–35, 59–60, 75–76, 146,
201, 202–3; their views of,
22, 35, 59–60, 146, 166, 168,
203–4
Montagnards, 157, 158, 170, 253

National Liberation Front (NLF),
224, 249, 253
New Economic Zones (NEZ):
description of, 12; former
political prisoners and, 48, 119,
158, 164, 253–54
Ngo Dinh Diem, 10–11, 18, 34,
254
Nguyen Cao Ky, 146, 183, 254
Nguyen van Linh, 254
Nguyen van Thieu, 183, 189, 254;
former prisoner's view of, 146
Nguyen van Thuan, 74, 77
Nha Trang, fall of, 77
Nixon, Richard Milhous: effects of
resignation on U.S. support for
Vietnam, ix, 37; and U.S. troop
withdrawals, 11
North Vietnamese Army (NVA),
185, 247, 254
Nui Voi (Elephant Mountain), 157,
158

Orderly Departure Program (ODP),
98, 120, 242, 254; bribery and,
96–97

Paris Accords (1973), 11, 21, 184;
and U.S. support for South
Vietnam, 37
personality changes after re-
education camps: in prisoners,
49, 64, 98–99, 128, 173, 189,
199–200, 211–12, 217–18, 226,
229–30; in prisoners' wives,
128–29, 176, 229–30
Pétrus Trương Vĩnh Ký, 34, 255
Pham van Dong, 25
Phan Rang, fall of, 77–78
Phoenix Program, 61, 255
Pleiku, 255; evacuation of, 111,
247
Popular Forces (Nghĩa Quân), 203
Post-Traumatic Stress Disorder
(PTSD): symptoms in former
prisoners, 6–7, 21, 25, 67, 100,
121–22, 163–65, 190, 199, 204,
211, 217–18, 236–37, 243,
244–45; symptoms in former
prisoners' wives, 200, 236–37
prisoners of war (POW): former
political prisoners' status as, 155,
157, 168; U.S., xx
psychotherapy, 236–37, 245

quốc ngữ (romanized script), 179

Red Cross, 187
re-education: People's
Revolutionary Government's

initial policy toward, 3; postwar
initiation of, 12; resistance to, 92;
techniques of, 24, 39–40, 42, 69–
70, 82–83, 91–92, 113, 150–55,
157–58, 167, 171
re-education camps: conditions in,
xii–xiii, 4, 24–25, 26, 41–43,
62–63, 81–85, 88–90, 93, 113,
114–15, 117–18, 150–57, 162,
185–89, 206–9, 222, 225–26;
escapes from, 84–86, 157; family
visits in, 43, 65, 82, 115, 150,
173, 186, 188; feelings of
prisoners on entry into, 39, 63,
81, 113, 149–50, 185, 206; guards
in, 91; in North Vietnam, 62–64,
76–77, 114–15, 119, 187–89,
207; killing of prisoners in,
208–9; lack of resistance on
entry into, 22–24, 38–39, 81–82,
113, 149–50, 206, 223–24; letters
from prisoners in, 115–16, 199;
number of prisoners in, 12;
numbers of, 86; ostensible goals
of, 23, 38–40, 149–50; prisoners'
initial expectations of, 4, 39, 149,
206–7; protests in, 85; radios in,
96; release from, 5–6, 25–26,
45–47, 64, 94, 119–20, 157, 189,
199, 209; self-criticism in, 83;
torture of prisoners in, 24–25,
43–44, 68, 84, 90, 116–17, 187,
207; types of prisoners in, 82,

86–88, 151; use of foreign
languages in, 83–84, 85, 187. *See
also* informers
refugee camps, 126, 137, 160,
161–62
Republic of South Vietnam, 255;
collapse of, ix–x, 3, 11, 23–24,
37–38, 61–62, 76–78, 109–12,
125, 147–49, 184–85, 204–6;
formation of, 10–11
resilience of former political
prisoners and their wives, 14,
67–68, 229
"righteous cause" (*chánh nghĩa*),
South Vietnam's lack of, 110,
146, 166, 232
Roman Catholics: migration
of from North Vietnam, 10,
73, 150, 247; and the Viet
Minh, 74; Vietnamese views of,
170–71
rural cadres (Black Pajama cadres),
60–61, 251

Saigon: fall of, 22–23, 38, 78, 79,
112, 133–34, 149, 161; postwar
conditions in, 26, 49–50
Second War of Resistance. *See*
Vietnam War (1962–1975)
Sông Hương (Vietnamese ship),
114, 186
Song Mao (re-education camp),
151–54

Southeast Asia Treaty Organization (SEATO), 109, 255

South Vietnamese Army Cemetery (Nghĩa Trang Quân Đội), 247–48

suicide: of former political prisoners, 7, 53, 156; of former prisoners' wives, 51

Tan Son Nhut (air base), 108, 125, 133

Trại Kiên Giang (re-education camp), 222

Tran Hung Dao, 246

Tran Trong Kim, 19

Trung sisters (Hai Bà Trung), 246

Truong Nhu Tang, 224

United Nations High Commissioner for Refugees (UNHCR), 161, 256

United States: failure to meet commitments to Vietnam, ix, 62, 110; postwar policies toward Vietnam, 13, 239–40; role in Vietnam War, 232–33; support for South Vietnam, 10–11, 37; trade embargo against Vietnam, 13, 239; withdrawal from Vietnam, ix, 8

Vessey, General John, role in release of prisoners, 5–6, 64, 93, 96, 256

Viet Cong (Việt Nam Cộng Sản), 182, 183, 185, 204–7, 218, 249, 256; former prisoners' appraisal of, 166, 167–68, 183–84, 195–96, 207, 215. See also Communists, Vietnamese

Viet Minh (Việt Nam Độc Lập Đồng Minh Hội), 72, 73, 256; and August Revolution, 9, 143–44; campaigns against land owners, 32, 106; conflicts with Roman Catholics, 72–73; formation of, 9

Vietnam, Associated State of, 10, 104; postwar conditions in, 11–13, 65, 99, 117–18, 212

Vietnamese National Military Academy (VNMA), 142, 146, 147, 148, 150, 256–57

Vietnamization, ix, 111

Vietnam War (1962–1975) (Second War of Resistance), 11, 246; U.S. withdrawal from, ix

Vo Nguyen Giap, 18

wives of former political prisoners: acculturation problems in, 128–29, 177; backgrounds of, 97–98, 123–24, 169–71, 192–95, 227–28; conditions of life in U.S., 126–27, 128–29, 176, 177, 200; coping strategies of, 173; departure from Vietnam, 119, 126, 174–75; depression in, 128,

173, 197, 198, 222, 225; effects of
status loss on, 176–77; feelings
about leaving Vietnam, 98;
feelings about war, 124–25; lives
after husbands' incarceration, xii,
xix–xx, 4–5, 46–47, 125–26,
171–73, 196–99, 218, 222–23,
224–25; means of supporting
themselves in U.S., 126–27, 221;
means of supporting themselves
in Vietnam, 47, 65, 124, 125–26,
170, 171–72, 196–97, 198, 200,

218, 222; reactions of
Vietnamese toward, 172,
196–97, 222–23; reactions to
war's end, 125; re-education of,
171; visits with husbands in re-
education camp, 173, 197–98,
225, 226

women's education in Vietnam, 18,
193

World War II, former prisoners'
recollections of, 103–4, 143,
180